THE UNIVERSITY OF MICHIGAN
CENTER FOR CHINESE STUDIES

MICHIGAN PAPERS IN CHINESE STUDIES
NO. 26

THE SIAN INCIDENT:
A PIVOTAL POINT IN MODERN CHINESE HISTORY

by
Tien-wei Wu

Ann Arbor

Center for Chinese Studies
The University of Michigan

1976

ISBN 0-89264-026-X

Copyright © 1976

by

Center for Chinese Studies
The University of Michigan

Printed in the United States of America

Grateful acknowledgment is made to the Viking Press, Inc.,
for their permission to reproduce two photographs, "Generalissimo
Chiang and the Young Marshal" (p. 132) and "Peasant Guards in
Armed Procession in Sian" (p. 133), from First Act in China: The
Story of the Sian Mutiny, by James M. Bertram, copyright 1938 by
The Viking Press, Inc.

To

My Mother

CONTENTS

LIST OF TABLES AND MAPS

PREFACE

Almost forty years after the melodrama enacted at Hua-ch'ing-ch'ih, the hot-spring resort of the celebrated Chinese beauty Yang Kuei-fei, the Sian Incident still absorbs much attention from both Chinese and Western scholars as well as the reading public. The Incident is doubtless one of the most sensational episodes in modern history and many people still view the event with excitement, regret and indignation. While the dramatic capture of Chiang Kai-shek and his abrupt release have already mystified many, the negotiated settlement and the aftermath of the Incident remain largely in speculation.

Apart from the coup itself, the Sian Incident was the pivotal point in modern Chinese history, so crucial in fact to the survival of the Chinese Communist movement that even today Nationalist writers and officials in Taiwan denounce the Young Marshal Chang Hsüeh-liang for having done unforgivable and irreparable damage to the nation. They argue, as did Chiang Kai-shek himself, that the Red Army, then numbering approximately 30,000 men and cornered in the inhospitable North Shensi, would have been doomed to destruction, had the Sian Incident not occurred to ruin the whole plan for its extermination.

In spite of so much that has been written, the Sian Incident--ranging from the CCP campaign for a "united front" against Japan, local suspension of civil war between the Red Army and the Tungpei-Hsipei Armies, the engineering of the coup, negotiations for a peaceful settlement, the aftermath of the coup, and the fate of the two chief actors, Chang Hsüeh-liang and Yang Hu-ch'eng--is only known in fragmentary forms. Writings either in the form of reminiscent account or from the approach of analytical study have continuously poured out from the Chinese press in Hong Kong and Taiwan. In one way or another, these publications have revealed crucial information which would otherwise have remained hidden, but few of them are without partisan bias, and at the same time they fail to give a conceptual framework to the subject.

Conversely, Western study of the Incident is somewhat one-sided, tending to place undue emphasis on the role of the CCP. To a great extent, Western scholarship has suffered from Edgar Snow's authoritative, pioneering works. As is well known, his account of the Incident is Communist-centered, partly because of his keen concern with the CCP and partly because of his journalistic account which relied heavily on interviews with a few people, particularly Chou En-lai and Miao Chien-ch'iu. This is by no means to minimize the important contributions Snow made to our understanding of many events involving the Chinese Communists. Admittedly, the importance of the Sian Incident lies primarily in its influence on the course of the Chinese Communist movement; it is viewed as a distant cause for the Communist takeover of China. It is easy to overlook the fact that eight years of the Sino-Japanese War and four years of the Chinese civil war had intervened between the Sian Incident and the Communist triumph in China. True, the Sian Incident led to the temporary suspension of the KMT campaign against the Red Army; yet there was no guarantee that the KMT or Chiang Kai-shek would not resume the campaign in spite of a verbal promise given to his captors upon leaving Sian. The forces that upheld the Sian accord must be scrutinized and assessed before a justifiable conclusion concerning the effect of the Sian Incident on the KMT-CCP relations can be reached.

In writing this book, I have attempted to bring together whatever information has been thus far gleaned about the subject, and to cover all aspects and controversies involved in it. This undertaking grew out of both personal concern and scholarly interest for many years, and it is built upon the labor of many scholars and writers from James Bertram to Lucien Bianco. In addition to the revelations made by the captive and his captor, Generalissimo Chiang and the Young Marshal, as well as by the two negotiators, Madame Chiang and William Donald, three participants of the Incident revealed valuable information in their interviews with me. They are Miu Cheng-liu, Commander of the 57th Tungpei Army, Wan Yao-huang, army commander who was detained at the Sian hostel, and Mao Ching-hsiang, Chiang's secretary who was with him at Hua-ch'ing-ch'ih. Further, Mr. Mao has generously provided me with two pictures related to the Sian event, which have been reproduced and inserted in this book.

At various stages of this study, many scholars gave great help and criticism that improved the quality of the work beyond the reach of my ability. Among those whose help should be specially mentioned are: Professors C. Martin Wilbur of Columbia University, Eugene Wu of Harvard University, Knight Biggerstaff of Cornell University, Lucien Bianco of Sorbonne of the University of Paris, and Eugene Trani of Southern Illinois University at Carbondale. I am deeply indebted to Mrs. Beth Haas and Mrs. Jennie E. Calonne of the

Department of History at Southern Illinois University for improving the style and typing the manuscript. Special thanks is due the Publications Committee of the Center for Chinese Studies at The University of Michigan, particularly its Director, Professor Albert Feuerwerker, without whose interest and support, this book may not have been published. Finally my profuse thanks to Jeannie Lin for providing me with invaluable editorial assistance and to Dorothy Perng for her excellent calligraphy.

T. W. Wu
New York
November 1975

LIST OF ABBREVIATIONS

CCC	Ch'en Ch'eng Collection
CCP	Chinese Communist Party
CCWH	Ch'uan-chi wen-hsüeh [Biographical literature]
CEC	Central Executive Committee
Comintern	The Third Communist International
CTTC	Chiang Tsung-t'ung chi [Collected works of President Chiang]
CWR	China Weekly Review
KMT	Kuomintang
KWCP	Kuo-wen chou-pao [National news weekly]
MPYK	Ming-pao yueh k'an [Ming-pao monthly]
NHBS	Northwestern Headquarters of Bandit Suppression.

I. CHANG HSÜEH-LIANG AND HIS TIME

After the epic "Long March," the worn, nervous, beaten, but not annihilated Communists at last reached their temporary destination, North Shensi, in the fall of 1935. It took another year for the two separated Communist groups--the one under Mao Tse-tung reaching North Shensi and the other under Chang Kuo-t'ao and Chu Teh remaining in Inner Tibet--to be reunited. In the new situation the Communist leaders must have realized that at best they could hope to establish and consolidate a new base bordering Inner Mongolia and Ninghsia, while at worst they could expect to seek asylum in Outer Mongolia or Sinkiang or even inside the Soviet Union.[1]

By all accounts, chances of survival for the Communists in North Shensi were rather slim because Chiang Kai-shek, in spite of the CCP (Chinese Communist Party) overture for peace and ever-increasing Japanese aggression in North China, was determined to continue his policy of "internal pacification before resistance against external aggression" (an-nei jang-wai). When Chiang arrived at Sian, and laid plans for launching his last campaign against the Red Army with an expectation of exterminating it in a month,[2] he badly misjudged the mood of the Tungpei (Northeast) Army and more so its leader, Chang Hsüeh-liang (1901-), better known as the Young Marshal. Refusing to fight the Communists, Chang with the loyal support of his officers staged a coup d'état by kidnapping Chiang Kai-shek for two weeks at Sian. Undoubtedly the Sian Incident of December 12, 1936, was one of the crucial events in modern Chinese history, certainly the pivotal point in the Chinese Communist movement. Yet, the CCP was not involved, not even informed of the premeditated coup before it took place, nor did its chief delegate, Chou En-lai, who later helped bring about the release of Chiang, play a decisive role in the negotiations during Chiang's detention at Sian. Throughout the entire episode--from the kidnapping of Chiang at Lintung to his triumphant return to Nanking--the Young Marshal remained its mastermind, so that it is altogether necessary to understand the man first.

1

The Young Marshal

In the words of John Gunther, "Young Marshal Chang Hsüeh-liang is, I think, the most difficult, the most refractory, the most engaging human being I have to write about."[3] Some traces of his early life tend to confirm these personal traits as attributed to him by Gunther.

Chang Hsüeh-liang, the eldest of the seven children of the Manchurian warlord Chang Tso-lin, was a born prince. When he was yet a small boy, his father had already achieved supremacy in Manchuria. Reared in bandit tradition and illiterate, the elderly Chang wanted his son to have all the benefits bestowed on a literate man and, therefore, put him into the care of a Confucian scholar. As a naughty and mischievous boy, the young Chang preferred to play around the barracks of his father's troops than sit at home to study. Incapable of enforcing discipline on his part, the tutor failed to make the boy literate in Chinese tradition. Consequently, his general education had been much neglected. He also missed his opportunity to mingle with the Chinese youths of his age. However, it was probably his good fortune to be exposed early to the Western way of life. He visited the YMCA regularly and enjoyed Western sports. He learned how to drive an automobile and to fly an airplane, both of which have been novelties in China until recently.[4] In the meantime, he had made acquaintances with European youths, particularly James Elder, who has become his lifelong friend. Reminiscing of his boyhood, the Young Marshal wrote that he was influenced more by his Western teachers and friends than by their Chinese counterparts.[5]

Like his compatriots from Manchuria, Chang Hsüeh-liang possessed the traits of generosity, straightforwardness, and temperament, which grew stronger as he rose to power. Destined to be the successor of his father's domain, he naturally pursued a military career. Soon after graduating from the first class of the military academy his father had organized at Mukden, he began to assist his father in conducting military campaigns as well as in managing governmental affairs of Manchuria, a region rich in natural resources and coveted by its two powerful neighbors, Japan and Russia.

In his midtwenties, the Young Marshal was made commander of an army of 50,000 men. In the ensuing Second Chih-Feng War between Chang Tso-lin and Wu P'ei-fu, he proved himself to be an able commander. But it was his sincerity and trust in his subordinates that won their loyalty. (During the critical hours of Kuo Sungling's revolt in October 1925 when the elderly Chang was ready to flee to Dairen, the young Chang stood firm outside Mukden to repel the rebels' advance and eventually succeeded in destroying the rebels from within.[6] (Later in May 1927, in fighting against the revolutionary army led by Chang Fa-k'uei in Honan, the Young Marshal showed himself to be not only a good general in battle but also a man of feeling in his concern for the sufferings of the people and abhorrence of civil war.[7])

By the time he succeeded his father as ruler of Manchuria (after the latter was killed by a Japanese bomb on June 4, 1928), he had acquired the title of the "Young Marshal." Like his father, he would not yield to Japanese pressure for further rights in Manchuria, but he had to tackle the delicate internal struggle for power created by the death of the strong man. With great dexterity he handled the situation. Shortly after his assumption of power, he accomplished two deeds so remarkable that they silenced those who were opposed to him and won over those who had doubts about his ability as a leader. (On the one hand, in a quick maneuver, he executed two of his father's leading lieutenants, Yang Yü-t'ing and Ch'ang Yin-huai, known as pro-Japanese and allegedly implicated in the killing of his father; and on the other hand, he raised the revolutionary banner in support of the Nanking government, a gesture that gave a nominal unification to China, for which Chiang Kai-shek rewarded him with the lofty position as his Vice-Commander-in-Chief.) Till then, the Young Marshal had been admired as much for his good fortune as for his clairvoyance.[8]

Intoxicated by power and wealth, the Young Marshal, who knew little hardship in life, readily indulged himself in pleasure-seeking. He soon became a narcotic addict, a condition that did more to damage his reputation than anything else. But he still possessed the characteristics of generosity, straightforwardness, and temperament. In his administrative policy, he continued to pursue his goal to build up Manchuria's economy. Within a few years, a gigantic stride was made in the development of railroads, industry, and education. He streamlined the Tungpei Army and buttressed it by an air force and a navy, the greatest that China had ever seen.[9]

However strong it became militarily and economically, Manchuria was no match for either of its two strong, ambitious, aggressive neighbors. While the Young Marshal was determined not to lean toward one side in the summer and fall of 1929, he was led into an undeclared war against Soviet Russia fought on the northwestern Manchuria-Siberia border over the control of the Chinese Eastern Railway. Despite its defeat, Manchuria had not lost any territory or civil rights, partly because of the international climate of peace prevailing in the wake of the signing of the Kellogg-Briand Pact, and in part because the new Socialist regime of Russia was still too weak to wage a full-scale war with China.[10]

The hidden Sino-Soviet war in 1929 also hastened the Japanese aggression in Manchuria. Clearly the military weakness of the Tungpei Army was exposed in the war, so that Japan's confidence in her capability to conquer Manchuria, which had long been in the making since the Tanaka cabinet inaugurated in 1927, had measurably increased. More important, Japan had viewed the new posture of progress and self-strengthening of the "Young Manchuria" with alarm; in the minds of Japanese radical officers, Japan would forever lose the opportunity to conquer Manchuria if she failed to carry it out soon.

As in the past, China's chaos and civil wars had always afforded good excuses and opportunities for foreign aggression. While the main forces of the Tungpei Army were engaged in fighting the warlord Shih Yu-shan, Japan struck Mukden on September 18, 1931.[11] Without proper counseling, the Young Marshal left the whole matter to the Nanking National Government for international negotiations but failed to offer resistance to Japanese attack. The failure of the League of Nations to restrain Japan from all-out aggression in Manchuria resulted in the fall of the whole of Manchuria to Japan. The loss of Manchuria brought national humiliation to all the Chinese; it was also a personal tragedy for the Young Marshal. He, together with the Tungpei Army, was driven from his home and began an exiled life. From that time on, the Young Marshal was ridiculed as a "nonresistant" general. There is no doubt that the loss of Manchuria was the root of the Sian Incident.

The worsening situation in North China caused by Japan's further aggression and China's defeat in Jehol compelled the Young Marshal to resign. After a brief conference with Chiang Kai-shek at Paoting, Chang announced his resignation on March 10, 1933, and handed over his army, planes and materiel to Chiang.[12] The courage and patriotism shown by Chang in laying down his power was so unprecedented in the warlord games of modern China that he drew praise from the press throughout China. In his farewell message to his troops, Chang said:

> We came into China proper to effect national unification, but the result is that we are now homeless. Our sacrifice is great, but it is worthwhile. After my departure, you must absolutely obey the order of Mr. Chiang [Kai-shek] and unanimously support the Government. It should be borne in mind that Mr. Chiang in allowing me to resign has shown special concern for me; unless I have a long period of recuperation, my health will never recover. After I have left, whenever you think of me, you should remember our common responsibility and hope which is to dedicate ourselves to the service of the country, to bring about the revival of our nation, and then to recover our lost territory so as to attain our goal of returning to our homeland. This time I am going abroad for the purpose of reforming myself, so that I shall be more worthy to lead you when I return. On your parts, you should also do your best to have improved yourselves before you see me again. Brothers! Do your best! Farewell![13]

After staying in Shanghai for about a month, during which the Young Marshal's narcotic habit was cured by Dr. Miller of the Seventh Day Adventists, the Young Marshal, accompanied by his Australian adviser and mentor, William W. Donald, sailed aboard an Italian steamer for Europe in the middle of April. Chang's eight-month tour in Europe turned out to be a successful one; he met many important personages, learned much of Western society and government, and immensely enjoyed the sightseeing. But what impressed the Young Marshal most was the resurgence of Germany and Italy. He became fully convinced that what had made Germany and Italy quickly revive might be the best remedy for China too. In a letter to a friend in China, the Young Marshal wrote that "the rejuvenation of Italy and Germany is due chiefly to their people's wholehearted support of their leaders, who, therefore, have sufficient strength to overcome the obstacles on the way to national salvation. . . . If our people wish to work for national salvation, they must have implicit faith in their leader and support him."[14]

What the Young Marshal urged in the above letter to his friend occurred in China. In late 1933, leaders of the famed 19th Route Army in the Shanghai battle with Japan revolted in Fukien and established the Fukien People's Revolutionary Government. Urged by Chiang Kai-shek and the Tungpei Army leaders to return immediately, the Young Marshal cut short his European tour and returned to China. Arriving in Shanghai on January 9, 1934, Chang immediately put himself at Chiang Kai-shek's service. [15]

Not only was the Young Marshal still a force to be reckoned with but his new support of the national leader pleased Chiang Kai-shek immensely. The latter immediately entrusted him with the mission of suppressing the Communists in the O-Yü-Wan (Hupeh-Honan-Anhwei) Soviet area. According to his own account, Chang, not enthusiastic about being involved in civil war, accepted the appointment as Deputy Commander-in-Chief of the Bandit-Suppressing Headquarters with some reluctance. [16] Setting up his headquarters at Wuhan, the second largest urban center of China, Chang presented himself as a new man; for a man of only 33, he had enormous vitality both physically and mentally and he was refreshed from his European tour. Impressed with the Fascist doctrine, the Young Marshal now championed the cause of Fascism and Chiang Kai-shek's dictatorship. Chang tried to build up Chiang as the leader of China in the image of Hitler and Mussolini, a movement that had already begun during Chang's absence. [17]

To emulate the <u>Li-chih she</u> (Moral Endeavor Corps) of Chiang Kai-shek, [18] Chang organized a <u>Szu-wei hsüeh-hui</u> (The Learning Society for Promoting Four Virtues) with Chang as chairman and Chiang Kai-shek as honorary chairman. The four virtues are <u>li</u> (propriety), <u>i</u> (righteousness), <u>lien</u> (honesty), <u>ch'ih</u> (humility), a program resonant with that of Chiang's New Life Movement (Hsin shenghuo yün-tung).

Despite success in liquidating the remnants of the Communist base in the O-Yü-Wan area, Chang began to doubt the wisdom of civil war for whatever reason while leaving Japan's aggression unchecked. [19] The Japanese steadily stepped up their aggression in North China in early 1935 by openly instigating revolt in Inner Mongolia and by manufacturing one incident after another that served as excuses for further pressure on the Chinese authorities in the Peking-Tientsin area. In his July 6 letter to General Umetsu, commander of Japanese troops stationed in North China, Ho Ying-ch'in, representing the Nanking government at Peking, was compelled to accept a series of unreasonable demands which had been erroneously known as the Ho-Umetsu Agreement.[20]

Among other concessions, the Nanking government, then led by Wang Ching-wei and Chiang Kai-shek,[21] agreed that Governor Yü Hsüeh-chung of Hopei Province and Yü's 51st Army must retire from North China and all anti-Japanese agencies and propaganda would be prohibited in North China. As the 51st Army was the Tungpei troops and Yü was Chang Hsüeh-liang's chief lieutenant, Chang took as his personal humiliation these concessions to Japan. In a conversation with his friend, Chang said, "My compatriots previously blamed me for not offering resistance to Japan; now I hope that the leader, Chiang Kai-shek, will change my appointment, not letting me fight the Communists but the Japanese, for I feel that to die in fighting the Communists is not as worthy as to die in fighting the Japanese."[22]

In contrast to the increasing aggression of Japan and her determination to divorce North China from the jurisdiction of Nanking was the sharp decline in the Chinese Communist movement. As long ago as 1933, the CCP work in the "white" areas had collapsed and most of its clandestine organizations were broken.[23] Everywhere the Communists were in retreat; not even one Soviet area was able to withstand the Nationalists' onslaught; and the Communist forces were either in hiding as in the case of Kiangsi after the "Long March" or driven from their bases.[24] To the great majority of Chinese living in 1935 and 1936 the Red Army was almost nonexistent, for it did not occupy even a single large city but rather took shelter behind the Great Snow Mountains (Ta-hsüeh shan) in Hsikang or in the caves of the hostile northern Shensi, as though the Communists were cut off from civilization. Yet by no means were the Communists disheartened; they were as dedicated and resolute as ever so far as their long-term goal of Communism was concerned, but their immediate objectives were their own survival and national salvation from Japan's aggression. This objective of resistance to Japan's aggression coincided not only with the goal of Chang Hsüeh-liang but with that of the Chinese people as well, particularly the intellectuals among the youth.

8

The Student Response

The consummation of the Ho-Umetsu negotiations in early July set the stage for removal from Hopeh province of all military and political persons and groups unfriendly to Japan and therefore ushered in a new era of Japanese control in North China. Japan's all-out "imperial" aggressive policy which was beginning to take shape in early 1933 had definitely manifested itself in the spring of 1935 when Japan launched the "self-government" movement of five provinces (Suiyuan, Chahar, Hopeh, Shantung, and Honan) in North China. After much solicitation for a puppet leader among the old and new Chinese warlords, from Wu P'ei-fu and Sun Ch'uan-fang to Yen Hsi-shan, the Japanese Army in North China, with the consent of the Kwantung Army in Manchuria, eventually settled on General Sung Che-yüan; he had a hero image gained at the battle of Hsi-feng-kou where his 29th Army slaughtered about 3,000 Japanese soldiers with Chinese big swords, and had just been relieved of the governorship of Chahar under the Japanese pressure. [25]

No sooner had Sung Che-yüan and his 29th Army taken over in late September the control of Peking and the Tientsin area than Major General Doihara Kenji, chief of the Kwantung Army's Special Service Section, and known as "the Lawrence of China," set out to engineer a series of incidents, particularly the "Hsiang-ho incident," behind the scenes and to confront Sung Che-yüan with open demands for immediate proclamation of self-government. Evidently the strong measures taken by the Japanese military had the full support of the Japanese government, for on October 28, 1935, the Japanese Foreign Minister Hirota announced the three principles of China policy: (1) thorough suppression of anti-Japanese thoughts and activities in China; (2) conclusion of a Sino-Japanese anti-Communist military pact; and (3) achievement of "economic cooperation" between Japan, Manchoukuo, and China, with a special position provided for North China. [26]

The open manifestation of Japan's aggressive policy hastened the development of the self-government movement on the one hand and, on the other, aroused a new surge of Chinese patriotism which had gained momentum since the Mukden Incident. The crowning success of Doihara's adventure was the separation of twenty-two counties in East Hopeh from Chinese jurisdiction by inaugurating the "East Hopeh anti-Communist and self-government council" with the notorious

Yin Ju-keng as chairman on November 24, 1935. Doihara also made headway toward establishing a "Mongolian military government" to be headed by Teh Wang, a design to sever Inner Mongolia from China.[27]

The startling advance of Japan in North China alarmed intellectual leaders and students alike in Tientsin and Peking. A strong protest was lodged by 2,600 members of the faculty and staff of colleges and high schools led by Chiang Meng-lin, Hu Shih, Mei I-ch'i, Yüan T'ung-li and others. The statement reads in part:

> Recently some people spuriously claiming to represent the people's opinion have instigated the so-called North China self-government movement so as to realize their design of treason. We are strongly opposed to it and, at the same time, firmly believe that all the people in North China unanimously oppose the movement. With all the power at our disposal, we will petition to the central government and local authorities to suppress this movement without delay so that our territory and sovereignty will be protected. We urge all our brethren to rise together to save our country from destruction.[28]

Sandwiched between the Japanese demands and the pressure of Chinese public opinion, the Nanking government (now wholly under the control of Chiang Kai-shek after Wang Ching-wei had been wounded by an assassin's bullets at the Fifth National Congress of the KMT), far from being prepared for war, tried to avoid military confrontation with Japan. Amidst the great crisis over North China, the KMT Fifth Congress convened at Nanking in early November 1935 and made no drastic changes of policy toward Japan which, since the Shanghai Incident in early 1932, had been characterized by the slogans, "only after internal security is accomplished, resistance against external aggression is possible," or briefly, "internal pacification before resistance against external aggression" (a slogan Chiang kept alive until the Sian Incident). However, the Nanking government indeed tried to apply a dual policy by which negotiation and resistance were to be used simultaneously as a means to slow down Japanese aggression. At the Congress, Chiang Kai-shek spelled out his well-publicized policy toward Japan for the next year and a half until the Lukouchiao Incident on July 7, 1937, when China decided to go to war with Japan: "We would never abandon our efforts for peace until the hope for peace is completely gone; nor would we lightly talk about sacrifice until sacrifice becomes our last resort."[29]

Under the circumstances, Sung Che-yüan and his 29th Army became the ideal power group to serve as caretaker of the Peking-Tientsin area. Not quite satisfied with the choice of Sung by the Nanking government, Doihara and the Japanese military leaders in North China saw a good chance to win him over to their side, basing their judgment on Sung's warlord and anti-Chiang background. But the establishment of the Hopeh-Chahar Political Council with Sung Che-yüan as chairman touched off the greatest student patriotic movement since the May Fourth movement in 1919.

The long dormant student movement was suddenly revived at Peking on November 18, 1935,[30] when delegates from various schools met to announce the establishment of the student union. At its meeting on December 3, 1935, it was resolved that a demonstration be staged on December 9. At dawn on December 9, students from Chung-kuo and Tungpei universities and a few high schools rushed out of their school gates in spite of blockades by the police. Outside the city, 5,000 students from Ch'ing-hua and Yenching universities and some high schools reached the west gate of the city at 9:30 a.m., only to find that the gate was shut. For the rest of the day they tried to get into the city by a detour through other gates without success. However, inside the city, the student crowd mounted to more than 5,000. The students bore signs with incendiary slogans such as "Down with Japanese imperialism," "Support the 29th Army in resisting Japan," "Oppose self-government in North China," and "Protect the territorial and administrative integrity of our Country."[31]

The demonstrators of December 9 aimed at presenting a petition to Ho Ying-ch'in. As Acting Chairman of the Peking Sub-Council of the Military Affairs Council, of which Chiang Kai-shek was the Chairman, Ho was the highest authority representing the Central Government in North China. Ever since his submission to the Japanese demands as embodied in the so-called Ho-Umetsu agreement, Ho had been labeled as pro-Japanese and had been the target of the student attack. When the demonstrators thronged in front of the Chung-nan-hai ("Central and South Sea" park), where Ho had his office, they were refused an audience. Later in the afternoon, they marched toward the Japanese legation, in front of which they were blocked by the Chinese police who turned water hoses on them, driving the students to flee. The police also beat the students with their clubs and arrested those who failed to escape.

Despite the fact that high-handed measures to suppress the student movement were used by Sung Che-yüan in order to comply with Japanese demands, the students were not to be intimidated, for the next day most students in universities and high schools throughout the city were on strike, demanding the release of those who had been arrested. Torn between sympathy for the students' demonstration of patriotism and the necessity to enforce discipline, presidents of six universities on December 13 issued a joint statement urging the students to return to their classes; however, they were met with a blatant refusal when the students staged a huge demonstration three days later. [32]

On the morning of December 16, students from nearly all high schools and universities in Peking succeeded in evading the police and the 29th Army soldiers armed with their renowned big-swords; they beat their way toward T'ien-chiao (Heavenly Bridge) at the south end of the city, half-running in their tight formation like troops and yelling patriotic slogans along the way. By 11 a. m. the crowd had grown to about 30,000 at T'ien-chiao where a rally was held. Then a demonstration parade ensued. The planned procession was to pass through the foreign legations area right inside Cheng-yang-men, (popularly known as Ch'ien-men or front gate), the south gate of the inner city. Reaching Cheng-yang-men, the procession was halted by the troops of the 29th Army in an attempt to prevent the students from clashing with the Japanese inside the legation. The students made a detour toward Hsuan-wu-men further west but found it closed too. In a severe northwest wind, the students stood outside the gate until 9 o'clock at night when they were charged and dispersed by the troops. However, not many students were injured, for the soldiers, apparently in sympathy with the students' cause, were unwilling to harass them. [33]

One of the professed goals of the December 16 demonstration was to disrupt the inauguration of the Hopeh-Chahar Political Council; this goal was accomplished, for the inaugural day was postponed until December 18. The real significance of this action is that it gave further impetus to the student movement which had been kindled by the December 9 demonstration. On the inaugural day of the Hopeh-Chahar Political Council, a student rally of 5,000 held at Nanking staged a demonstration and presented a petition to the Executive Yüan. It was followed by another demonstration held by a greater crowd the next day, and the students declared a strike a week later to dramatize their patriotic cause. [34]

Demonstrations and strikes by students soon spread to most major cities in the country--Tientsin, Hankow, Hangchow, Canton, and Shanghai. The Shanghai students, with the Futan University at the lead, answered the call of the Peking students as early as December 12, when they issued two circular telegrams giving their full support. At a student rally on December 19, seven demands were adopted and immediately presented to the mayor of Shanghai, Wu Tieh-ch'eng. Later, 2,000 students set out to Nanking to petition the National Government directly to take a strong stand against Japanese aggression in North China. [35]

Back in Peking, more than 500 students, some from Tientsin, were organized into a propaganda team in the countryside. The two-week propaganda trip in January 1936 took the students beyond Kuan county, where they were denied entry into the city of Kuan for three days. Despite its minimum impact on the peasants, the propaganda team led to the formation of the Chinese National Liberation Vanguard, [36] an organization definitely having Communist overtones.

Communist influence in the December student demonstration was substantial. Probably more than two or three Communists were present at the Peking demonstration in December 1935, contrary to what Helen Snow believes. [37] There were many more, like Ning Ku-shih (alias Hsiang Nai-kuang) and Ma Shao-chou, who were students of Tungpei (Northeastern) University. Furthermore, the most militant students did not come from Yenching University but from Tungpei University as borne out by the fact that Wang Yü-chang, a political science major at Tungpei University, became the head of the Chinese National Liberation Vanguard. [38]

The student movement took a new turn after the return of the propaganda team from the countryside. The Peking authorities, apparently urged by the Nanking government, took some stern measures against the students. As a result, many student leaders who took part in the December 1935 demonstrations or in the January 1936 propaganda tour were arrested. But the repression was not so great as is generally believed, for all the arrested students from Tungpei University and the Chung-shan Middle School were released after a few weeks' imprisonment through the intercession of the Young Marshal. [39] On the other hand, the Peking student movement suffered from suppression and internal conflict between the rightist and leftist students and it lost its leadership to Shanghai.

13

A Nation in Awakening

In early 1936 the student movement quickly spread to many
parts of the country and a general national awakening was kindled
by the December student demonstration in Peking. The nation's
awakening to the exigencies of Japanese aggression was slow but
real. The impact on two powerful groups of Chinese society was
discernible and important: the intellectual and militarist groups,
both of which were as responsible for having caused much domestic
confusion as they were indispensable for uniting the nation to face
a common foe.

The surge of national movement in early 1936 coincided with
the transfer of the center of the student movement from Peking to
Shanghai, where the national salvation movement led by some prominent members of the KMT Left Wing like Mesdames Sun Yat-sen
and Liao Chung-k'ai had remained viable. In the meantime the slow
recovery of the leftist writers' activity at Shanghai certainly served
as a catalyst for this upsurge. It was at Shanghai that the national
student association was born; its initial meeting was held on March 28
and its formal inauguration took place on May 29. Two days later,
in the same city, the All-China Federation of National Salvation was
established. [40]

The literary activities at Shanghai, and in many other large
cities of China, centered around the theme of "national defense literature," a slogan consonant with the "united front" spelled out by
the CCP since August 1, 1935. [41] The new literature was initiated
by the Communist writers, some of whom had recently made their
way back to Shanghai from northern Shensi. In spite of Lu Hsun's
suspicion of the new CCP line--a shift from proletarian literature
to "national defense literature"--it won the day, [42] for writers of
various political convictions did rally to the banner of the China
Writers' Association which was organized on June 7, 1936. The
essence and appeal of the "united front" against Japan were effectively and clearly spelled out in the manifesto of the Writers' Association:

> We are literary men and hence we are of the opinion
> that all our literary colleagues of the country should
> unite together for national salvation against Japan with-
> out making any distinction between the old and new

schools. . . . But, regardless of these differences, they
are all Chinese and they are all unwilling to be slaves in
a destroyed nation. . . . In literature, we do not force
an artificial unity, but in national salvation against Japan,
we should be united together so as to make our action
more powerful. [43]

The symbiosis that existed in the literary movement was even
more so in the whole national salvation as revealed in the five-point
proposals embodied in the manifesto of the All-China Federation of
National Salvation: (1) immediate cessation of civil war; (2) release
of all political prisoners; (3) through the National Salvation Front,
delegations from all parties and groups meet to negotiate and formulate a joint anti-enemy program and to establish a coalition government; (4) the National Salvation Front assist in formulating the joint
program and guarantee its fulfillment; and (5) the National Salvation
Front use sanctions against any party or group that violates the joint
program. [44]

The cessation of civil war mentioned in the manifesto was
addressed not only to the fighting between the Nationalists and the
Communists in the northwest but also to the civil war just erupting
between the Central Government and Liang-Kuang (Kwangtung and
Kwangsi) in the south.

Kwangtung had been the base of opposition to the Nanking government since the return of Hu Han-min from Nanking after his
eight and a half months' house arrest by Chiang Kai-shek in 1931. [45]
Through his organ, the San-min chu-i yüeh-k'an, Hu, without ceasing
from 1933 until his death in May 1936, expounded his political views
and launched his most vociferous attack on the Nanking government,
particularly its leaders Chiang Kai-shek and Wang Ching-wei. With
his able pen, Hu almost single-handedly shaped much of the opposition opinion against Nanking. True to his claim, Hu opined that
"China's only hope lies in her resistance to Japan," a view he had
held since the Mukden Incident in 1931.

Immediately following the December 1935 demonstrations at
Peking, Hu and his journal gave their full support to the students
as did the authorities of the Liang-Kuang. On the eve of the latter's
revolt against Nanking, Li Tsung-jen, in the May 1936 issue of the
San-min chu-i yüeh-k'an, published his article under the title, "War

of Resistance Is the Only Way," in which he praised the stand taken by the students and the All-China Federation of National Salvation.

Li's open support of the students, coupled with the pronounced goal of fighting against Japan, made the rebels of Liang-Kuang more acceptable to the students than the Nanking leaders. Not without some misgivings about their motives however, the National Student Association in its inaugural declaration on May 30, 1936, endorsed the rebels instead of the Nanking leaders by demanding that the Nanking government should immediately end its military operation against the army of the south and allow the latter to march northward to fight the Japanese. Further, the declaration gave strong support to the request of Li Tsung-jen, Feng Yü-hsiang, Chang Hsüeh-liang and others to suspend the campaigns against the Communists.[46]

With civil war looming ahead, the All-China Federation of National Salvation made its utmost effort to stop the civil war on the one hand and, on the other, to unite the nation to cope with Japan. It adopted a "Preliminary Platform for War of Resistance against Japan and for National Salvation." In line with this platform, four leaders of the Federation issued an open letter on July 15, 1936, setting forth the basic conditions and minimum demands for a "united front." They openly challenged Chiang Kai-shek's policy of achieving "internal pacification before resistance against foreign aggression" but praised the leaders of Liang-Kuang in the south and General Sung Che-yüan in the north. They asked Chiang to do three things: (a) cease hostilities against the southwest; (b) conclude an armistice with the Red Army for the purpose of joint resistance to Japan; and (c) freely carry on anti-Japanese propaganda for the national salvation movement.[47]

Emphatically, the four leaders of the Federation viewed the inclusion of the Chinese Communists in the "united front" as indispensable as that of the KMT. They went even further to say that there can be no grounds for rejecting "even traitors when they realize the necessity of taking part in the movement to save the country and resist Japan.[48]

This open letter was immediately answered by Chairman Mao Tse-tung. He welcomed the conditions and demands set forth by the leaders of the National Salvation Front and was glad to comply with them for the purpose of forming the "united front":

We are in agreement with your manifesto, program and
demands and earnestly desire to cooperate with you and
all other parties and groups, either as organizations or
as individuals. . . . We, not only in word but in deed,
sincerely desire unity for the purpose of fighting for the
existence of our country. . . . We have no interest
whatever in continuing a civil war in which Chinese fight
against Chinese. We shall never attack the troops of
the central government or any other armed forces unless
they attack us or hinder the Chinese troops from fighting
Japan. [49]

In conclusion Mao wrote, "all representatives who desire to
conduct negotiations with us are requested to come to the Soviet
districts where their safety will be guaranteed. If our safety is
guaranteed, we, in turn, agree to send our representatives to other
sections of the country to set up negotiations."[50]

II. THE UNITED FRONT IN THE NORTHWEST

True to its claim, the CCP policy of opposing Japanese aggression had been of long standing. As early as April 12, 1932, the Chinese Central Soviet Government in Kiangsi formally declared war on Japan. In subsequent years the CCP continuously poured out statements demanding that the Red Army be allowed to march north ward to fight the enemy. During the Fukien Incident the CCP and the 19th Route Army reached and signed an agreement under the title "Anti-Japan and Anti-Chiang Preliminary Agreement."[1] On the occasion of dispatching the Northward Anti-Japanese Vanguards shortly before the Long March, the CCP also issued a declaration on the "Northward Anti-Japanese Movement of the Chinese Red Army."[2]

The CCP "United Front" Strategy

Equally cogent is the CCP claim that they had long advocated the "united front." The earliest evidence was a manifesto jointly issued by the Central Soviet government and the Red Army on January 10, 1933, laying down some conditions for signing an agreement with any armed units for opposing Japanese aggression. Later, they had circulated the so-called "five great programs for war against Japan" and "six programs for military resistance to Japan."[3] So far the CCP attempt at forming an alliance had been a "united front from below," chiefly confined to the military sphere. The real turning point came with the August 1, 1935 Manifesto which formally introduced a "united front" policy on a national scale, but which was designed and proclaimed in Moscow without the knowledge of the CCP leaders then in China.

The gist of the Manifesto is summarized here:

1. Chinese affairs should be solved by the Chinese. However criminal and treacherous the KMT and the Blue-Shirt Club have been, Japan has absolutely no right to meddle with them.

2. All parties and groups and all walks of life should put aside their divergent political views and inter-

18

ests, suspend the civil war, and unite themselves in the struggle against Japan and for salvation of the nation.

3. An anti-Japanese allied army will be organized.

4. A national defense government composed of all parties, groups, and professions will be established to carry out the responsibility of resisting Japan and saving the country by implementing the following measures:
    a) Resist Japan and save the country by the recovery of lost territory.
    b) Relieve famine, prevent floods in order to stabilize people's livelihood.
    c) Confiscate all the properties of the Japanese in China in order to finance the war with Japan.
    d) Confiscate all the properties, grains and land of the Chinese traitors to be handed over to the poor brethren and anti-Japanese fighters for their use.
    e) Abolish onerous taxes and fees, regulate currency and finance, and develop industry, agriculture, and commerce.
    f) Increase salaries and wages and ameliorate the life of workers, peasants, soldiers and officers, and students and teachers.
    g) Practice democracy, liberty and free all political prisoners.
    h) Promote free education and provide jobs for unemployed youth.
    i) Carry out the policy of equality for all nationalities in China and protect the freedom of life, property, residence, and the business of overseas Chinese in China and in foreign countries.
    j) Unite with all antiimperialist masses (toiling masses inside Japan and peoples of Korea and Taiwan) as our allies and unite with all nations who are sympathetic to the Chinese liberation movement, and establish friendship with all those nations which maintain goodwill and neutrality in the anti-Japanese war of Chinese people's liberation. [4]

The full text of the August 1 Manifesto, and the background in which it was written were not known to Mao Tse-tung and his CCP Central until the arrival of Chang Hao, the CCP delegate to the Comintern, in November 1935 and not known by Chang Kuo-t'ao and his CCP Central, who had remained in Hsikang, until January 1936.[5] On the basis of the August 1 Manifesto, the CCP at its Politburo meeting held at Wayaopao, North Shensi, in December 1935 adopted the "Resolution on the Current Political Situation and the Task of the Party," which in the main served as the official party line from that time onward. This resolution, while maintaining intact the ten programs of the August 1 Manifesto just quoted above, differed from it on a few crucial points.[6]

First, the united front enunciated in the December 1935 resolution was to be formed both "from below" and "from above," as all those, including the national bourgeoisie, who were opposed to the Japanese imperialists, were included regardless of individual origin, parties, groups, and classes. However, it singled out Chiang Kaishek as traitor along with the Japanese imperialists to be opposed.

In the second place, the peasant policy of the resolution showed a marked departure from the past radical policy of the "poor peasant line" prevalent throughout the Kiangsi Soviet period. Under the new peasant policy, "rich peasants in the Soviet territory would enjoy the same rights as the poor peasants in the distribution of land." Although landlords as a class were automatically included in the united front and landlords were specifically given full political rights, yet no mention was made concerning the land the landlords owned, nor their right to own land. Ironically, the resolution repeatedly stressed the importance of the solution of the land problem as well as the fundamental principle of linking the land revolution and the national revolution together.

In the third place, not only was the CCP determined to retain the Soviet--a point which was not touched upon in the August 1 Manifesto--but it also wanted the Soviet to be expanded so as to serve as the base of resistance against Japan and to vie for the CCP leadership in the people's united front. But the name of the "workers' and peasants' Soviet republic" was slightly changed by substituting the word "people's" for "workers' and peasants'" in order to include the whole Chinese people.

Under the slogan of resistance against Japan and promotion of the "united front," in spite of the fact that a more important reason may have been the solution to the food shortage, the main force of the Red Army crossed the Yellow River in western Shansi on February 20, 1936. In connection with the February eastern expedition, the CCP issued a circular telegram entitled "Convocation of a National Congress for War of Resistance against Japan and National Salvation," calling for immediately convening the national congress, formally establishing a national defense government, and joining all forces in fighting Japan.[7]

Shansi was the home and power base of the warlord, Yen Hsi-shan. This sophisticated warlord made some hasty preparations to fend off the enemy, appealed to Nanking for more troops to help defend his territory, and introduced some social measures to fight Communism. Yen adopted the "Regulation for Common Land-Ownership in Villages," "Follies of Communists and the Critique of Communism," and "Distribution of Land According to Labor and Assurance of Products." He also organized the people into a "Group for Justice" and a "Group for Protection against Communists."[8] Unfortunately for Yen, all these improvisatory measures were either too late to bring about the expected effect or too radical to be implemented; he failed to stop the Communists.

Not until after the Red Army had invaded forty-eight counties of Shansi and eight divisions of the Central Army of Chiang Kai-shek had arrived on the scene, did the Red Army make a successful withdrawal to the west of the Yellow River, taking with them the provisions they had seized in Shansi.[9] But upon crossing back to Shensi, the CCP issued a passionate declaration under the title "Armistice and Negotiation for a Joint Resistance Against Japan" on May 5, 1936. Unlike previous declarations, this declaration was addressed to the Nanking national government, all parties, groups, and armed forces of the whole nation, and all Chinese who were unwilling to become slaves. It is important to note that the declaration revealed a fundamental shift in CCP strategy. Whereas in the December 25, 1935 Resolution, Chiang Kai-shek was considered the enemy of the Chinese people and equated with the Japanese imperialists, the May 5, 1936 declaration sounded like a direct appeal to Chiang himself, as shown in its central passage:[10]

The Soviet central government and the Red Army, after
repeated deliberations, recognize that in the face of national exigency, no matter who is victorious in the decisive battle, the result will be the loss of strength in
Chinese national defense, a result which will only please
the Japanese imperialists. . . . In order to urge Chiang
Kai-shek and his patriotic military subordinates to awake
at last, we, though having won many victories in Shansi,
have still withdrawn the People's Anti-Japanese Vanguards to the west bank of the Yellow River. This move
was intended to show to the Nanking government . . .
and the whole people of China our sincerity. . . . We
solemnly urge the leaders of the Nanking government to
consider our views: at the critical turning point of national extinction, it is only reasonable that we should
suddenly repent and let the spirit of unity in fighting
foreign aggression prevail over "the fighting between
brothers outside the wall." In the country as a whole,
we must first stop fighting in the Shensi, Kansu, and
Shansi area and on both sides must send representatives to discuss and formulate concrete methods for
national salvation. This will be the fortune not only
of your gentlemen but also of our country and people.
Should you continuously refuse to repent your role as
Chinese traitors, then your days and rule will certainly
be numbered as you will be cursed by the people of the
whole country.

Apart from public statements like the May 5, 1936 Declaration
appealing to Chiang Kai-shek and the Nanking government to terminate civil war, the CCP also sent its representatives to approach
the KMT leaders personally. Chiang himself revealed that the CCP
representative made the first contact with the KMT at Hong Kong in
the fall of 1935. About the time when the CCP issued its May declaration, negotiations between the KMT and the CCP virtually had
started between Ch'en Li-fu, Chiang's protégé in charge of party
affairs, and P'an Han-nien, the CCP negotiator with the 19th Route
Army during the Fukien Incident. The KMT-CCP negotiations then
taking place at Shanghai and Nanking may not have led to a successful conclusion because the KMT put forward some exorbitant demands:
(1) believe in the San-min chu-i [Three principles of the people];
(2) obey the command of Generalissimo Chiang; (3) abolish the Red

22

Army which will be reorganized into the national army; and (4) abolish the Soviet which will be changed into a local government.[11] On the other hand, however, the CCP's incessant propaganda and passionate overtures gradually took effect on the Tungpei Army, particularly its commander the Young Marshal who was responsible for terminating the Red Army in the northwest.

The New Base for the Young Marshal

Even before the Communists ended their Long March and settled in North Shensi in late October 1935, Chiang Kai-shek had transferred the Young Marshal and his Manchurian army to Shensi, then still the base of the warlord Yang Hu-ch'eng (1883-1949). Yang, a bandit in origin, had a long revolutionary career, being a general of the 2nd Kuominchun (People's Army) commanded by Hu Ching-i in the early 1920s. Yang gained fame in the defense of the city of Sian under an eight-month seige by another warlord Liu Chen-huan in 1926. Later Yang curried the favor of Chiang Kai-shek, especially in the latter's contest with Feng Yü-hsiang in 1930, and thus succeeded in maintaining his semiindependent status while paying Chiang his allegiance.[12]

Earlier in 1927, when Yang's army was nominally under Feng Yü-hsiang's command, it had undergone internal transformation from a typical, feudal force into a more progressive, revolutionary army under the influence of political workers sent by the Wuhan Left regime. One noticeable result was the penetration of the Communists into his army. Despite the fact that Yang followed Feng Yü-hsiang in purging the Communist elements from his army, some Communists managed to survive until 1936, even holding important posts.[13] Further, Yang, in spite of his lack of education, was not at all resistant to revolutionary ideas, as long as they did not limit his power.

With the arrival of the Long Marchers in North Shensi, Chiang Kai-shek immediately turned his attention to Sian, the center of the northwest whose political and military structures were to be reorganized and geared to the needs of punitive war against the Reds. Whatever the change, it was certainly at the expense of Yang's power and interest. Yang conceded the governorship of Shensi to Shao Li-tzu, a long-time friend of Chiang Kai-shek; in the military realm he retained his post as Pacification Commissioner of Shensi but his prestige and power were overshadowed by the newly created North-western Headquarters of Bandit Suppression (NHBS).

While Chang Hsüeh-liang was vacillating in accepting the appointment as Vice Commander-in-Chief of the NHBS, Yang showed some goodwill toward Chang by dispatching a message of welcome to him. [14] Moreover, Chang also saw the opportunity of using the northwest as his base to regroup his scattered forces in North China and to give his leadership to his fellow men from Manchuria. In the reshuffling of the Shensi and Kansu provincial governments, Chang's man, General Yü Hsüeh-chung, was made governor of Kansu. Indeed, before long, Chang had made Sian the haven of those exiled from Tungpei (Northeast or Manchuria).

Since the Tungpei Army was transferred to the northwest, not only had the families and relatives of the troops followed and moved to Shensi, but many Tungpei people from other parts of China, mainly from North China, had also come to seek new opportunities in jobs or business. The Young Marshal had no choice but to try to help these people resettle in the northwest. He therefore undertook a gigantic construction program; villages for Tungpei refugees, hospitals, schools, and factories were built by funds out of his own pocket. He also moved the engineering school of the Tungpei University with a view to transferring the whole university to Sian. [15]

Naturally the Young Marshal found his situation in Sian quite different from that at Hankow in 1934-1935, during which period he was surrounded by Chiang Kai-shek's men, his own force was scattered, he had no political base, and most of all, he lacked mass following. Now in the northwest, his situation had improved greatly, for the Tungpei people began to play a dominant role in many phases of life in the two provinces of Kansu and Shensi. As for Chang himself, he was still only a man in his midthirties with tremendous energy and imagination; he had his responsibilities, difficulties, and burdens, but he also drew consolation from helping people, from leading his troops and the Tungpei people, and from his destiny and ambition to recover his homeland and to become great. But his great mission and ambition had to be put off for the sake of immediate duty--to destroy the Reds.

Chang had never been interested in fighting the Communists. During the Hopei crisis in June 1935 when Yü Hsüeh-chung, governor of Hopei who was also the commander of the 51st Army of Tungpei, was forced to quit Hopei by the Japanese demand, Chang was greatly aroused and said: "My compatriots previously blamed me for not offering resistance to Japan; now I hope that the leader, Chiang Kai-shek, will change my appointment, not letting me fight the Communists but the Japanese, for I feel that to die in fighting the Communists is not as worthy as to die in fighting the Japanese."[16] As long ago as in his Hankow period, the Young Marshal recommended to the Central Government that the policy of "internal pacification before resistance to external aggression" should be changed. He was convinced that "the success of German and Italian Fascism did not lie so much in their ideology as in their expansive policy which restored national rights and gained glory for the people; in so doing, their leaders won strong support from the people. Conversely, the Chinese government recovered territory inch by inch in a civil war, while it lost its territory to the foreign aggressors 'province by province'; certainly it would lose the support of the people; and as a result the government and the people must perish together."[17]

Disenchanted with the policy of suppressing the Communists as he had been, the Young Marshal was optimistic and gladly assumed his post as acting Commander-in-Chief of the NHBS in the hopes that the few thousand remnants of Communists in the area would be easily liquidated in a short time and that the consolidation of the new base for the war of resistance against Japan could be started soon.[18] To his dismay, the first encounter between the Tungpei Army and the Red Army came as a surprise. In late October 1935 when the 67th Army commanded by Wang I-che marched toward North Shensi along the line from Fuhsien, Kanchuan to Yenan (then called Fushih), his two divisions were waylaid by the local Shensi Red Army at Loshan near Kanchuan. Commander Ho Li-chung of the 110th Division was killed, and more than three thousand soldiers and officers in the lower ranks were taken prisoners; among them was a regiment commander of the 107th Division named Kao Fu-yüan, who later turned out to be instrumental in linking the Tungpei Army with the CCP. Less than a month later, in mid-November, another Tungpei division, the 109th, commanded by Nu Yüan-feng, was routed by the Red Army at Chihlochen in western Shensi. Nu was captured and he as well as several regiment commanders later committed suicide.[19]

One might wonder what gave the spectacular victory to the Red Army? Though the Red Army was better trained in guerrilla war-

fare, suitable for the mountainous terrain of North Shensi, the Tungpei Army was much better equipped and the ranking officers of both
divisions in question were strongly dedicated to their goals. By virtue of the fact that all the high-ranking officers of the two divisions--
except one who was captured and another who escaped back to Sian--
gave up their lives, their high morale cannot be doubted. It was not
the fighting strength of the Red Army that overwhelmed the two divisions, but rather the propaganda that disarmed them. When the Red
Army propaganda team sang the song, "My Home is on the Sungari
in the Northeast," it had an instant nostalgic effect on these homesick men. The rank and file were even more moved by the slogans
of the Red Army, such as "Chinese must not fight Chinese!" and
"Unite with us and fight back to Manchuria!"[20] All those Tungpei
Army men captured in these two campaigns became the first members of the training school for captives.[21] It had been the policy of
the CCP that those captured KMT soldiers and low-ranking officers
were given the choice between remaining in the Red Army and returning to the KMT areas. Those who decided to leave were set
free with some pocket money. Understandably special efforts were
made to indoctrinate the Tungpei captives, particularly the regiment
commander, Kao Fu-yüan, who was received by Chairman Mao Tse-
tung and other CCP leaders. Upon their return, Kao and most of
those captured became willing propagandists of the CCP "united
front" line.

Even before the repatriation of the captives from the Soviet
area, the Young Marshal took the stunning defeat and the loss of
two divisions and one regiment with a heavy heart and began to toy
with the idea of seeking a "peaceful" solution as he wrote:

> First the 110th Division was annihilated and its command-
> er Ho Li-chung was killed. This was followed by the
> total defeat of the 109th Division and its commander Nu
> Yüan-feng died in refusing to surrender. These two
> division commanders were among the best in the Tung-
> pei Army. Twice terrible defeats have inflicted great
> pain on my heart; they further reinforced my belief that
> it was regrettable that outstanding generals had to sac-
> rifice their lives for the sake of civil war. At the
> same time I no longer disparage the fighting strength of
> the Communist bandits. Thus, the thought of using
> "peaceful" means to solve the Communist issue was
> kindled in my heart.[22] (Emphasis mine.)

26

Indeed the Tungpei Army was never again engaged in such a life and death struggle with the Red Army as in these two campaigns. One reason, of course, was that the Tungpei Army was wise enough not to be trapped again. Also there no longer seemed a need for such hard fighting, inasmuch as the CCP was determined to win over the Tungpei Army to the united front. In January 1936, the CCP organized the White Army Work Committee with Chou En-lai and Chang Hao (alias Lin Yü-ying) as secretary and deputy-secretary respectively, a group mainly devoted to penetration and propaganda work in the Tungpei and Hsipei Armies.[23] It was clear to the CCP leaders that the mere survival of the Communists in North Shensi, let alone victory in fighting Japan, hinged upon how successful they could be in winning over the Tungpei Army, the largest non-Chiang force in the northwest, a prize the CCP was determined to win.

On January 25, 1936, the Red Army issued "An Open Letter to All the Officers and Soldiers of the Tungpei Army," in which it pointed out that "Chiang Kai-shek transferred the Tungpei Army to Kansu and Shensi with the intention that the two willing and resolute anti-Japanese armies, the Tungpei and Red Armies, would make great sacrifice and suffer colossal losses." It further pointed out that "Chiang sent his own stooges to spy on, supervise, or split the Tungpei Army from within. Therefore, the Tungpei Army have no other choice but resistance against Japan and opposition to Chiang. The workers' democratic government and the Red Army are willing to unite with the Tungpei Army and to organize the national defense government and the allied army in order to fight the Japanese jointly."[24]

Riding the tide of the national movement generated by the December 1935 student demonstrations, the CCP appeal to the Tungpei Army to end civil war and unite with the Red Army in order to resist Japan had a greater result than had been anticipated. Further, the Red Army moved into Shansi in February for the purpose of marching northward to face the Japanese aggressors, a duty which the Tungpei Army could not help feeling was its own. In fact, not only were most of the young officers of the Tungpei Army aroused and prepared to accept the "united front" doctrine, but even the Young Marshal himself was quite moved. Here he recalled the situation:

It was then that the Communists roared out the song of
ending civil war and resisting Japan together. This did
not merely win my heart, but it captured the minds of
the majority of the Tungpei Army, particularly the young
officers. As no progress had resulted from further campaigns against the Communists, I began to think myself
that my own policy had failed, and therefore I consulted
with my subordinates for their views. As a result, proposals for making contact with the CCP and Yang Hu-
ch'eng for cooperation, suspending the bandit-suppression
campaign, conserving our own strength, and uniting with
others in the resistance against Japan were advanced.[25]

The Young Marshal had many reasons to see the wisdom of
ending civil war which he had always abhorred. His view of the
Chinese Communists deserves some elaboration. While far from
being a scholar, the Young Marshal had learned a great deal from
his advisers and secretaries, many of whom were professors and
returned students from Japan and Western countries. In addition,
through the years of fighting the Communists, actually since 1926,
he had acquired some knowledge of Communism and had been familiar with the Chinese Communist issues. In his view, the surge of
Communism in China must be attributed to imperialist aggression.
It was the imperialist oppression of China that drove the Chinese
intellectual elite to Communism. For Chang knew this by his own
experience. Earlier in 1932, when two professors along with several students of the Tungpei University were arrested by the Central
Government on the charge of being Communists and were brought to
Nanking, the Young Marshal as president of the University intervened
and brought about their release.[26] As for the poor people who joined
the Communists, Chang blamed the imperialists. Imperialist aggression had reduced China to the status of a semicolony. China had
lost her tariff autonomy, and foreign goods were inundating the mar-
kets. That not only prevented her infant industry and commerce
from normal growth but even helped create widespread economic
depression and rural bankruptcy, a result that drove thousands of
people to the Communist ranks. Indeed, he was convinced that "if
the Communists are the greatest enemy of China, their origin is
still the imperialists."[27]

With his long view of the Chinese Communists as has been
described, Chang had no difficulty in convincing himself that the

CCP overture was sincere. He would not mind taking the initiative in approaching the Communists. Still in Hankow in 1934 he gave support to General Li Tu, an anti-Japanese hero, for his return to Manchuria where he would carry on partisan warfare. Chang assigned Ying Te-t'ien, his secretary, and Chao I, formerly a brigade commander, to accompany Li to return to Manchuria via the Soviet Union. In Manchuria they would have to make contact with the Communists who had been fighting a guerrilla war there. Although Li's group did not reach Manchuria but instead returned to China, the Young Marshal knew that Li had connections with the Communists. Now he asked Li to contact the Communists on his behalf. Li sent a certain Liu Ting, a Communist, to Sian.[28] Liu told Chang that the Communists wished to come to Sian to talk with Chang in person but were afraid for their safety. Finally Chang decided to go to Shanghai himself. Probably in late February 1936 the Young Marshal met Pan Han-nien in a Western restaurant in Shanghai. Nothing came out of the meeting, partly because of Chang's imposing posture as though he demanded nothing short of Communist surrender, and in part because of Pan's ambiguity in presenting the CCP position.[29] But there was no question that the CCP leaders at Paoan, North Shensi, realized that the Young Marshal was willing to negotiate with the CCP.

While the Young Marshal's personal attempt to reach some understanding with the CCP may have failed in late February and early March 1936, the CCP took the diplomatic offensive, so to speak, by releasing the Tungpei captives, including nearly all the officers. The impact of their return, though the full extent is still difficult to judge, must have been tremendous. What they had learned during their captivity probably had little to do with Communism or revolution. It is safe to say that they must have become well versed in the language of the "united front" which had gained popularity since the December 1935 student movement. This language could have been reduced to a simple formula such as the following: "Japan wants to terminate the existence of China and all Chinese will become slaves of the Japanese. No matter how deep and intolerable our hatred and enmity may have been, we Chinese must no longer fight each other, for we must be united to fight the enemy and to save our country. Those who are rich give their money; those who are powerful give their strength. Once we are united, not only shall we be able to drive the Japanese out of North China, but we shall recover our three lost northeastern provinces!" The plain truth as represented in this argument would have been sufficient to convince any Chinese soldier, had he not been denied the opportunity to listen to it. The effectiveness of this argument would have been magnified when presented to the homesick, disappointed, and alienated Tungpei officers and soldiers whose hope had been exactly the same as shown in the argument.

The first convert of the Tungpei high-ranking officers to the "united front" doctrine was no other person than Wang I-che, the defender of Mukden during the "September 18 Incident" of 1931 which led to the fall of the whole of Manchuria to Japan. As already noted, Wang's 67th Army, to which the bulk of the repatriated captives were returning, suffered a stunning defeat and colossal losses at the hands of the Red Army. It was not unnatural that Wang, more than any other Tungpei high-ranking officer, was willing to lend his ears to the accounts of the Soviet episodes given by his returned comrades-in-arms, notably his regiment commander Kao Fu-yüan.[30] Like Edgar Snow who visited the Soviet area a few months after the release of the Tungpei captives, Kao and other returned captives needed only to tell Wang what they actually had seen and heard. That the Communists desperately wanted to save themselves from destruction by the KMT suppression campaigns was beyond doubt, but that question seemed as irrelevant to Wang as it is to us today. The crucial fact that their immediate goals--to resist Japan--were identical and that their mutual need--to cease killing each other-- was real must have occupied the mind of Wang. Without delay he sent Kao to the Young Marshal to report the same to him.

Chang, of course, listened to Kao and other returned captives attentively, but being the head of the Tungpei Army, Chang in all his activities in the northwest was under close, constant watch by Chiang Kai-shek's men who were all over the northwest. There was another consideration on his part, i.e., to maintain the morale of his army still facing the Red Army at the front. Chang was extremely cautious and thus revealed no sign whatever that he was persuaded or influenced by Kao's and others' reports. On the contrary, as for those returned captives who talked vociferously or tended to spread rumors, Chang without hesitation punished them severely. It looked as if the Young Marshal had put the "united front" issue to rest for the time being. His overt negative response to the reports of the returned captives and his punishment of some of them were quite understandable under the circumstances. But all this had aroused much resentment among his young followers whose faith had been cherished by him.

Among Chang's young followers, two groups stood out as influential: the small civilian bureaucracy under Chang was dominated by the graduates from the Tungpei University who held most of the middle-ranking posts; in the military, nearly all officers except a few top-ranking generals were graduated from the Tungpei Chiang-wu T'ang. These like-minded young officers, most of them inclined to the left, some of them Communists, formed a coterie which exerted a great influence as the summer of 1936 wore on.[31]

This elite group was enlarged by the arrival of two Communists from Peking. Shortly after his arrival at Peking in February 1936, Liu Shao-ch'i sent Ma Shao-chou and Sung Li as student representatives from Peking to Sian. Their mission was to sound out the Young Marshal's attitude toward the "united front." Ma, though a graduate of the Tungpei University, thought that they really risked their lives when they approached the Young Marshal and asked him to support the "united front." To their surprise, Chang received them with great calm; not only was he undisturbed by the idea of the "united front," but he was even pleased with their appeal. At once they were asked to remain in Sian to work for him. Later, Ma was responsible for the establishment of the political training school, a haven of refugee students from North China. As this nucleus grew in strength, it took an organizational form called the "Society of Comrades for Resistance against Japan" (K'ang-Jih t'ung-chih hui). All its members were young and middle-ranking civilian and military officers, except one who was a division commander.[32] Their names as far as we know included Kao Ch'ung-min, Tsou Ta-p'eng, Ying Te-t'ien, Li Yu-wen, Tu Wei-kang, Kao Fu-yüan, Ch'en Hsü-tung, Chang Ch'ien-hua, Miao Chien-ch'iu, Ma Shao-chou, Sung Li, Chieh Ju-chuan, Liu Lan-po, Sun Ming-chiu, and Hsiang Nai-kuang. Although the group was non-Communist, Communist influence must have been very great. Besides Ma and Sung, who were Communists, there were other Communists in this group, namely, Li Yu-wen, Chang Ch'ien-hua, Chieh Ju-chuan, Liu Lan-po, and Hsiang Nai-kuang. An invisible hand to direct the policy of the "Society of Comrades for Resistance Against Japan" was the newly organized CCP Tungpei Army Work Committee of which Liu Lan-po was secretary, succeeded by Hsiang Nai-kuang later.[33]

The Young Marshal was not unaware of the existence of the Society; important organizations of such secret nature would never have been tolerated in a provincial and personal army. Probably the Young Marshal did not care who were Communists or non-Communists. One thing was clear--they were all young men from Manchuria; their way of life was common, as was their fate. Instead of discouraging its growth, Chang saw that the Society fit into the general scheme which he was forming.

By the middle of March 1936 the Young Marshal was able to make direct contact with the CCP. According to his own account, shortly after the lifting of the siege of Kanchuan by the Red Army on March 10th, a clear indication of showing goodwill toward the Tungpei Army, the Red Army dispatched a representative to the headquarters of the 67th Army to express its genuine desire for co-operation with the Tungpei Armies in the resistance against Japan. Wang I-che, in turn informed the Young Marshal requesting that he receive the representative himself. With little hesitation the Young Marshal flew to meet the Red Army representative, Li K'o-nung, a secret leader of the CCP. But Chang did not know Li nor especially had contacts in the CCP. Nevertheless, Li proposed some conditions on which the united Front was to be based. In fact, his proposals were similar to those eventually advanced by the CCP. Because of his lack of confidence in Li, Chang said to him that "if the CCP has faith in the united front, it should send either Mao Tse-tung or Chou En-lai here." To Chang's great surprise, shortly after L's departure, word was sent from the CCP that Chou would come. The Young Marshal trusted Chou Fu-ch'eng, commander of the 25th Division of the 53rd Army then stationed at Yenan, with the task of a cordial reception for Chou.[35]

One night in late April or early May at a Catholic Church in Yenan, Chang and Chou met for two or three hours. Among many other things discussed in relation to the united front against Japan, the role of Chiang Kai-shek became the central issue. While both readily agreed that given the general situation, China could not achieve unification through Fascism, they differed greatly over Chiang Kai-shek. Hot debate ensued. At one point, Chou raised the issue of Hirota Koki's three principles to which Chang assured Chou that Chiang would never accede as a price for peace. The dilemma with which the CCP and Chou were confronted was that heretofore the CCP official position had not included Chiang in the united front. Moreover, not only had the CCP advocated a united front against Japan without Chiang, it had even insisted on "opposition to Chiang for the sake of a united front." In its view, until

Chiang's rule was overthrown, it would be impossible to form a
united front. Conversely, Chang believed that it would be unthinkable that resistance against Japan could be brought about without
Chiang whose leadership was absolutely necessary. To him, support for Chiang was prerequisite to resistance against Japan. Chang
tried to convince Chou that Chiang was anti-Japanese and was making preparations for a war with Japan. [36] At last Chou recognized
that Chiang was devoted to the country and willing to resist Japan;
he also believed that in a war with Japan Chiang ought to assume
the leadership. He pointed out that, as in the past, he and other
Communists would be glad to serve Chiang again. However, Chou
still did not trust the men surrounding Chiang. Indeed he argued
that had the Central Government been determined to resist Japan,
why would it still want to exterminate the Communists who were
most hated by the Japanese for their enthusiastic resistance to them?
Despite all misgivings the CCP was prepared to restore the old relationship with the Kuomintang and again to put itself under the
leadership of Chiang, under the proclaimed "Platform of War of
Resistance against Japan." Then a nine-point agreement was reached:

1. The Communist armed forces will receive inspection,
reorganization, and concentration for training to prepare
for resistance against Japan.

2. It is guaranteed that the Communist army will never
be deceived or disarmed.

3. Communist forces in Kiangsi, Hainan, and Ta-p'ieh
Mountain will also receive inspection and reorganization.

4. The title of the Red Army will be abolished, and it
will receive the same treatment as the national armed
forces.

5. Communists are no longer allowed to work in the
army.

6. Communists will stop staging all kinds of tou-cheng
(struggle).

7. Communist prisoners, except those who are opposed
to the government and attack the leader, will be released
and given freedom of activity.

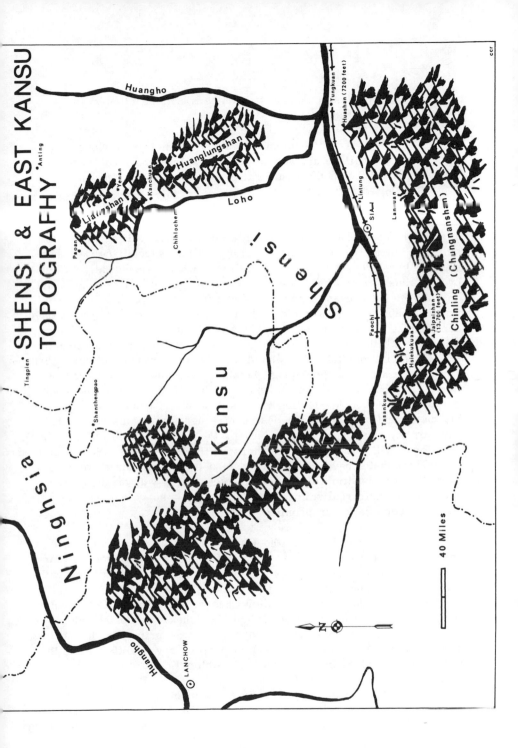

SHENSI & EAST KANSU TOPOGRAFHY

Huangho

Anting

Huanglungshan

Tingpien

Yenan

Kanchuan

Liaunshan

Loho

Paoan

Chihlocher

Shanchengpao

Ninghsia

Kansu

Shensi

Huangho

LANCHOW

Tungkuan

Huashan (7200 feet)

Lintung

SIAN

Lan uan

Paochi

Chinling (Chungnanshan)

Hsiekukuan

Taipaishan (13,700 feet)

Tasankuan

N

40 Miles

ccr

8. Nonmilitary Communist members will be allowed to live in North Shensi.

9. After war of resistance against Japan is victorious, the CCP will be allowed to become a legal political party like those in the democratic countries of England and the United States.[37]

In addition, Chou proposed that if the Young Marshal harbored any doubt about what Chou had said, he would be willing to put himself and others under his direct command and surveillance so that they could be reproachable at any time. Chang was greatly moved by the sincerity of Chou. As a matter of fact, Chou had spent his boyhood in Mukden and later attended school in Tientsin. Since he was only about two years older than Chang, their meeting must have been marked by soul-searching for ways to save the country, intermingled with the joy over reconciliation, nostalgia and mutual admiration for their youthful achievements. The meeting had a tremendous emotional impact on the Young Marshal. He was overwhelmed by Chou's personality and the sincerity of the CCP in the united front; he later described his feelings: "At that time I generously accepted his views and expressed the desire of vengeance against Japan not only for injuries to my family but for the national humiliation. I, therefore, will not lag behind others in fighting Japan. Yet, I pointed out to him that I have my superior, and there are things which I am not in a position to decide; nonetheless, I will do my best to recommend their realization to Chiang. We also vowed that we should never break our promise to each other."[38]

From its knowledge of the Chang-Chou conference and their agreement, the CCP Politburo met to formulate a new policy. After a hot debate, the CCP recognized the necessity of "allying with Chiang" and "supporting Chiang." Although there is no document available to account for this policy change, the May 5, 1936 Declaration of the CCP clearly urged Chiang Kai-shek to stop the civil war and to lead the nation to resist Japan. It was primarily due to this policy change that Chiang acceded to preliminary negotiations with the CCP carried on by his close aide Ch'en Li-fu.[39]

Also as a result of the Chang-Chou meeting, Chang extended some material aid to the Red Army and allowed the CCP to set up a liaison office at Sian headed by the famed CCP security chief Teng

Fa. In the meantime, General Yeh Chien-ying, formerly Chief of Staff of the Red Army, was invited to Sian to improve political training and organizational work in the Tungpei Army, preparations necessary for fighting Japan.[40]

III. THE CHAMPION OF A CAUSE

The united front between the Tungpei Army and the CCP brought about phenomenal changes in the Northwest. Not only was a tacit, local armistice accomplished, but also Sian was made the center of the united front movement while the Young Marshal became its virtual leader. The first step he took in espousing the cause, of course, was to rejuvenate his Tungpei Army. An officers' corps, known as the Wangch'ü Officers' Training School, with General Wang I-che as dean was formally opened on June 15, 1936. Members of the school were middle- and low-ranking officers drawn from all outfits of the Tungpei Army for one month training. At its height the school had about four hundred cadets.[1] As time progressed, the school became dominated by the left-wing groups, and became the center of the united front movement in the Tungpei Army.

The Development of a Revolutionary Ideology

The establishment of the officers' corps, which was not military-oriented, marked a turning point in Chang's career. In words as in deeds he began to build up his own power base in Shensi and intended to strengthen the northeastern political group which heretofore had only a vague existence. Now he assumed the leadership and gave it a definite direction with his slogan, "Resistance against Japan is the only way for China. "

Chang's new doctrine was further reinforced by the Liang-Kwang revolt. On June 1, 1936, Ch'en Chi-t'ang of Kwangtung and Li Tsung-jen and Pai Ch'ung-hsi of Kwangsi openly revolted against the Nanking government, moving their forces into Kiangsi and Hunan and demanding that they be allowed to march northward to fight against Japan.[2] Although the revolt was resolved within three months without bloodshed, the effect on China's political climate was very great. Because of their strategic location, their status as a singularly powerful group, and their long standing opposition to the Nanking government, the revolt not only weakened the leadership of the Nanking government especially in the eyes of some provincial leaders, like Chang Hsüeh-liang, Liu Hsiang, Sung Che-yüan, and Yen Hsi-shan, but also reflected the general feeling and attitude toward Japanese aggression. Like the Red Army, the Liang-Kwang leaders also

37

issued a declaration of war on Japan. Whatever the motive, the anti-Japanese stand taken by the Liang-Kwang leaders was a great challenge to a young man who above all took upon himself the responsibility for recovering the lost northeastern provinces. Chang was hypersensitive to the slogan of "revenge against Japan." On the one hand, he supported wholeheartedly whoever wanted to fight against Japan and, on the other, felt ashamed of his failure in resisting Japan during the Mukden Incident of 1931 for which he had gained the stigma of a "nonresistant" general. Now the more he heard of the outcry for fighting Japan, the more he was resolved to lead his Tungpei people among the first to fight back for their lost homeland, and the less he had faith in Chiang's "internal pacification first and then resistance to external aggression." His position was unequivocally spelled out in his speech to the officers' corps at Wangch'ü on June 22, 1936. The speech was later published in a 57-page pamphlet under the title, "The Only Future of China is Resistance against Japan."[3] The pamphlet was restrictedly circulated in the Tungpei Army.

Chang began his speech by saying that in the past divergent opinions had existed in the Tungpei group chiefly because he had not made his determination and attitude known. But Chang hastened to point out that his views could have been easily discerned from his earlier pronouncements. Now it was time for him to enunciate clearly and frankly his determination and attitude which would serve as the guiding principle for open discussion among the officers. This principle was that "the only future of China is resistance against Japan." What Japan feared most was a unified China. By resisting Japan, China could achieve internal unification, and therefore unification and a war of resistance against Japan could not be separated. Now resistance against Japan was the corollary of unification.[4]

Secondly, by revealing his determination and attitude the Young Marshal felt that the doctrine of war of resistance against Japan was to be indeed realized. Chang reminded his audience that they should not take the matter lightly, "for Japan had been determined to bring about the extinction of China and would never allow us to make unhurried, full preparations for a war against her." It was all logical that the war against Japan was the greatest mission of the Tungpei Army, a mission which could be accomplished only if

the Tungpei Army itself is totally unified: i.e., to unify and concentrate on its goal, to establish a cen-

tral thought, and to become a true political faction for
the people and the country in a new era. [5]

There was always a kind of altruism in the Young Marshal.
He took the blame for the loss of Manchuria without complaint, as
he told his young followers, "with military forces Japan seized Tungpei from our hands, and we must use our own power to take it back.
To recover our homeland is our duty, and our Tungpei Army must
stand on the front line of the war against Japan for sacrifice should
belong solely to us. "[6]

Thirdly, the Young Marshal conceived that China would not be
able to enter into war with Japan without a strong leader, nor could
she fight Japan without being totally mobilized. He saw that the war
was to be long but China would come out of a protracted war victorious. That China needed a strong leader had been Chang's slogan
since he returned from abroad. But the relationship between the
leader and his followers, he conceived, was not the one of a master
and slave relation. Here Chang followed the Chinese tradition, as
he envisioned that true loyalty would transcend absolute obedience:

> Our support for the leader is to offer our opinion as
> well as our strength to him. Basing our action on
> truth and justice, we may make remonstration to him,
> even to the extent that like men of old, subordinates
> without hesitation and regret staged their remonstra-
> tions which may have resulted in their death. [7]

One might say that here already lay the seeds of the Sian coup
d'état. What he conceived and said in June 1936 was precisely what
he did six months later.

Fourthly, prerequisite for a protracted war was mobilization of
the strength of the whole country. It was imperative that the people
of the whole country awaken and organize themselves. The Young
Marshal was optimistic that China would defeat Japan in a protracted
war. He gave reasons for his optimism along these lines: (1) the
Japanese could not be united in a war of aggression; there was the
tendency of forming an antiwarlord, capitalist, and aggressive
"united front"; (2) Japan was primarily a weak nation in terms of
resources, so that she could not afford a war of attrition; (3) the
conflict between China and Japan must have been viewed by Japan
not as the last great war she had to fight in her grand scheme of

world conquest; on the contrary, Japan must have considered the
Soviet Union a greater enemy; and (4) in a national self-defensive
war, China had the advantage of terrain, support and morale of the
people, and the use of guerilla tactics, all of which put together
would be enough to overcome the inferiority of Chinese weapons; it
was important to reject the mistaken view that weapons alone could
bring about victory. [8]

Lastly, Chang exhorted his audience by saying that "we must
take into consideration the 'great self' but never the 'small self.'"
There was no time for empty talk in the face of the life-and-death
struggle against Japan. Disunited as sand, the people of China must
be united, awakened and forged into a strong force behind their leader to meet the Japanese in the front line. As for the suppression
of the Chinese Communists, Chang said it would be a mistake to
confuse the two issues--suppression of the Communists and resistance against Japan. The former was a temporary order of the leader, while the latter was the greatest mission of the Tungpei Army.
Furthermore, the strength of the Communists was rapidly waning,
as if a powerful arrow had spent its force at the end. Conversely,
the enemy was as powerful as the noon sun, so that the sole issue
was resistance against Japan. In concluding, the Young Marshal
made a personal commitment by saying that "Chang Hsüeh-liang had
long ago made a decision that he would never do anything detrimental
to the interest of the people and the country. Further, I would never
regret my sacrifice. If the severing of my head would profit the nation, thereby reviving itself, I would sacrifice myself without a single
thought for my life. "[9]

Chang's June 22, 1936 speech not only disclosed much of his
frame of mind at the time but also typified his revolutionary ideas
as regards the question of the war of resistance against Japan, particularly the role of the Tungpei Army in that war, the need for a
national leader, and the issue of the Chinese Communists. All these
constituted the fundamental doctrines of the Young Marshal and his
Tungpei Army. More important was Chang's personal commitment
to carrying them out. To begin with, the Young Marshal was far
from being a politician, but rather a military man or even a warlord of a provincial army. Once his pronounced views and policies
ran counter to those of Chiang Kai-shek, he had no alternative but
to force Chiang to accept them or at least some of them, for otherwise Chang would have to deny himself as a man of principle and

the leader of the Tungpei Army or to give up the revolutionary doctrine which he enthusiastically held and believed could save the nation. Furthermore, the later unpredictable turn of the Sian Incident could also be found in this speech, because the Young Marshal indeed put the interest of the nation above his personal interest, the "great self" above the "small self" as exemplified by the dramatic episode of his release of Chiang.

Alienation from Nanking

As a political group, the Tungpei Army was greatly strengthened by the development of a new revolutionary ideology. The Tungpei Army was unique in its constituency, social background, and peculiar aspiration, the features which were further accentuated by the discriminatory treatment of the Tungpei Army by the Central Government. Up to the Sian Incident, the Tungpei Army had never received any military supplies, such as arms and ammunition. Its navy and air force which were stronger than those of the Central Government were handed over to it after the Mukden Incident. In the meantime, the three brigades of artillery were also appropriated by the Central Army for temporary duty.[10] The Tungpei Army began to be funded by the Central Government after the Mukden Incident, but its officers and soldiers were paid 20% less than their counterparts in the Central Army. This reduced pay was known as "national humiliation pay." Probably this bad practice did not exasperate the rank and file of the Tungpei Army much, for, after all, they had lost their base and, therefore, seemed to have no right to claim equal pay.

In 1936, the Tungpei Army was composed of five armies (51st, 53rd, 57th, 67th, and the Cavalry). Except for two divisions of the 53rd Army and the three artillery brigades, all the Tungpei troops were dispatched to Shensi and Kansu. Of the fourteen divisions then stationed in the northwest, only the 105th Division, the former guard division with Liu To-ch'üan as commander, was well equipped and numbering more than 20,000 men, while other divisions were relatively small; each was composed of three regiments.[11] A fair estimate of the total strength of the Tungpei Army in the northwest was around 130,000 men. Now these scattered forces of the Tungpei Army for the first time since 1933 had a base of their own. Moreover, throughout the years of exile generals and officers of the

Tungpei Army had learned much and grown to maturity, both militarily and politically. Undoubtedly, the esprit de corps must have been extremely strong.

The crisis came with the annihilation of the 109th and 110th Divisions by the Red Army in the winter of 1935. Now the Young Marshal requested the Central Government to rebuild the two lost divisions. Surprisingly, the Central Government not only refused to make any appropriation but it went even so far as to eliminate their titles. According to Miu Cheng-liu, commander of the 57th Army, and Tung Yen-p'ing, brigade commander of the 105th Division, Nanking's decision to eliminate the titles of the two divisions, the 109th and the 110th, had greatly alienated the Young Marshal and the Tungpei Army and must be viewed as one of the most, if not the most, important causes of the Sian Incident. [12]

Worse still, the Central Government refused to give adequate pension for the families whose husbands and sons were killed in fighting the Red Army. When the Young Marshal's request that the two division commanders' families be given a handsome pension of $100,000 each was rejected, he was so infuriated that he was reported to have said: "My prestige has reached so low as not to be worth even $100,000."[13] Many families of those killed were left without any means of making a living and scattered along the Sian-Tienshui highway; many had to sell their daughters to keep from starvation. Naturally, their plight aroused the sympathy of the Tungpei officers who were ashamed of the bad fortune of their friends' and comrades-in-arms' families. Probably there was also some self-pity on their own part, for what had happened to their friends' families might one day happen to them too.

Under the circumstances, the feeling of alienation ran high in the Tungpei Army. Some questions may have been readily posed: "Why and for what does our Tungpei Army fight the Red Army? Are the Communists our real enemies? If we are killed, who will take care of our families? After all, both the Red Army men and the Tungpei military men are poor people. Why do poor people fight against each other? Why do we kill our brothers, while leaving our true enemy--the Japanese--free to devour North China? Why do we not join hands with the Red Army to drive the Japanese out of North China and to recover our homeland?" The slow awakening of the fact that they had not fired a single shot to repel the invaders, but merely continued to kill their own people, at last dawned on the Tungpei Army. The suspicion of a policy that "one stone hits two birds" gradually became persuasive and won over proselytes among the young officers as well as among the generals, even the Young Marshal himself.

As early as October 1935 when the Young Marshal was appointed Deputy Commander-in-Chief of Bandit Suppression in the north-west, the San-min chu-i yüeh-k'an reported that rumors had spread that the assignment of the Tungpei Army was designed to eliminate that army as had been done to other provincial armies on previous occasions. The editor of the magazine then enumerated how Chiang Kai-shek had disarmed other non-Chiang troops such as Sun Lien-chung, Kung Ping-fan, Chang Chen, Chang Ying, Chang Yin-hsiang, and Wang Chia-lieh.[14]

Certainly there was some truth in the allegation. Since the Red Army set out on the Long March from Kiangsi, it had traversed eight provinces and "25,000 lees," but the Red Army and the pursuing Central Army rarely met. Among other things which accounted for the Red Army's success in evading the pursuing forces, one paramount reason undeniably lay in the halfhearted fighting of the provincial warlords' troops. However, it was equally undeniable that Chiang's deep concern about the elimination of the warlords' troops made them unwilling to fight so as to preserve their strength. In fact, Chiang was accused of using the Communists to extend his control over the provinces. As is well known, the Kwangtung and Kwangsi leaders had always been at odds with the Nanking government, particularly Chiang Kai-shek, their defense line against the Communists on southern Kiangsi being weak where, as it turned out, the Red Army successfully made its major drive to break through the blockade for the Long March. When the Red Army entered Kwangsi, the well-trained troops of Li-Pai (Li Tsung-jen and Pai Ch'ung-hsi) simply tried to fight off the Communists and to drive them out of the province. The case was even worse with the war-lords of Kweichow, Yunnan, and Szechwan, who were unable to take any concerted action to cope with the Red Army because of their constant bickering and clash of interests. Usually with the Commu-nist entry into their provinces came the arrival of the Central Army of Chiang Kai-shek. It looked as if the Red Army blazed the way by which the Nanking government extended its influence in remote provinces. Chiang had good reason to look upon the campaigns against the Communists as an opportunity to eliminate many provincial armies, a gigantic step leading to a true unification of China. As the Long March ended, the Central Government had full control over Kweichow and secured a dominant position in Szechwan. In fact, from the beginning of 1935 until the outbreak of war with Japan the struggle between Liu Hsiang and Chiang Kai-shek for control of Szechwan dominated much of its provincial political life.[15] Hu Hanmin, Chiang's greatest critic, summarized Chiang's suppression campaigns in this way:

> Before September 1931, his policy was to use the Reds as a means of destroying those troops not of his own. After September 18, 1931, he has used the suppression of the Communists as a pretext for his mistake of submission to the Japanese. In the meantime, he has adopted the slogan, "Suppression of the Communists must precede resistance against Japan," aimed at winning the understanding and support of the people. But in reality he continued his policy of eliminating his rivals so as to build up his own personal army.[16]

To criticize Chiang's policy of suppressing the Communists as Hu did would have had a strong appeal to all provincial armies in general but to the Tungpei Army in particular, which was engaged in suppressing the Communists and had suffered colossal losses. It should be borne in mind that despite some progress in social and economic life, China in the mid-1930s was not better than in the 1920s, which was characterized by warlordism. Although Chiang Kai-shek's own power and prestige had risen measurably, his virtual control or power had not extended beyond eight provinces, namely, Kiangsu, Chekiang, Anhwei, Kiangsi, Fukien, Honan, Hupei, and Hunan. In North China, Sung Che-yüan was half-loyal to Nanking; so was his long-time colleague, Han Fu-ch'ü, warlord of Shantung. In Shansi, except for a brief period in 1930, Yen Hsi-shan had ruled with an iron hand since the founding of the Republic. In western China, the Ma families, led by Ma Hung-k'uei and Ma Pu-ch'ing, still held Ninghsia and Tsinghai as their feudal fiefs. However, the two Mas with their Moslem subjects, being strongly anti-Communist, helped to secure the northwest for Chiang Kai-shek. Far in the west lies Chinese Turkestan, or Sinkiang, where a Tungpei man and a former officer of Chang Hsüeh-liang named Sheng Shih-ts'ai seized power in April 1933 with the support of the Tungpei partisan force of a few thousand men just evacuated from Manchuria through Siberia. Sheng maintained his de facto independence from Nanking and leaned totally toward the Soviet Union. He himself had joined the Communist Party of the Soviet Union and accepted the predominant position of the Soviet Union in Sinkiang in return for Soviet military and economic aid. [17]

Most of the warlords just mentioned were opposed to Chiang, but they opposed the Communists even more. While a majority of them were anti-Japanese and wished to see civil war ended, some like Han Fu-ch'ü, and, to some extent, even Sung Che-yüan and Yen Hsi-shan, were ambiguous in their attitude toward resistance against Japan. As individuals they were all older than the Young Marshal and less progressive and western-oriented too. Among the half-dozen or more warlords in China, Yen Hsi-shan's position was extremely crucial, partly because of the presence of a Communist threat on the border, and partly because of his close relationship with the Young Marshal. Furthermore, they both were faced with the same problem--how to deal with the Red Army in peace or in war.

At Nanking, the Central Government, particularly Chiang Kai-shek, seemed to ignore utterly the problems and sentiment of those regional warlords. Probably Chiang had only one objective in view, i.e., to continue his drive for the unification of the whole country under his personal hegemony. At the 5th National Congress of the KMT held in November 1935, Chiang spelled out his foreign policy with special respect to Japan:

> Until the time when peace has utterly disappeared, we should not give up our efforts for peace; similarly, until such time that sacrifice is called for as the last resort, we should not lightly talk about sacrifice. Sacrifice of an individual is not so important as the sacrifice of a nation which is of paramount importance. Also the life of an individual is rather limited, but the existence of a nation is infinite. Just as peace has its limitation, so sacrifice requires determination. We must use our determination of sacrifice to make our utmost endeavor for peace. [18]

Chiang's policy toward Japan was also shared by Wang Ching-wei, then President of the Executive Yüan. With Wang, Chang

Hsüeh-liang had been disenchanted since 1930, when Chang's intervention brought about Chiang's victory over Yen-Feng with whom
Wang sided. The relationship between Wang and Chang was worsened after the Mukden Incident, chiefly because of their disagreement
and even personality clash over policy toward Japan with Chang's
reputation declining. On the last day of the 5th Congress of the
KMT, Wang was shot and severely wounded by an assassin's bullets.
Chang was on the scene and helped to subdue the assassin, Sun Feng-
ming. Nevertheless, Chang was greatly disturbed by the internal
struggle in Nanking; for he was convinced that the corruption and
impotency of the Central Government had driven many able persons
out of governmental service and that there was not enough enthusiasm
among the government leaders for resistance against Japan. Despite
Wang's removal from the political scene, his cowardly policy of
"offering resistance on the one hand and carrying on negotiations on
the other," which was designed to deal with domestic foes rather
than to repel the external enemy, would linger on and had the support of powerful pro-Japanese military and political leaders, such
as Huang Fu, Chang Ch'ün, and Ho Ying-ch'in.[19]

Having once reached Shanghai, Chang had quite a different
experience; there he witnessed the surge of a patriotic movement
that caught his imagination. He plunged himself into close association with radical intellectuals, young and old, such as Madame Sun
Yat-sen, General Li Tu, Shen Chün-jui, and Wang Chao-shih, under
whose spell he was drawn closer to the national salvation movement,
thereby strengthening his views on the suspension of civil war and
the formation of a united front against Japan.[20] As it turned out,
the Young Marshal became the only man of power who had patronized the cause of the students and the national salvation movement.
The formal establishment of the National Salvation Union at Shanghai
coincided with the Liang-Kwang revolt in early June 1936. Both had
served as catalysts to shaping Chang's mind over China's domestic
issues and policy toward Japan. As the Central Government grew
more repressive to the national salvation movement, the Young Marshal appeared to move to the other extreme by giving it tacit protection. Though still clandestinely, he had virtually transformed
Sian into a base of the national salvation movement and the united
front. And yet, with civil war looming ahead, he began to turn to
his good neighbor Yen Hsi-shan for alliance.

An Undependable Ally

The Young Marshal's good relationship with Yen Hsi-shan dated back to the period of Pei-fa (Northern Expedition), when in the summer of 1928 the revolutionary army reached the Peking-Tientsin area. Before its withdrawal, the Tungpei Army preferred to transfer the area to Yen instead of the Christian General, Feng Yü-hsiang, against whom it fought hard and still harbored enmity. Later in 1930, with his defeat followed by temporary exile, Yen had lost his base in Shansi only to have it restored with the aid of Chang Hsüeh-liang, who controlled the whole of North China at the time. Since the Red Army invaded Shansi in early 1936, Chang and Yen had frequently contacted each other in order to coordinate their campaign strategy.

At a banquet given in his honor in Taiyuan, metropolis of Shansi, in March or April 1936, Chang without reservation spoke his mind on the issue of resistance against Japan. Present at the banquet was a division commander, Kuan Lin-cheng, graduate of the first class of Chiang's Whampoa Military Academy, who presently said that the Young Marshal was in so great distress that his words naturally became provocative. Chang responded to him by saying that "if any Chinese of today does not feel in great distress, there must be something wrong with him. There is nothing which we see and hear which does not make us feel distressed."[21] Chang concluded that the only future of China lay in her resistance against Japan, a suggestion which was also welcome to his host, Yen Hsi-shan, who was equally obsessed with the problems of how to deal with the Communists and the Japanese.

In early 1936 Doihara Kenji called on Yen at Taiyuan to demand economic cooperation between the two countries, to which Yen responded: "Economic cooperation between China and Japan is necessary and welcome, provided that it is based upon fairness and mutual needs." In answer to an invitation by a Japanese news agency, Yen wrote an essay to discuss the mutual benefits of Sino-Japanese cooperation. A little later, the Japanese cabinet dispatched Jikawa Nobuji, President of the Yuchu Company, to approach Yen again, expressing the view that Japan did not approve military action in China but she was interested in economic cooperation between the two countries. Yen reiterated his position as he had replied earlier to Doihara.[22] As the Japanese aggression in North China was intensified, Yen resolutely advocated the slogan, "Defend our territory and

resist the enemy." Like Chang Hsüeh-liang, Yen began to see that
the Japanese menace in North China was real and that a war of resistance against Japan could hardly be avoided if North China was to
be saved.

To sound out Yen's stand on the issues of resistance against
Japan and the suspension of civil war, the Young Marshal sent his
personal secretary Li Chin-chou to Taiyuan. The selection of Li
for the mission could not be more fitting, for Li was not from Tungpei and moreover he was well acquainted with Yen, under whom he
had worked for two years at Taiyuan. Li's secret mission, which
probably took place in July 1936, brought back important information
about Yen's attitude toward the two issues in question. First, Yen
was worried about Japan's pressure in North China and doubted the
wisdom of continuing the policy of suppressing the Communists. He
believed that if all the energy and power were used to fight a civil
war, there would not be enough strength left to deal with the external enemy. Second, Yen had no intention of opposing Chiang Kai-
shek but was willing to join with Chang to make recommendations to
Chiang at some opportune time. [23]

Chang was elated with the report from Li that Yen was resonant with his views despite the fact that Yen was still noncommittal.
To follow up the fruition of Li's initial contact with Yen, Li was
sent to Taiyuan for a second time. But this time Li was accompanied by a more authoritative representative from the Young Marshal, Chi I-ch'iao. Chi was Chang's former chief of staff and had
then retired to Peking. Chi was the classmate of Yen Hsi-shan and
his chief of staff, Chu Shou-kuang, at the Military Officers' School
in Japan. The mission was conducted in complete secrecy. The
two crossed the Yellow River at Tungkuan and took the third class
train from there to Taiyuan. Certainly Yen gave them a warm reception. Yen reiterated the position to Chi as he had earlier spoken
to Li alone. Evidently this was less than what was desired by the
Young Marshal and he intended to send Chi on a second mission.
Chi was too old to enjoy the hardship of traveling and returned to
Peking directly, leaving his report to the Young Marshal with Li to
bring back to Sian. After reading Chi's report, Chang's confidence
in his own views was strengthened, and said to Li that he would
await a time that he and Yen would make a joint recommendation to
Chiang.

However, Chang and Yen did have an intimate talk at the end of October 1936. On his way to Loyang to celebrate Chiang Kai-shek's 50th anniversary, Yen and his staff first flew to Sian to talk with Chang Hsüeh-liang and Yang Hu-ch'eng. After spending a full day in Sian, Chang and Yen together took a night train for Loyang. At Loyang the plan for presenting a joint recommendation to Chiang never materialized, because Chiang, in his speech delivered after the review of troops, made a vituperative attack on those who toyed with the idea of uniting with the Communists.[24] Chiang is reported to have said: "The Communists are our greatest traitors. And those who think of allying with the Communists are even less worthy than Yin Ju-keng."[25] Chiang's speech was enough to preclude the presentation of the joint recommendation as planned. The Young Marshal was extremely saddened and secretly shed tears.

On the evening of October 31, 1936, when ceremonies for the celebration of Chiang's 50th anniversary were almost over, Chang and Yen alone took a walk and had a long discussion. Both Chang and Yen later confirmed this talk. According to one version, Yen at last said to Chang: "Ah! Han Ch'ing [Chang's other first name]! Considering the attitude of the Generalissimo, we cannot speak more. What we may be able to do in the future is to take some discreet action at some opportune time."[26]

What was discussed and agreed upon in the secret talks between Chang and Yen may never be known, but one thing seems certain--the two, only a little over a month before the Sian Incident, had reached some understanding that they would support each other in some independent action aimed at ending civil war so as to cope with Japan's aggression in North China. Evidently when he staged the coup of December 12, 1936, Chang counted on Yen's support in his effort to end the campaigns waged against the Chinese Communists and to bring about a union with the latter in a war of resistance against Japan. On the other hand, Chang needed a collaborator in the coup, which he readily found in General Yang Hu-ch'eng, without whose participation the coup would not have been initiated, much less successfully staged.

IV. AN INEVITABLE NEMESIS

When the Young Marshal was appointed acting Commander-in-Chief of Northwestern Headquarters of Bandit-Suppression, he was very reluctant to assume his office. At first he was doubtful as to whether Yang Hu-ch'eng would welcome his presence in the northwest, especially as he had brought with him a military force four or five times larger than that of Yang. Only after Yang sent his welcome message to Chang did the latter agree to accept the new appointment. In the reorganization of the Shensi government, Yang stepped down from the governorship to become Commissioner of Shensi Pacification Headquarters. Shao Li-tzu, a close friend of Chiang Kai-shek, was made governor of Shensi.

In transferring to the northwest, Chang Hsüeh-liang seems to have had one aim in mind which he had not had in Wuhan, that is, he hoped to make the Northwest his base, a second home for the Tungpei people who had been in exile since the loss of Manchuria. While failing to take over the reign of the Shensi government, his man Yü Hsüeh-chung was appointed to the governorship of Kansu and practically controlled the Kansu provincial government. At Sian, Chang was extremely cautious in dealing with Yang Hu-ch'eng. Their early relations were marked by tension and mutual suspicion. To allay Yang's fear, Chang deployed all his forces to the front, while keeping only one guard battalion of 100 men at Sian and leaving the garrison duty of the city to Yang. This situation continued up to the Sian Incident. Another interesting incident which may help to illustrate the Chang-Yang early relations occurred in the allocation of office buildings. Yang had occupied a new building in the city, and he refused to give it up to Chang, who was his superior, for his headquarters. Fortunately, Chang's friendly posture helped iron out many irritations.[1]

The Chang-Yang Union

At the outset, Chang conducted the anti-Communist campaigns with vigor and resolution until his force suffered from defeats that gradually slowed down his offensive. Yang, nurtured in the warlord tradition, saw the peril that his force would be eliminated in fighting against the Communists, so that he, by giving all kinds of excuses, tried to avoid any engagement of his force with the Red Army and frequently complained about the fruitless campaigns. He once said that troops assigned to fight the Communists were comparable to a person sentenced to life imprisonment. At one time, he refused to move his army to the front, using the shortage of funds as a pretext, and Chang was obliged to advance him $100,000 to have his troops move.[2]

Before long, Chang also accepted Yang's view that in suppressing the Communists Chiang had two purposes to achieve--one stone hits two birds--to destroy the Communists as well as to eliminate non-Chiang forces. In fact, the same kind of propaganda was only too familiar to the Young Marshal, but not until he was disillusioned with Chiang and had established close contact with the Communists did he begin to look askance at Chiang's policy and his real intention. Gradually he appreciated Yang's viewpoint while Yang no longer looked at Chang as a rival but a friend.

As already mentioned, in the camp of Yang there had been Communist elements since the Pei-fa, probably at first not well organized for active work but nevertheless having a salient influence on Yang. For instance, it is reported that Yang's wife, Hsieh Pao-chen, was a Communist. Some of the important posts had been held by Communists: Shen Po-shun served as director of the political department of the 17th Route Army; both Nan Han-ch'en and Mi Tsan-ch'en were Yang's one-time secretary-general; and lastly, Wang Ping-nan, who with his German wife Anna had just returned from Moscow, joined Yang's entourage in the spring of 1936.[3]

Communist infiltration into Chang's Tungpei Army was intensified after his conversion to the "united front" and his agreement with the CCP. While Chang had a secret understanding with the Communists from above, Communists and their sympathizers worked hard from below. Led by Kao Ch'ung-min and others, the Society of Comrades for Resistance against Japan was most active. Members of the Society who dominated the coterie of Chang had exerted great influence on him, not so much in decision-making as in preparing his frame of mind for implementing the united front strategy and in instilling in him anti-Chiang feelings. Among several organizations and programs that sprang up as a result of their activities, the special regiment and the political training school with some two hundred students from Peking as their nucleus under Sun Ming-chiu and Ma Shao-chou would play important roles in the months ahead.[4]

The united front should have been as broad as it was inclusive. The union between Chang and Yang as well as between their respective armies was indispensable to its success.   Neither Chang nor Yang knew exactly the other's relations with the CCP.   At least Chang knew nothing about the CCP's relations with Yang, but he admitted that in the course of time Yang also learned of his contact with the CCP.   The initial contact between the two camps was carried out by Chang Ch'ien-hua, Chang's secretary, who was a Communist and a schoolmate of Yang's wife at the College of Law of the Peiping University (not to be confused with the Peking University).   The purpose was simply to improve friendship between Chang and Yang.   With the united front under way, the two camps drew closer to each other.   The man who served as liaison between them was none other than Kao Ch'ung-min.[5]

At the height of friendship between the Tungpei and Hsipei Armies, Huo-lu [Way of survival] and Hsi-pei hsiang-tao [Northwest guide] were published to promote collaboration between the two armies.   The Huo-lu also advocated opposition to suppression of the Communists and suggested toleration of the Communists and the formation of a united front against foreign aggression.   More than any other literature, the journal created a rallying point for the two armies; for most of the time, Kao Ch'ung-min was its editor.[6]

The Gathering Storm

Since June 1936 Sian had become a haven of left-wing intellectuals and the center of patriotic movement.   Most vociferous of all patriotic organizations was the Northwestern Association of National Salvation established in early June 1936 immediately following the inauguration of its parent organization at Shanghai.   Assuming the leading role in the patriotic movement, the Association distributed declarations and a "Preliminary Political Platform for the War of Resistance against Japan" issued by its national headquarters at Shanghai.   Suddenly the Sian press was dominated by left-wing writers.   Sung I-yün, Yang Hu-ch'eng's secretary, became the head of Wen-hua chou-pao [Cultural weekly] and Chang Chao-lin, president of the Yenching student body during the December 1935 demonstra-

tions, and Han Tzu-cho were assigned to work with the Si-ching
min-pao [People's daily news of Sian], whose chief, Chao Yü-shih,
a veteran newsman, was imprisoned on account of his attack on the
leftists. On the occasions of the "September 18" and "October 10"
anniversaries, the press launched a propaganda drive on the united
front against Japan. The Wen-hua weekly since its initial issue in
early November virtually became the organ of the united front.
Equally active was the student union of Sian which did much to support the student strike as in the case of the Sian Normal School.
At this time there emerged many cultural organizations; among
those well known were The Preparatory Society of Cultural Exchange,
Association of High School Teachers and Staffs, and Association of
All Professions for Supporting War of Resistance in Suiyuan. The
last certainly was most popular, as some eighty cultural groups
participated in it and its branch offices were established in many
counties of Shensi province. Evidently a general awakening throughout the country, at least among the intellectuals, was created by
the burning issue of Japanese aggression, an issue so pressing that
it had become far greater than the Communist menace.[7]

Japan's new diplomatic offensive centered around the issue of
the Chinese Communists; it began with Chiang Kai-shek's interview
with the Japanese Ambassador Shigeru Kawagoe on October 8, 1936,
at which time Chiang expressed his interest in readjusting Sino-
Japanese relations and in solving the outstanding problems. This
was followed by a series of eight secret talks between Kawagoe and
Chang Ch'ün, Chinese Minister of Foreign Affairs, which ended with
an abrupt breakdown in early December. The Japanese demand was
composed of two parts: (1) joint military cooperation in the area
from Shanhaikwan to Yumenkwan, covering the whole span of the
Great Wall; and (2) Sino-Japanese political cooperation against the
Communists in the rest of China. As negotiations wore on, Chang
Ch'ün consistently refused the Japanese demands as unacceptable.
However, after the seventh meeting the Japanese envoy suggested
that the second part of the proposal might be waived, but he pressed
for the acceptance of the first part. The Chinese foreign minister
was reported to have accepted a scheme for cooperation of the Manchurian provinces, Jehol, East Hopei, and northern Chahar to fight
the Communists, while China would take care of the Communist
problem in the remainder of the country.[8]

The fact is that the Central Government had no objection to
suppressing the Communists in China, as suggested by the Japanese;

on this issue the interests of the two governments coincided. What was totally unacceptable to Nanking was Japan's design to extend her aggression in North China under the pretext of suppressing Communism. In reality, negotiation with Nanking was only one part of the Japanese game, for simultaneously Japan launched an invasion in Suiyuan, a design which was well underway in July 1936. By late October, puppet troops of "Manchukuo" and Mongolia led by Wang Ying, Li Shou-hsin, and a Mongolian prince, Teh Wang, and backed up by Japanese airplanes and tanks started an all-out offensive. The local force defending Suiyuan was the Shansi provincial troops commanded by General Fu Tso-I who put up a strong resistance. Later, the Central Army commanded by General T'ang En-po was also dispatched to the front, while the 7th Cavalry Division of the Tungpei Army was allowed to take part in the fighting. The Chinese resistance in Suiyuan generated a great patriotic fervor; it also strengthened Chang Ch'ün's stand at the negotiation table. Earlier, Yang Yung-t'ai, governor of Hupeh, was assassinated, ostensibly for being pro-Japanese. The anti-Japanese feeling was further exacerbated by the strike of Chinese workers in a Japanese cotton mill at Tsingtao in early November. To sustain the striking workers, the Young Marshal made generous contributions. While the feeling of the Chinese people ran high, seven leaders of the national salvation movement were arrested at Shanghai on November 23, for whose release the Young Marshal took up the cudgels before Chiang Kai-shek. [9] Consciously or unconsciously the Young Marshal took upon himself the cause of the people or the weak. It is to be expected that sooner or later he would clash with his superior to whom he owed allegiance.

Back in Sian, Chang's relations with the agencies and leaders of the Central Government had deteriorated rapidly since he took up the cause of the united front. Chang's distrust of Chiang was to some extent aggravated by the ill will of Chiang's men in Shensi, particularly those attached to his headquarters. The chief of staff of the Northwestern Bandit-Suppression Headquarters was Yen Tao-kang, who served as Chiang's chief of aides-de-camp. Unlike his predecessor, Ch'ien Ta-chün, who served the Young Marshal at Hankow well by mitigating and ironing out irritating issues between Nanking and the Young Marshal, Yen reversed the approach by taking issue with him at every turn. He spied on the activities of the Tungpei Army and on every occasion imposed his authority as a proxy of Chiang. At times he even openly criticized the Young Marshal. Whether he acted on his own or by order of Chiang cannot be verified. His failure to mitigate and stave off the Sian Incident not only cost him his position but led to his subsequent imprisonment by Chiang. [10]

Another expected consequence of Chang's defense of the student and national salvation movements was his conflict with the KMT Headquarters at Sian. In September 1936, Ma Shao-chou was arrested on the charge of instigating a student riot by the KMT Headquarters without consulting with the Young Marshal in advance. Failing to obtain his release by verbal order, the Young Marshal dispatched a company of troops to storm the KMT Headquarters. Not only did the troops force the release of Ma but they seized a large number of documents. All the staff members of the Headquarters were crowded into one room for the night. On the following day, Chang lifted the siege only through the mediation of Shao Li-tzu. The episode heightened the tension between the Tungpei Army and the agencies of the Central Government then stationed in Sian. [11] The Young Marshal had a lengthy interview with Helen Snow at the time. The interview was released to the Chinese press on October 3 and later translated into English and published in the North China Star on October 9 and in the China Weekly Review on the 24th. It left no room for doubt that the Young Marshal had categorically committed himself to the cause of the united front:

> If the government does not obey the will of the people, it cannot stand . . . ; only by resistance to foreign aggression can the real unification of China be maintained. . . . The Northeastern Army must stand on the first front for national defense, and history gives the great mission of restoring our lost territory. . . . The will of the Chinese people must be my will. . . . If my determination wavers, the rifle is in your hand. You can kill me at any time. [12]

It would be naive to argue that Chiang was not well informed of what had been going on at Sian, for divide et impera had always been Chiang's method of governing and that was the way in which the triangle power structure of Chang Hsüeh-liang, Yang Hu-ch'eng, and Shao Li-tzu was set up to begin with. Indeed, the Young Marshal complained that the Generalissimo had paid too much attention to inaccurate intelligence reports made by his men from Sian. [13] Certainly Chiang had failed to grasp the true situation at Sian, but his greater mistake still lay in his failure to understand the two men, Chang and Yang, in whom he had put his trust.

Chiang's Visits to Sian

Shortly after the celebration of the "Double Tenth," Chiang returned to Hangchow, Chekiang, for a few days' rest. There he summoned several provincial military leaders for consultation on national affairs, including Han Fu-ch'ü of Shantung, Hsü Yung-ch'ang of Shansi, Yang Hu-ch'eng of Shensi, and a representative of Sung Che-yüan. This conference occurred only a week before his trip to Sian on October 21, 1936. It is reported that Chiang, realizing the restive situation developing within Sian, confided his planned Sian visit to Yang with the hint that Yang should make precautious necessary preparations for the visit. Obviously for this reason, Yang was later charged with disloyalty. [14]

In the midst of tension and rumors, Chiang Kai-shek arrived at Sian on October 21. Despite his information about fraternization between the Tungpei and Red Armies, the chief objective of his visit was to build the morale of the Tungpei Army to carry on the punitive campaigns against the Communists. Up to this time, the Young Marshal had not told him about his contact with the Communists. According to his own account, during his visit to Nanking in early June 1936, while riding with Chiang on their way to the gendarme school, Chang decided to reveal to Chiang his meeting with Chou En-lai, but missed the opportunity. Later when he had gone to Nanking on one or two occasions, once in early July and another time in October, he did not have the opportunity to approach Chiang. [15]

In order to let Chiang sense the mood of the Tungpei and Hsipei Armies and the feelings of the rank and file, Chang and Yang summoned the midranking officers above the level of regiment commander from both armies to Wangch'ü for a conference with Chiang. At the conference, many spoke out in opposition to Chiang's policy. The overall feelings of the officers were summarized in one account as follows: (1) they believed in support of the leader, i.e., Chiang Kai-shek, to unite the nation in resistance against Japan, and to end civil war so as to preserve national strength; (2) they requested equitable treatment in terms of pay and supplies between the Tungpei Army and the Central Army as well as the question of pension for

those who were killed in fighting the Communists; and (3) the Generalissimo's policy of "internal pacification first and resistance against
Japan later" would have little hope of success simply because the
enemy would not await the completion of internal pacification before
launching her further aggression. [16]

Chiang was adamant. In his speech to the officers with his
leading lieutenants around, notably Chiang Ting-wen and Ku Chu-t'ung,
Chiang referred to all the talk about fighting Japan as madness. He
argued that the enemy close at hand was not the Japanese but the
Communists, against whom the Tungpei Army must fight. Equally
he chided the idea of forming a "united front" against Japan by saying that "resistance against Japan requires the suppression of the
Communists first; those who do not suppress the Communists are
the same as those who do not fight the Japanese; and the Communists
are great traitors." [17] Chang was greatly embarrassed by Chiang's
remarks which were equivalent to a direct blow to him, for those
ideas under attack were his own which he had preached all along.
It was reported that he was so saddened that he was found in tears.

After Chiang left, Miao Chien-ch'iu, then Chang's counselor,
addressed the same audience including all the cadets of the Officers'
Corps in most inflammatory language. He went so far as posing a
question, "Are all our Tungpei young officers really such cowards
that not even one of us equals the Japanese hero of February 26?" [18]
In other words, Miao suggested that someone should be heroic enough
to kill the Generalissimo. That was why the Young Marshal ordered
Miao immediately to leave Sian, to which he did not return until December 28, 1936, with James M. Bertram. In the meantime, the
Young Marshal placed several officers into custody because of their
vociferous attack on Chiang, among them Kao Ch'ung-min. One
might speculate that if Miao could openly propose the assassination
of Chiang, why had he not also toyed with the idea of kidnapping
him? Indeed he claimed he did just that. [19]

It is evident that the Young Marshal, since he spelled out his
views on the united front to the cadets of the Officers' Corps on
June 22, 1936, and assumed the leadership of the patriotic movement, had found himself in a dilemma between championing the cause
of the national salvation movement and disowning the anti-Chiang and
antigovernment pronouncements and activities promoted by his followers. In fact, he tried to restrain his followers from going too far

and becoming too antagonistic toward Chiang and the Central Government, for he had not intended to hurt his already strained relations with Chiang, much less to sever these relations. It is clear to us today as it was to Chang in his days that to break with Chiang could only lead either to his resignation or his defiance of Chiang; neither course was conceivable during Chiang's first visit to Sian. On the other hand, the issue of the "united front" was brought into the open. Needless to say, the Young Marshal had failed to persuade Chiang to his views. Instead of vacillating in the face of Chiang's rebuttals in public as well as in private, Chang was resolute to carry on the struggle, for it was a cause he considered more important than any other.

Only a few days after his visit to Sian, Chiang celebrated his 50th birthday at Loyang, during which Chang Hsüeh-liang and Yen Hsi-shan jointly asked Chiang to consider the suspension of civil war in order to unite the nation to face Japan's aggression as discussed earlier. Returning to Sian, the Young Marshal immediately informed the CCP that he was unable to request the Generalissimo to realize the plan for a cease fire, but that he would continue to try. In the meantime, General Yeh Chien-ying brought forth the plan for a temporary armistice in the areas of the Red and Tungpei Armies drafted by Mao Tse-tung, to which the Young Marshal acceded:

> Under the proposition of resistance against Japan, the
> CCP is willing to bring about mutual cooperation with
> the Tungpei Army and to put its troops under my com-
> mand. I asked the CCP to make a temporary with-
> drawal to the north so as to create a buffer zone and
> to give me time for maneuvering. They replied that
> the land of the Ordos area is meager, coupled with a
> severe climate, so that they need winter clothes and
> supplies. I personally donated a huge amount of mon-
> ey with which they could make their purchases.[20]

The CCP fulfilled its promise to Chang and accordingly withdrew from Wayaopao to the north and settled only in the three Piens (Chingpien, Anpien, and Tingpien) just inside the Great Wall.[21] By this time, the mutual understanding between the CCP and the Tungpei Army, particularly the Young Marshal, was greatly enhanced. On his part, Chang saw that the Communists, except for their belief in Communism, were as trustworthy as any other patriotic Chinese.

Also he regarded his verbal promise and written agreement with the CCP as binding as his personality, and as such could not be easily broken or retracted.

With the Japanese advance in Suiyuan and the negotiation sessions between Chang Ch'ün and Kawagoe proceeding at Nanking, the anti-Japanese sentiment rose to unprecedented height across the country. The heroic resistance of the Chinese troops in Suiyuan kindled the patriotic fervor and restored much of the lost confidence of many Chinese. Moreover, it caught the imagination of the Tungpei Army and the Young Marshal, who had always viewed the fighting against the Japanese as their primary duty. The slogan, "Support Suiyuan and resist Japan," permeated the whole Tungpei Army. Some of the high commanders told the Young Marshal that "even if the Central Government does not allow us, we will have to act on our own and march to Suiyuan to give our support."[22] For this reason, the Young Marshal tried to quiet down his subordinates and advised them to be patient; at the same time, he made repeated requests to Chiang that the Tungpei Army be dispatched to the front to face the enemy, only to be rejected on the grounds that "the time is not ripe for it." Finally a division of cavalry of the Tungpei Army was dispatched to Suiyuan as a token of its participation in resisting Japan. In his parting speech to the 7th Cavalry Division, the Young Marshal admonished the rank and file that it was the great glory of the 7th Cavalry Division to march to the front line of national defense in eastern Suiyuan and to undertake the sacred mission of resistance to Japan. "We should bear in mind," he continued, "that at the present time the most urgent and immediate task of the Chinese people is to resist Japan, thereby to save the nation. Until such time that the influence of Japanese imperialists is driven out of China, no work can be started and no hope for national recovery can be anticipated."[23]

The pivotal turning point came with the capture of Pailingmiao by General Fu Tso-i's Shansi Army on November 24, 1936. However, the Central Government and Chiang Kai-shek were not prepared to pursue the war with Japan further, but rather hoped to accommodate with Japan for a modus vivendi. Any negotiated settlement with Japan at that time would involve a quid pro quo that China would stop anti-Japanese agitation and prosecute suppression of the Communists. To show its goodwill toward Japan, the Central Government on November 23, 1936, openly suppressed the anti-Japanese movement by closing down fourteen magazines followed by the arrest of seven leaders of the national salvation movement at Shanghai.[24]

The arrests infuriated the Young Marshal, simply because their cause was the same as his, their motives were pure, patriotic, and above partisan politics, and their programs were appealing to him. In the recent strike of Chinese workers at a Japanese cotton mill in Tsingtao on November 8, 1936, these leaders had given their strong support by staging a demonstration at Shanghai; to the same strikers the Young Marshal had made generous donations. Furthermore, some of the seven had become his friends. It would be unthinkable that, as a leader of the national salvation movement in the north-west, he had failed to come to their defense.

The Young Marshal must have viewed the suppression of the anti-Japanese movement as a signal of China's leaning toward Japan. His fear was further substantiated by the signing of the anti-Comintern Agreement between Tokyo and Berlin on November 25, 1936. Chiang had been very much intoxicated with Fascism; he had recently sent his second son, Wei-kuo, to Germany to study military science and on his side there was still a group of German advisers headed by General Alexander von Falkenhausen, successor since 1935 of General Hans von Seeckt,[25] whose chief mission was to exterminate the Communists. The bond between Japan and Germany could have only forced China to move closer to Japan. The rapprochement between China and Japan was a corollary of China's de facto recognition of "Manchukuo" and prosecution of suppression campaigns against the Communists, both of which were intolerable to the Young Marshal and his Tungpei Army. In the throes of his career, Chang found himself torn between personal loyalty to Chiang and commitment to principle. Still hoping to preserve both, he wrote an emotional letter to Chiang on November 27, 1936, a fortnight before the Sian Incident:

> The situation in Eastern Suiyuan becomes more and
> more critical. . . . For the period of nearly half a
> year, I have continuously laid before Your Excellency
> my principle and program of struggle against Japanese
> imperialism for national salvation. . . . Now the war
> against Japanese imperialism is beginning. . . . I
> have therefore waited patiently for Your Excellency's
> order. . . . Pressed by the zealous sentiments of
> my troops and urged on by my personal convictions,
> I ventured to present my recent appeal, but Your
> Excellency instructed me to wait for an opportunity.

Since then I have ordered my troops to wait patiently,
although their desire to fight against Japanese imperialism was already flaming. . . . In order to control
our troops, we should keep our promise to them that
whenever the chance comes they should be allowed to
carry out their desire of fighting against the enemy.
Otherwise, they will regard not only myself but also
Your Excellency as imposters, and will no longer
obey us. Now is exactly the right time. Please give
us the order to mobilize at least part, if not the
whole, of the Tungpei Army to march immediately to
Suiyuan as reinforcements to those who are fulfilling
their sacred mission of fighting Japanese imperialism.
If so, I as well as my troops numbering more than a
hundred thousand will follow Your Excellency's leadership to the end. [26]

The passionate appeal of the Young Marshal failed to move the
Generalissimo whose set goal remained unchanged. The issue between the Generalissimo and the Young Marshal had been of nearly
half a year's standing; unification had to be achieved before any kind
of resistance against Japan could be effectively carried out and unification meant the extermination of the Communists. Fully convinced
of his correct reasoning, Chiang sent his most trusted lieutenant
Ch'en Ch'eng, Commander-in-Chief of Bandit-Suppression Headquarters in Shansi, Shensi, Suiyuan, and Ninghsia Border Areas, to the
Suiyuan front to make a personal investigation of the war situation
on the spot. It was largely based upon Ch'en's report--that Japan
had no intention of expanding the existing conflict into a full-scale
war and the Chinese troops there were sufficient to handle the puppet
forces--that Chiang was determined to prosecute the campaign against
the Communists to the finish. [27] In this state of mind, Chiang ignored the plea put forth by Chang in his letter of November 27, 1936.

On December 3, 1936, the Young Marshal flew to Loyang in a
military plane. He came with two purposes in mind; the first and
most important was to report to Chiang that the anti-Japanese feeling in the Tungpei Army was running too high to be restrained,
whereas the campaign against the Red Army was too unpopular to
be continued. The second was his personal plea for the release of
the "six gentlemen" of the national salvation movement. Concerning
his plea for the release of the "six gentlemen," the Young Marshal
gave a vivid account:

I pleaded for their innocence by saying that "if they are found guilty, that guilt must be described as love for the country as Shen Chün-ju claimed." The Generalissimo fell into a fury and said to me: "You are the only one in the whole country who sees things as you do. I am the revolutionary government; what I do is revolution." I did not respond but said to myself: "Revolutionary government is not merely empty words; revolution must be accompanied by action."[28]

While the Generalissimo and the Young Marshal had an intimate talk over the crucial issue of suspending civil war and uniting all forces in a war against Japan, the situation at Tsingtao was worsened with the landing of a large number of Japanese marines. Since Tsingtao was a naval base, a former commander-in-chief of the Tungpei navy, Shen Hung-lieh, was appointed mayor of the city, following the transfer of the Tungpei Navy to the Central Government in 1932. It was natural that the Young Marshal had special concern for the Tsingtao situation, for he had maintained good relations with his former lieutenant, now mayor of Tsingtao, and his navy comrades stationed there.[29]

Now it was at Tsingtao that Japan's posture appeared to be most militant and aggressive. Dissatisfied with the progress of negotiations conducted between the conflicting parties in the strike through the intermediary of the municipal government authorities, the Japanese Cottonmill Owners Association suddenly enforced the lock-out of the nine Japanese mills on December 2. As a coordinate step, the Japanese Marines landed at Tsingtao on the morning of December 3, and they immediately started a vigorous roundup campaign against the agencies of anti-Japanese agitators. They raided the railway branch of the Kuomintang, the municipal library, and several other public places and arrested many people including the editor of the Pei hua pao, a vernacular daily. Not only did Haruhiko Nishi, Japanese consul-general at Tsingtao, and representatives of Japan's war and navy ministries ignore the protest lodged by the mayor of Tsingtao and the Central Government, but they even made some intolerable demands on the Chinese mayor.[30]

At Nanking, the Kawagoe-Chang Ch'ün talk entered its eighth session on December 3, 1936, which again ran into an impasse. Japan continued to put strong pressure on the Nanking government for its acceptance of the three-point principle advanced by Hirota, for Tokyo repeatedly announced that Japan's China policy remained unchanged. The most sensitive issue during the 8th session of the Kawagoe-Chang talk was the employment of Japanese advisers by the Chinese government, a demand similar to one contained in the fifth group of the 21 Demands of 1915. [31]

In north China, Japan spurred the Mongolian and Manchoukuo puppet troops led by Teh Wang and Li Shou-hsin to launch a counter-offensive against the Chinese forces in Suiyuan with the recapture of Pailingmiao as its immediate goal. As many of the Manchoukuo puppet troops once served in the old Tungpei Army, the Young Marshal dispatched General Chang Cheng-te to Chahar to defeat them, thereby destroying the insurgent force. [32] In the meantime, he hoped to lead the Tungpei Army to confront the enemy. Judging from the tempo of the anti-Japanese movement and Japanese aggression, China's forebearance was nearly exhausted. A veteran American journalist commented on the critical situation a few weeks before the Chiang-Chang talk at Loyang as follows:

> Japan and China are rapidly nearing a showdown and the
> next few weeks will determine whether the outcome is
> to be war or peace. There are strong indications that
> Japanese aggression in China has reached its peak. . . .
> Today's indications in China are that there will be war
> with Japan shortly or a basis of lasting peace. [33]

The full extent of the Chiang-Chang talk at Loyang may never be known, but it is quite certain that their talk centered around the issue of the dispatch of the Tungpei Army to fight against the Japanese and the suspension of civil war. By that time, the CCP's direct appeal to the Central Government for ending hostility had been well known in high governmental circles. [34] The Young Marshal tried to convince the Generalissimo that the CCP was sincere and prepared not only to cooperate with the Central Government but also to support Chiang Kai-shek's leadership to lead the nation to war with Japan. Conversely, in line with his thinking, he may also have reminded the Generalissimo that the Red Army could not be easily annihilated as he believed. Probably he also cited his own experience and the recent setback of Hu Chung-nan's army, the crack troops of Chiang, at Yuwang bordering Kansu and Ninghsia. [35]

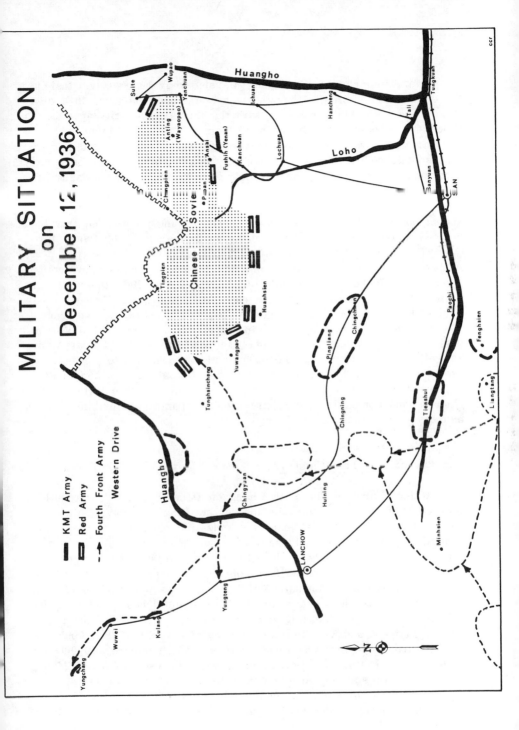

MILITARY SITUATION
on
December 12, 1936

Huangho

Loho

Chinese Soviet

Legend:
- KMT Army
- Red Army
- Fourth Front Army
- Western Drive

Huangho

Wupao
Suite
Yenchuan
Anting (Wayaopao)
Chingpien
Ansai
Fushih (Yenan)
Kanchuan
Ichuan
Hancheng
Tali
Tungkuan
Lochuan
P—an
Tingpien
Huanhsien
Yuwangpao
Tunghsincheng
Sanyuan
—AN
Pingliang
Chingchow
Paochi
Fenghsien
Chingning
Tienshui
Liangtang
Chingyang
Huining
Minhsien
LANCHOW
Yungteng
Kulang
Wuwei
Yungchang

N

ccr

More importantly, the Young Marshal may have argued that
the enormous sacrifice of human lives and money incurred in a civil war should be used in a war with the true enemy. If Japan is
China's archenemy, not the Chinese Communists, all Chinese,
whether members of the Red Army or Central Army, should join
forces with each other to fight Japan. Reasonably, it may be con-
jectured that after having been rebuked by Chiang over the issue of
ending civil war, Chang insisted on his troops being sent to the
front to fight the Japanese, a battle cry that had been unanimously
supported throughout the Tungpei Army. Chiang pointed out that it
seemed unfeasible for the Tungpei Army to march to the front, for
General Yen Hsi-shan would refuse it passage through Shansi. [36]
At last Chang probably told Chiang that judging from its prevalent
mood, the Tungpei Army could not be expected to fight the Red
Army, and that he was no longer capable of enforcing Chiang's order. Chiang immediately decided to convene a military conference
at Sian instead of Loyang as originally planned. Earlier Chiang had
issued urgent summons to all high commanders of his Central Army
as well as some provincial military leaders to hasten to Loyang.
Now only commanders of the Tungpei and Hsipei Armies and those
high-ranking officers of the Central Army who would be involved in
planning and conducting the suppression campaigns against the Communists were summoned to Sian. [37]

The Layout of a Last Campaign

Chiang came to Sian with Chang on December 4 with the full
knowledge of what was going on inside the Tungpei Army. Also
clearly known to him was Chang's clandestine contact with the Communists. [38] Yet he probably had no knowledge of Yang's relations
with the CCP, much less of the Chang-Yang collaboration. For one
thing, Chiang's men were well entrenched in Sian; Shao Li-tzu
served as governor of Shensi, Ma Chih-ch'ao as police chief of Sian;
Kuo Tzu-chün as chairman of the KMT provincial headquarters. In
the military realm, Tseng K'uo-ch'ing was the director of the political department and Yen Tao-kang the chief of staff of the Northwestern Bandit-Suppressing Headquarters. Furthermore, 40,000 or
50,000 Central Army troops commanded by Hu Tsung-nan and Mao
Ping-wen were stationed in eastern Kansu, while another crack
troop, the 25th Division, commanded by Kuan Lin-cheng, was in
northern Shensi. In the ancient city of Hsienyang, only twenty miles

west of Sian, the 13th Division under Wan Yao-huang, was being deployed. In the meantime, most of the bombers of the Chinese Air Force were transferred to Sian for action.

Apart from the presence of his military forces in the northwest, Chiang had unwavering confidence in Chang Hsüeh-liang and Yang Hu-ch'eng whose loyalty had never been questioned. Chiang's relationship with Chang was one of intimacy such as had not been shared by any other military leaders in China at the time. Chang used to proudly say in public that he treated Chiang as if he were his father. With Yang, Chiang had maintained good comradeship and honest dealings. Yang, in spite of having a long tradition in the revolutionary rank especially since casting his fate with Chiang in 1929, was still an insignificant local warlord whose poorly equipped and ill-trained troops numbering no more than 30,000 would never pose a threat to Chiang. In fact, Chiang probably anticipated that Yang would keep some vigilance over the Young Marshal. Such being the case, Chiang ignored the advice of his brother-in-law, Dr. H. H. Kung, then Vice-President of the Executive Yüan and concurrently Minister of Finance of the Central Government, that Chiang should not go to Sian where the "united front" reigned.[39]

A week before the Sian Incident, Chiang at Hua-ch'ing-ch'ih, the hot-spring resort of the celebrated Chinese beauty Yang Kuei-fei some twenty miles east of Sian, was interviewed by Chang Chi-luan, reputed editor of Ta-kung pao. A native of Shensi, Chang had wide contact with provincial leaders. He cautioned Chiang that Sian was fraught with rumors and that the prevalent political atmosphere was marked by "ending civil war" and "united front against Japan." Chiang voluntarily told his visitor that

> the so-called rumor he had heard was the news that
> Chang Han-ch'ing [Chang Hsüeh-liang] met the Communists at Yenan and decided to support the Central
> Government and to unite all forces for resistance
> against Japan.[40]

Asked about what Chiang's opinion was on suspension of the suppression campaign against the Communists and the formation of a united front against Japan, Chiang replied:

> Union of forces for resistance against Japan has always
> been the policy of the Central Government, an adopted

policy since the completion of the suppression of Communists in Kiangsi last year. However, everyone should
bear in mind that the purpose of the Communists is not
"united resistance against Japan" but rather "cessation
of suppression campaign against the Communists." The
so-called "united resistance against Japan" is nothing
more than a transitional measure. [41]

Since Chiang was convinced that the Communists would never
become true comrades in the war against Japan, his coming to Sian
could have no other purpose than to silence any dissenting voice in
the Tungpei and Hsipei Armies. There is every reason to believe
that Chiang had made up his mind that the anti-Communist campaign
must be prosecuted to its finish.

No sooner had he settled at Hua-ch'ing-ch'ih than he began to
tackle the issue of the morale of the Tungpei and Hsipei Armies.
Instead of speaking first to Chang Hsüeh-liang and Yang Hu-ch'eng,
he went directly to the Tungpei and Hsipei commanding generals.
He summoned for individual interview every division commander
without the presence of either Chang or Yang. [42] Aside from giving
a personal touch, Chiang must have exhorted the generals that they
were approaching the "last five minutes" of the campaign and that
a complete victory was in sight. The time was as crucial for the
future of the country as for that of the generals, so that everyone
must dedicate himself to bringing about a successful conclusion of
the last campaign. Indeed Chiang believed that "eight years of bandit suppression could be accomplished in two weeks, within a month
at the most. "[43]

But did the Tungpei and Hsipei generals look at the Communist issue in the same way as Chiang did? Probably they did, at
least concerning the strength of the Communists: as an independent
force, the Communists were not strong enough to challenge or shake
the power of Nanking or Chiang. The generals certainly doubted
the wisdom that more killing in civil war had to be done before
China could turn against her real enemy--Japan--unless Chiang harbored quite a different intention aimed at eliminating the independent
forces of Tungpei and Hsipei. The issue at stake seemed not so
much the extermination of the remnants of the Communists as the
unification of the country. Like Chiang, Chang equally minimized
the strength of the Red Army in spite of the earlier defeats of the
Tungpei Army. [44] Chiang, having learned the close contact between

the CCP and the Tungpei Army, was probably more obsessed with the latter than with the former.

It was obvious to Chiang that the issue of the Tungpei Army was more pressing and must be resolved before the renewal of the campaign against the Communists. Although the Young Marshal had been cooperative, the Tungpei Army was still a warlord army and as such must be eliminated sooner or later. This both Chiang and Chang knew. Yet the Tungpei Army was Chang's only capital which he would not give up without a worthy cause--that is fighting against Japan. To the clever mind of Chiang, the first step he had to take was to neutralize the Tungpei Army and the Red Army so that he decided to transfer the Tungpei Army to Anhwei and northern Kiangsu, a proposition which the Young Marshal had strongly resisted from the beginning.[45] Chang and Yang felt suspicion concerning Chiang's motive aroused by the latter's direct interviews with the Tungpei and Hsipei generals; their suspicion abruptly turned into real fear as Chiang proposed the transfer of the Tungpei Army from the Northwest to the east. Such a transfer would have been necessary in view of the fact that the Tungpei Army, having collaborated with the Communists, ought to have been neutralized and moved out of the Northwest. Also such a transfer was desirable from the logistic point of view that the Tungpei Army, being no longer capable of fighting the Communists effectively, ought to have been deployed elsewhere so as to clear the field for the Central Army to move in and to maneuver freely. To coordinate the forthcoming campaign against the Communists, in which the Central Army would play a major role, Chiang Kai-shek appointed Chiang Ting-wen Front Commander-in-Chief of Bandit-Suppression in the Northwest. Chiang's appointment was not to replace the Young Marshal as has been misconstrued.[46]

Although no record concerning the private talks between Chiang Kai-shek and Chang Hsüeh-liang in the few days that preceded the Sian Incident is available, all indications show that the outstanding issue of transferring the Tungpei Army to the east had not been resolved on the eve of the Incident, whereas preparations for launching an all-out campaign against the Communists were well underway. Confronted with a crucial dilemma between submission and defiance to Chiang, the Young Marshal must have made the most difficult decision in life. If his choice were to support Chiang's policy, he would have to follow Chiang's order either to prosecute the suppres-

sion campaign in earnest or to transfer the Tungpei Army to the
east. It meant that he would at once break his promise and agreement with the CCP, a thing which he would least want to do because
not only had he promised the CCP to stop fighting so as to bring
about a united front against Japan but also he had found nothing
wrong in that policy. Secondly, he also made that policy explicit
to his subordinates, especially the cadets at Wang-ch'ü. Thirdly,
by this time the officers and soldiers of the Tungpei Army had been
well indoctrinated by the Young Marshal himself that their goal was
to fight the Japanese, not the Communists. Even though there was
no question of loyalty of his troops, many of his followers would not
hesitate to challenge him, not his authority but his failure to fulfill
his promise. The Young Marshal was too honest to break his promise with the Communists and he was too proud to revoke his pledge
with his Tungpei followers whom he would lead to recover their
homeland.

But to defy a man--whose leadership the Young Marshal had
helped to build up, to whom he publicly and privately paid his hom-
age, and whom he had revered as if he were his father--must have
created insurmountable difficulties even to think about. To the Young
Marshal or to anyone, the consequences of such a move would have
been prohibitive, for it certainly would result in open rebellion,
a course full of adventure and danger not only for himself but for
the whole nation. Probably his mood at the time and the decision
which he eventually made, were best accounted for in Chang's
speech to the whole staff of the Northwestern Bandit-Suppression
Headquarters given only one day after the outbreak of the Sian
Incident:

> The conflict between Generalissimo Chiang and myself
> over political policy had developed to such an extent
> that it had to be brought to an end as neither of us would
> give up his own views. Consequently, I had laid down
> for myself three alternatives: (a) to bid farewell to
> Chiang and to quit my post; (b) to make a last attempt
> at a verbal recommendation in the hopes that he might
> change his views; and (c) to use the method similar to
> ping-chien [remonstration with military force], the one
> that was eventually chosen. [47]

The Young Marshal argued that he could not take the first alternative by tendering his resignation because of his peculiar personal

reasons, notably his determination for revenge upon the Japanese who killed his father, and his profound concern for the plight of the nation, as well as his acceptance of the opinion and criticism of his subordinates.[48]   As for his last appeal to Chiang, the Young Marshal had been trying his utmost for a full month preceding the Incident, but to no avail.   Since Chiang settled at Lin-t'ung on December 4, serious dialogue between the two had taken place and the Young Marshal had had the opportunity to speak his mind and present his case.[49]   According to Chang, Chiang was stubborn and spoke contemptuously of Chang's opinion as he went so far as to say that "except in the Northwest and except for you, Chang Hsüeh-liang, no one dares talk with me in the manner as you did and none dare criticize me.   I am the Generalissimo; I do not err; I am China; and China cannot do well without me."[50]

With the first two alternatives ruled out, the only option open to Chang was the ping-chien, an idea with which Yang Hu-ch'eng toyed first.   Shortly after his return from Loyang in early November, the Young Marshal in a conversation with Yang expressed his great disappointment with Chiang's policy as well as his unwillingness to continue fighting against the Communists.   Then he sought Yang's advice.   The conversation, as the Young Marshal later recalled, ran as follows: "Are you really determined to resist Japan?" inquired Yang.   Chang then swore to him that he was.   Yang replied: "Await Generalissimo Chiang's visit to Sian; we can hold the emperor hostage to demand submission of all feudal princes in the nation."   Upon listening, Chang was so astonished that he remained silent.   Noticing that Yang was somewhat fearful of his silence, Chang began to comfort Yang by saying, "I am not the kind of person who would betray his friend.   Please feel assured!   Yet as to your suggestion, that is something that I am unable to do."   Feeling relaxed, Yang said sarcastically: "So much so that the emotional factor and personal consideration are put above concern for the nation."   Replied Chang, "Let me think first and then discuss it.   Please be assured that I will not mention your suggestion to anybody."[51]   Thus the idea of kidnapping Chiang was hatched in the Chang-Yang talk.   It did not require long-term planning, for Chang possessed all the facilities to stage the coup.   However, the plan was shelved for the time being.   What rekindled the idea in Chang's mind and precipitated the fateful event were some unexpected developments.

One of the things that alienated the Young Marshal from Chiang was the arrest of the seven leaders of the national salvation movement, as already discussed. Another thing, according to Chang's own account, that contributed greatly to hastening his decision on the ping-chien was Chiang's demand for punishment of some of Chang's subordinates whose conduct was considered improper obviously for their open advocacy of terminating the civil war and forming a united front against Japan. Chang said that he was unable to do that, for he would rather sacrifice himself if he were found unacceptable to the authorities than victimize his innocent subordinates. [52]

Yet the most important development that precipitated Chang's decision to act was the student demonstration on December 9, 1936. In the few weeks prior to the Sian Incident, the city of Sian was overshadowed with the uproar of "suspension of civil war for a united front against Japan," a scene too familiar in Peking and Shanghai. To commemorate the December 9 demonstration at Peking a year earlier, students at Sian planned a huge demonstration. Chang, Yang, and Governor Shao tried to avert the student demonstration, apparently feeling that such a demonstration would be looked upon as unfriendly toward Chiang, and even embarrassing to him during his presence in Sian. They failed to persuade the students to hold memorial meetings instead of street demonstrations. Upon learning of the demonstration, Chiang ordered the police to fire on the students who resorted to violence. As a result, two students were shot and wounded. But the students were by no means intimidated, and they insisted on marching to Lin-t'ung to see Chiang. At this juncture, the Young Marshal rushed to the scene and successfully persuaded the students to return by promising that he would present the case to Chiang on their behalf. Further, he assured them that "the question of resistance against Japan would be answered by fact within a week." [53]

To his dismay, when the Young Marshal brought the students' petition to Chiang, not only did Chiang show little appreciation for his part as intercessor between Chiang and the students, but he even blamed Chang for taking up the cudgel for the demonstrators. Chiang gives his version of the rebuttal to Chang that

> the other day, Han-ch'ing reported to me that at Pa-chiao he said to the demonstrators: "I can serve as your representative; if you have anything to say, please

say it to me. At the same time, I am also a representative of the Generalissimo, capable of considering your request." He seemed very proud of what he did. I presently pointed out his wrongs by saying that a person will never be able to serve as representatives of two opposing parties, while standing in the middle. Should one who has faith in his leader do like that?[54]

According to the Young Marshal, he argued with Chiang, saying that the students were patriotic, pure youths. Chiang rebuked him by saying that "there is no way to deal with patriotic youths save shooting them with machine guns."[55] True to their claim, both Chang and Yang in their public speeches and radio broadcasts immediately following the Incident asserted that they were fully convinced that Chiang could not change his policies as shown by his attitude toward the students of the December 9 demonstration. As all hope of moving Chiang with written petitions and verbal supplications vanished, the Young Marshal must have realized that a showdown with Chiang was inevitable. However dreadful, the idea of ping-chien naturally reemerged and took hold of his mind.

V. THE DECEMBER 12TH COUP D'ÉTAT

Since the idea of the coup originated with Yang, Chang was assured of his cooperation. All he needed to do was to inform Yang that he now had made up his mind. Apparently this was done during the night of December 9 or on the morning of December 10. On December 10, Yang dispatched an airplane to Ninghsia with a message to invite Governor Ma Hung-k'uei to come to Sian. But Ma refused on the grounds that he had not received an order from the Generalissimo.[1] It is still not clear as to whether Yang intended to invite Ma to participate in the coup or to lure him to Sian to hold him as hostage so as to relieve the rear threat of the Sian rebels.

The following day, the Young Marshal sent his airplane to the Kansu front to bring back to Sian brigade-commander T'ang Chün-yao who would have the hazardous but historical mission of taking the Generalissimo into custody. The day of December 11 was full of events for both the captor and the captive. In the afternoon, Li T'ien-ts'ai accompanied by several high officials came to see Chiang without previous appointment. During the conversation, Chiang severely reprimanded them for negligence of duty. He is reported as having said that "Sian has already turned into a Red city; what have you political workers been doing, by allowing the state of affairs to drift to such a low degree?" That evening Chiang invited Chang, Yang and Yü Hsüeh-chung and several top commanders of the Central Army for dinner, but Yang and Yü failed to appear. Asked why Yang and Yü did not come, Chang answered that they served as hosts in the city to entertain the Nanking high officials who came with Chiang. The dinner and the conference that followed were apparently intended to wind up everything in the Northwest, particularly the launching of the bandit-suppression campaign, before Chiang's departure. When the dinner was over, the Young Marshal with several Nanking generals, including Ch'en Ch'eng, Ch'en Chi-ch'eng, Ch'en Tiao-yüan, and Wan Yao-huang, joined the farewell party in the city.[2]

It was nearly midnight when the Young Marshal said good-bye to the Nanking dignitaries at the hostel. Then he returned home and called a top-level meeting of the Tungpei Army. Except Wan Fu-lin who was at Peking and Ho Chu-kuo who could not be located in Sian on short notice, all army commanders were there. Also attending the meeting were Liu To-ch'üan, Commander of the 105th Division, Pai Feng-hsiang, a division commander of cavalry, and T'ang Chün-yao. Other senior officers without actual command were present at the meeting: Tung Ying-pin, the new chief of staff, Mi Ch'un-lin, chief of general administration, Huang Hsien-sheng, dean of the Wang-ch'ü Officers' Corps, and Pao Wen-yüeh, senior adviser. There were also a few civilian officials at the meeting: Wu Chia-hsiang, secretary-general, Lu Kuang-chi, director of political and party affairs, and Li T'ien-ts'ai, deputy director of the political department, all of the Northwestern Bandit-Suppression Headquarters.[3]

The Fateful Day

According to one account given by a participant of the meeting, there was a terrible silence in the conference room when the Young Marshal announced his decision and asked for some suggestions. Leading commanders like Yü Hsüeh-chung and Miu Cheng-liu are reported to have raised some questions along the line of "How and what will be the next step after Chiang is seized?" and "Is the Vice Commander determined to carry the whole episode through?" The Young Marshal replied repeatedly that his first step was "to support Chiang in resistance against Japan" and so were his second and third steps. The die was cast; no one dared raise an objection which might imperil his own life. They unanimously endorsed the plan by saying that "since Vice Commander has already decided, we are glad to obey his order." Afterwards, the Young Marshal assigned T'ang Chün-yao to take charge of the whole mission of seizing Chiang at Hua-ch'ing-ch'ih. He was to be assisted by Pai Feng-hsiang, Liu Kuei-wu, a regiment commander, and Sun Ming-chiu, commander of the 2nd guard battalion. It was Sun who led his 2nd Company to carry out the operation. The Young Marshal gave his direct order something like this: "Bring the Generalissimo to the city. There will be no bloodshed. Unless absolutely necessary, no shot should be fired. The Generalissimo must be taken alive and unharmed at all cost. If he gets hurt, I will shoot you two [T'ang and Sun]!"[4]

While T'ang and all others who were involved in the operation at Lin-t'ung departed, those remaining at Chang's house began to devote themselves to the drafting of the declaration which would be released as soon as the Lin-t'ung operation was completed. Until

TABLE 1

Organizational System of the Tungpei Army

51st Army	Commander Yü Hsüeh-chung	113rd Division	Commander Li Chen-t'ang
		114th Division	Mou Chung-hsing
		118th Division	Chou Kuang-lieh
53rd Army*	Wan Fu-lin	129th Division	Chou Fu-ch'eng
57th Army	Miu Cheng-liu	108th Division	Ch'ang En-to
		109th Division	Huo Shou-i
		111th Division	unknown
67th Army	Wang I-che	106th Division	Shen K'o
		107th Division	Wu K'o-jen
		117th Division	unknown
Cavalry Army	Ho Chu kuo	3rd Division	Kuo Hsi-p'eng
		6th Division	Pai Feng-hsiang
		7th Division	unknown
		10th Division	T'an Tzu-hsin
105th Division**	Liu To-ch'üan	1st Brigade	Tung Yen-p'ling
		2nd Brigade	T'ang Chun-yao
		3rd Brigade	Kao Fu-yüan
		112th Division	unknown
		115th Division	unknown
		120th Division	unknown

*The 53rd Army had three divisions, only the 129th division was stationed in Shensi under the command of the 67th Army, while the other two divisions were stationed in Hopeh province.
**The 105th Division used to be the Young Marshal's guard division; numbering over 20,000 men, it was equivalent to two regular armies in size.

then, they all nervously sat up the whole night, waiting for the de-
nouement of Chiang's captivity. [5]

Sun's battalion had been responsible for the garrison duty from
Lin-t'ung to Sian since Chiang took his abode at Hua-ch'ing-ch'ih,
the security of which was undertaken by Chiang's bodyguards, numbering about 50 men, some in uniform and others in plain clothes.
Sun's 120 men loaded in four trucks were bound for Lin-t'ung which
they reached at 5:30 a.m. Failing to persuade the sentries to open
the gate, Sun's men tried to force their entrance and a skirmish
ensued. The Tungpei troops fought their way directly to Chiang's
room after having killed most of Chiang's bodyguards. To their
dismay, they found the room empty. [6]

Chiang had already gotten up when he heard the first shot
coming from the gate. As the fighting intensified in the front,
Chiang thought that it must have been a minor mutiny of the Tungpei Army instigated by the Communists. In the nick of time, he
slipped out the back door with three aides and scaled the wall. Unfortunately, in jumping down on the other side of the wall he was
slightly injured but still managed to climb up the mountain for some
distance until he found a cave beside a huge stone for shelter. For
nearly two hours, the Tungpei troops were at a loss as they sought
in vain for the Generalissimo. While examining Chiang's room,
they picked up his diary and some documents, along with his false
teeth. They sent some of the wounded to the hospital including General Ch'ien Ta-chün, Chiang's chief aide-de-camp. They also shot in
revenge Chiang Hsiao-hsien, the notorious commander of the 3rd
gendarme regiment, archenemy of the students of Peking. [7]

Twice they searched the mountain and twice they failed to lo-
cate Chiang. They wondered whether Chiang had made good his
escape, a situation which seemed unlikely considering that the mountain was virtually sealed from all directions. It was not until nine
o'clock that they found Chiang. Sun Ming-chiu immediately rushed
to Chiang and prostrated himself in front of him, saying while shed-
ding tears that "this is not a revolt of the Tungpei Army, but support for Chiang to lead it in a war of resistance against Japan." [8]
Having suffered from exhaustion and injury, Chiang was no longer
capable of walking. Sun and others carried him on their backs all
the way down the mountain to the gate of Hua-ch'ing-ch'ih, where a
car was in waiting. Sitting between T'ang Chün-yao and Sun Ming-

chiu, Chiang somewhat regained his strength and carried on some casual conversation with T'ang. Entering the city, Chiang noticed that all the troops belonged to the 17th Route Army; he even suspected that the Tungpei troops had disarmed Yang Hu-ch'eng's troops and put on their uniforms so as to deceive the people. He was further perplexed when the car was driven directly to the "new city building," the headquarters of Yang instead of Chang. In his mind, Yang, having a long tradition in the revolutionary rank, would not have joined the Tungpei Army in revolting against him.[9]

Upon his arrival at the "new city building" Chiang was received in full dignity, for the Young Marshal and Yang lined up all the senior officers and a military band to welcome him. Seeing the Young Marshal, Chiang understandably flew into a fury and said, "Don't salute me, you are not my subordinate, and I am your captive!" However, the Young Marshal aided Chiang to his room and immediately called in Doctor Tso Ti-ju to tend his injuries. As usual, the Young Marshal paid his superior reverence throughout his two weeks' captivity.[10]

Simultaneously inside Sian, Yang Hu-ch'eng's force was entrusted with the mission of seizing all the Nanking establishments and personages at Sian, most of them accompanying Chiang on the trip and staying at the Sian hostel. The plight of those dignitaries who were captured at the hostel is vividly described by noted writer Agnes Smedley, who was also the guest of the same hostel at the time. Detained in the hostel were Ch'en Ch'eng, Ch'en Chi-ch'eng, Ch'en Tiao-yüan, Chiang Ting-wen, Chiang Tso-pin, Chiang Po-ch'eng, Chu Shao-liang, Chang Ch'ung, Wan Yao-huang, and Wei Li-huang. In the midst of confusion, Shao Yüan-ch'ung, a veteran KMT leader, while trying to escape by jumping out through the window, was shot, and later died in the hospital. All the important Nanking appointees in Shensi were under house arrest: Shao Li-tzu, P'eng Shao-hsien, commissioner of civil affairs, Chou Hsüeh-ch'ang, commissioner of education, Yen Tao-kang, chief of staff, and Tseng Kuang-ch'ing, director of the political department, both of the Northwestern Bandit-Suppressing Headquarters. Also detained in Sian were several hundred air force personnel along with 50 airplanes.[11] Beginning at 5:30 a.m., General Sun Wei-ju, Yang's right-hand man who was entrusted with the operation in Sian, moved his garrison brigade and artillery regiment. First, they seized by surprise the gendarme headquarters, symbol of the Central Government power in Shensi, and many of the gendarmes were killed since they were greatly hated by the soldiers of the 17th Route Army whose poor discipline had been the target of gendarmes' punishments. Then they turned to the police headquarters, another stronghold of the invisible power of Nanking. They easily disarmed all the police but failed to catch the police chief, Ma Chih-ch'ao, who made good his escape by disguising himself as a rickshaw puller. For more than two hours, Yang's soldiers ran amuck, killing and shooting indiscriminately; even the deputy commander of the Tungpei 53rd Army T'ang Feng-chia and exmayor of Tsingtao Hu Jo-yü, who was visiting the Young Marshal, were wounded. The situation was not brought under control until 9 o'clock, when an extra news bulletin was issued to account for the coup, and handbills listing the eight demands of the Sian rebels were distributed throughout the city. [12]

Equally regrettable as the wanton killing was the three-day looting following the Incident. The bandit-oriented troops of Yang saw the coup as a golden opportunity to make a fortune. Now the city of Sian became their prize. Except for the area controlled by the Tungpei Army, the whole city was affected. Nearly all banks were robbed, including the Young Marshal's Tungpei Border-Developing Bank, and its manager was killed. Many warehouses of the Central Government were ransacked, particularly the Central Army's provisions train loaded with flour worth $1,500,000 (Chinese dollars). Looting continued for three days without ceasing until five soldiers were put to death in a public display. [13]

Outside Sian, the Young Marshal tried to carry out two co-ordinate actions: one was at Lanchow, metropolis of Kansu, and the other at Loyang. One of Chang's three artillery brigades, the 6th Brigade, commanded by General Huang Ta-ting, was stationed at Loyang. Shortly before the Lin-t'ung operation, the Young Marshal secretly telegraphed Huang with the following instructions: (1) seize the Central Bank of Loyang; (2) work with Commanding Officer Chao of the cadet detachment of the Loyang Military Academy; (3) attack the two military schools, army and air force; and (4) blockade the airport of Loyang. [14]

Instead of obeying Chang's order, Huang handed over the telegram to General Chu Shao-chou, garrison commander of Loyang. Huang's failure to carry out Chang's order had an important bearing on the outcome of the Sian Incident. Not only did it deprive the

Sian rebels of the control of Loyang--which could have served as a link between Sian and Hopeh where Chang still had two divisions-- but also the leaking out of the news of the Sian coup gave to the Central Army the opportunity to capture Tungkuan, the most strategic point commanding Shensi. Without delay, General Chu did two things: he immediately sent the 46th Army under the command of Fan Sung-pu to move westward to beat the rebels for the control of Tungkuan. Indeed Yang Hu-ch'eng had ordered his division commander Feng Ch'in-tsai to move from Tali, cross the Wei River, and occupy Tungkuan. Feng's troops were four hours late, and Tungkuan was taken by the Central Army.[15]

Chu's second action involved a salvage mission. Informed of the Sian Coup, Mao Pang-ch'u and Wang Shu-ming, commanders of Chiang's air force, made a futile attempt at saving the Generalissimo by dispatching an airplane to Lin-t'ung to bring him out of danger. The pilot, Ts'ai Hsi-ch'ang, made a successful forced landing in front of Hua-ch'ing-ch'ih, but he was immediately taken prisoner. Ts'ai was successful in deceiving his interrogators, and his mission was not discovered. It was too late anyway, for by the time he landed there, it was already 10 o'clock and Chiang was already safely situated inside Sian.[16]

In pursuance of the Young Marshal's order, the 51st Army at Lanchow staged a coup. On the afternoon of December 12, the 113th Division of the 51st Army together with the special service battalion seized the whole city and disarmed one regiment and one artillery battalion of the Central Army. The whole city was put on a war footing never before experienced at Lanchow. Looting and killing were so widespread and persistent that they resulted in great loss of lives. For several days communications with the outside were cut. The tension at Lanchow was not relaxed until the return of Governor Yü Hsüeh-chung from Sian a week later.[17] Unlike Loyang, which was strategic, the control of Lanchow would not have changed the military situation; at best it may have served as a rear base for the Sian rebels. Conversely, had the Tungpei Army failed to seize Lanchow, its morale would have been shaken. So far as the Sian rebels were concerned, their initial goal was accomplished with the detention of Chiang. What lay before them, particularly the Young Marshal, was how to persuade Chiang to change his policy--to transform the civil war into a war of resistance against Japan.

Chiang in Captivity

In the early morning of December 12, the Sian rebels issued a declaration in the form of a circular telegram to which 19 signatures were attached: eight of the Nanking dignitaries under arrest, three of the 17th Route Army, Yang Hu-ch'eng, Sun Wei-ju, and Feng Ch'in-tsai, one Ma Chan-shan, hero of anti-Japanese fighting in Manchuria, and seven of the Tungpei generals headed by the Young Marshal. The declaration, addressed to the chairman of the National Government, all leaders of the central and provincial governments, people's organizations, the press, and schools, began with the enumeration of China's humiliating agreements with Japan since the Mukden Incident. It then mentioned an international conspiracy underway, designed to sacrifice the Chinese people. It praised the gallant fighting of Chinese soldiers in east Suiyuan, while deploring the appeasement of the Central Government toward Japan in its efforts to destroy patriotic movement, particularly in the shooting of students at Sian. In order to urge the Generalissimo to make some reflection and to change his policy, it made the signers' last remonstration to him, but guaranteed his personal safety. In conclusion it put forth eight demands:

1. Reorganize the Nanking Government, and admit all parties to share the joint responsibility of saving the nation.

2. Stop all kinds of civil war.

3. Immediately release the patriotic leaders arrested in Shanghai.

4. Release all political prisoners throughout the country.

5. Emancipate the patriotic movement of the people.

6. Safeguard the political freedom of the people to organize and call meetings.

7. Actually carry out the will of Dr. Sun Yat-sen.

8. Immediately call a National Salvation Conference.[18]

The declaration of the Sian rebels that contained the eight demands was not presented to Chiang at first. Realizing that Chiang was injured from the fall and that he was so upset by the events of the day, the Young Marshal dared not mention the demands to him. [19] During the first two days of his captivity, Chiang refused to eat and for most of the two weeks at Sian he lay in bed. On the second day, the Young Marshal tried to move Chiang out of the "new city building" to a safer and more comfortable home of a division commander named Kao Kuei-chih, but Chiang refused to move. Though still having some misgivings about Chang's intention, Chiang late in the afternoon of December 14 acceded to move after the arrival of William Donald; there he remained for the next eleven days until on Christmas Day he flew out of Sian.

During his whole captivity, Chiang was treated by the Young Marshal with the same respect and courtesy as before. Half an hour after settling down in the "new city building," Chiang had his first talk with Chang, during which he furiously reprimanded Chang and demanded that he either be sent back immediately to Loyang or killed. He said that under duress he would neither accept any terms nor enter into any negotiations. Chang claimed that the coup was revolutionary in that by staging it he made the plea on behalf of the people. He merely spoke for the public opinion which demanded the suspension of civil war and the union of all forces in resistance to Japan. The coup was not intended to overthrow Chiang but rather to force him to change his erroneous policy. Nor was Chiang's leadership challenged. He had no intention of taking Chiang's place, although Chiang accused him of trying to do so. Chiang reports what the Young Marshal then said to him:

> Now the staged coup will be judged by the people. If the people approve our policy, then it is proven that we have represented the public opinion, and in the meantime you will clearly understand that there is nothing wrong with my policy. Therefore, please retire and let me take over. If public opinion proves to the contrary, I shall admit my mistake and ask for your help to patch up the affair. I am confident that I always have owed a great deal to your instructions. Please don't be angry and take time to consider the matter. [20] (Emphasis mine.)

Chiang's suspicion of Chang's motive--that he wanted to seize the leadership from Chiang--was not totally groundless.[21] Following Chang's talk as quoted above, Shao Li-tzu, who saw Chiang on the morning of December 12, did suggest to Chiang that

> judging from your uncompromising attitude toward Chang,
> it seems rather difficult to get your release or return
> to Loyang, even though [the rebels] dare not do any
> harm. However, with the passage of time, things might
> get out of hand. As the future of the nation is laid on
> your shoulder, you should first consider your own safe-
> ty. Please recall that on two occasions, in 1927 and in
> 1931, you had resigned, but before long came back as
> the Party and nation needed you. Could it be possible
> for you to make the same consideration this time?[22]

As is well known, Shao's advice was rejected as unacceptable under the circumstances. It should be noted that Shao gave the advice to Chiang voluntarily without being instigated by the Young Marshal or anyone.[23] Only one of the above two instances in which Chiang's retirement was mentioned is related to Chang. Probably out of anger in his argument with Chiang, Chang said to Chiang: "Please retire and let me take it over"; otherwise Chiang had no reason to put this in his book, written shortly after his release.[24] However, given the circumstances, Chang's words cannot be taken as a considered statement, much less his standing posture. Throughout the writings and public pronouncements made by Chang before and after the Sian Incident, there is no trace that would lead to the impression that he wanted to seize the leadership from Chiang. On the contrary, all evidence tends to confirm that the Young Marshal from the beginning had hoped: (1) that Chiang would have only to carry out some, not all, of the eight demands; (2) that Chiang should be set free as soon as possible; and (3) that he would accompany Chiang to Nanking so as to take upon himself the full responsibility for the detention of the national leader.

On the morning of December 12, the Young Marshal received General Wan Yao-huang, one of the captives at the Sian hostel. Wan, an army commander, had just had his 13th Division deployed at Hsienyang, 20 miles west of Sian. Evidently Chang's purpose of summoning Wan was purely military since he wanted to know the exact location of the 13th Division. But at the same time, Chang did tell Wan that as soon as some of the eight demands were accepted, he would send Chiang back to Nanking.[25]

In line with the spirit of the December 12th declaration issued to the outside world, the Young Marshal also dispatched a personal telegram to Dr. H. H. Kung, Vice-President of the Executive Yüan and Madame Chiang Kai-shek's brother-in-law, reassuring Kung of Chiang's safety at Sian. In fact, it was this message which raised Kung's hope and confidence that the Sian Incident could be solved by peaceful means.[26]

As in his "Confession," the Young Marshal himself claims his intentions in the coup could not be better proven than his public statements made during the Sian Incident. Many still living in Taiwan today were present during his speeches. True to his claim, on December 13, he found time to gather all the staff of the Northwestern Bandit-Suppressing Headquarters to present his account of the Incident, in which he described his attitude toward Chiang and envisioned the consequences of the Incident:

> Now Generalissimo Chiang is very safe. We cherish no
> personal vengeance against him; absolutely we are not
> opposed to him personally, but to his policies and
> methods. By opposing his policies and methods, we enable
> him to make a self-examination; this is just because we
> support him. Our action will not do any harm to him.
> Should he give up his past policies and resolutely lead the
> work for the war of resistance against Japan, we would im-
> mediately support him and obey him. Then, even if
> he regards our present action as rebellious and will
> therefore punish us, we would willingly accept it with-
> out regret. This is because what we contend is our
> policies. As long as our policies can be adopted and
> our goal can be accomplished, we do not care for any
> other thing.[27]

In the same vein, the Young Marshal gave his views in a broadcast to the nation on December 14, though not in so many words.[28] While neither the prime goal of his coup nor his sincere attitude toward Chiang can be doubted, there is evidence that reflects some changes in Chang's attitude toward Chiang as well as his views on the future course of the Sian Incident. In the entry of Chiang's diary on December 14, there is a crucial passage recorded:

> Early in the morning, Chang came, standing behind the
> door and shedding tears as if he repented. . . . At
> noon, he came back again, insisting on my moving . . .
> which I resolutely refused. Then Chang said: "Having
> perused the Generalissimo's diaries and some impor-
> tant documents, we now come to an understanding of
> the Generalissimo's great personality and loyalty to
> revolution as well as your painful devotion to the task
> of national salvation. . . . Had I known ten or twenty
> percent of what is written in the diaries, I would not
> have done so frivolous, so rude, a thing. . . ."[29]

The above passage does not reveal exactly what Chiang wrote in his
diary; all we can say is that the Young Marshal was convinced of
Chiang's loyalty to the revolution and dedication to national salvation.
However, Chiang did mention that in his diary on December 10, he
criticized Chang by saying that when the Young Marshal was assigned
to the Northwest, he was expected to use the opportunity to render
his best service to the country. Quite to the contrary, he had almost turned the great Northwest into another Manchuria. Chiang
regrettably felt how unwise and impotent he had been in not knowing
his people and in assessing their abilities.[30] He epitomized his
criticism of the Young Marshal in the December 10 diary entry:

> Han-ch'ing is clever in trifles but foolish in great
> matters; he cannot hold to things steadfastly, nor
> are his mind and will stable. These are indeed
> deplorable.[31]

Chiang's criticism of the Young Marshal as written in his diary was
cogent enough to dispel both the suspicion of Chiang's good will on
the part of the Young Marshal and to allay his fear that Chiang may
have tried to eliminate him. At least one source goes into some
detail concerning Chiang's diaries showing such suspicion and fear
as groundless. First, when Dr. H. H. Kung was dispatched on the
mission to attend the coronation of King Edward VIII in May 1936,
he was also entrusted with a secret mission--to negotiate with Krupp
of Germany for the purchase of arms and ammunition in preparation
for war with Japan, a great part of which had reached China by the
end of 1936. Second, Chiang ordered Ch'eng Ch'ien, then chief of
staff of the Chinese army, and others to draft a comprehensive plan
for a war of resistance against Japan. In the planned military oper-

ation, the Young Marshal was to command one of the seven front armies to fight Japan. [32]

With the revelation of Chiang's diaries, the intended ambiguity of Chiang's attitude toward Japan under the growing collusion of Fascist nations, which had naturally caused the alarm and suspicion of many Chinese intellectuals, now was cleared up in the minds of the Sian rebels. Writing in confinement twenty years later, the Young Marshal confirmed that after reading Chiang's diaries he and Yang Hu-ch'eng were convinced that Chiang was determined to fight Japan. [33] Yet the fact remains that while many sources corroborate Chiang's claim, after reading his diaries Chang changed his attitude toward Chiang; this probably had little effect on the outcome of the Sian Incident. There were far more important factors than his knowledge of what was written in Chiang's diaries not at first anticipated which compelled the Young Marshal to channel the development of the course of the coup. Seeing the immediate results of the coup, the Young Marshal was in great despair. He was as much disappointed with the impotence of his own men as he was shocked at the poor discipline of Yang Hu-ch'eng's troops. [34]

First, the Hua-ch'ing-ch'ih operation turned out to be a tragedy. Although the Generalissimo was captured alive, the operation took a heavy toll of lives with over twenty of Chiang's men killed and a dozen of Chang's soldiers losing their lives. [35] Next, Huang Ta-ting, the artillery commander of the Tungpei Army at Loyang, failed to carry out the Young Marshal's order. Understandably, it was a very difficult mission, but still not an impossible mission. The disloyalty of Huang must have meant more to the Young Marshal than his inability to accomplish the mission. However, had he tried, he would have gained some advantage for the Sian rebels. The control of Loyang by a friendly force or the destruction of the Loyang airport would have freed Sian from the threat of an air raid which proved to be real. By merely delaying the disclosure of the Sian coup, Huang would have helped the Sian rebels to secure Tungkuan, a result which would have relieved Sian of a land attack by the Central Army.

Shortly before the launching of the coup, General Yang Hu-ch'eng ordered Feng Ch'in-tsai, commander of the 42nd Division of the 17th Route Army, to make a forced march to Tungkung from Tali, thirty miles away. Since Feng was too slow to move his troops, Tungkung was invaded by the 28th Division of the Central Army commanded by Fan Sung-pu. [36] Realizing that his chances of success in fighting the Central Army were very few and that he had no faith in the Sian leaders, particularly the Young Marshal, to whom he would not offer help, Feng cast his fate with the strong side. Feng's force represented one-third of Yang's total strength and therefore his defection not only dealt a heavy blow to Yang Hu-ch'eng but also set a precedent for other recalcitrant generals.

Alarmed by the initial failures, the Young Marshal must have realized that the military situation was not favorable, if not peril-ous. With Tungkuan in the hands of the Central Army, toward which Nanking concentrated some eleven divisions, an invasion of the Central Army in Shensi was imminent. In the Northwest, i.e., in Shensi and Kansu, in addition to the 13th Division of Wan Yao-huang which had been entrenched at Hsienyang, the Central Army commanded by Mao Ping-wen, Hu Tsung-nan, and Kuang Lin-cheng, must have numbered 50,000 men. [37] Had a military conflict become inevitable, the war would have been very bloody, and without the participation of the Red Army, the Tungpei and Hsipei Armies alone could not withstand the Central Army's onslaught. In view of the difficulties that lay ahead, the Young Marshal decided to invite Chou En-lai and other Communist leaders to come to Sian. [38]

VI. NANKING: DIVIDED IN INTENTS AND POLICIES

The news of the Sian coup reached Nanking early on the morning of December 12 through Loyang. By the afternoon, Nanking received the Sian rebels' circular telegram setting forth the eight demands. Madame Chiang Kai-shek and Kung Hsiang-hsi, Vice-President of the Executive Yüan, were both in Shanghai at the time. Kung learned the news at 4:00 p.m., and was briefed on the Incident by telephone by Ho Ying-ch'in, Minister of Military Affairs, from Nanking at 8:00 that evening. Kung immediately got in touch with Madame Chiang and a family conference including Madame Chiang, T. V. Soong, and William H. Donald was held at his residence. Then the party took the night train bound for Nanking. [1]

Two Opposed Groups

Shortly before midnight on December 12, a temporary joint conference of the Standing Committee of the CEC of the KMT and the Central Political Council of the Central Government was convened without awaiting Kung's return. It adopted the following provisions: (1) Vice-President of the Executive Yüan will be Acting President in the absence of Chiang Kai-shek; (2) standing members of the Military Council will be increased to seven, including Ho Ying-ch'in, Ch'eng Ch'ien, Li Lieh-chün, Chu Pei-te, T'ang Sheng-chih, and Ch'en Shao-k'uan; (3) Vice-Chairman Feng Yü-hsiang and standing members will be responsible for the affairs of the Military Council; and (4) Ho Ying-ch'in, Minister of Military Affairs, and members of the Military Council will be responsible for conducting troops. The joint conference further resolved that Chang Hsüeh-liang be shorn of all official positions and apprehended for military trial by the Military Council, and that his army be brought under the direct command of the Council. [2]

In its December 13th mandate, the Central Government declared that adequate measures were being taken to cope with the situation resulting from the Sian revolt. It also pointed out that all governmental agencies both in and outside the capital were carrying on their functions as usual in accordance with previously determined policies. [3]

When Madame Chiang and H. H. Kung arrived at Nanking on the morning of December 13, they found that the Nanking leaders were divided into two groups over the issue of how to suppress the Sian mutiny and how to save Chiang Kai-shek. One group led by Tai Chi-t'ao and some military leaders, notably Ho Ying-ch'in, believed that the Young Marshal, in staging the coup, must have had some support, which may have been drawn from two sources: domestically from such militarists as Han Fu-ch'ü of Shantung, Li Chi-shen of Kwangsi, Sung Che-yüan of Hopeh, and Liu Hsiang of Szechwan, and externally from the Chinese Communists and even the Third International. In order to achieve political demands, Chang and Yang undoubtedly would try to hold Chiang hostage as long as they could. The Central Government could not yield to force: doing so would result in great damage to the country. These leaders could not make up their minds to launch an attack on Sian which certainly would endanger Chiang's life; nor could they tolerate the Sian rebels going unpunished. They were convinced that the Central Government must remain firm by a show of force to Sian; in so doing if Chiang were alive he would be safer. Conversely, Nanking's delay in launching an expedition against Sian would be interpreted as one of weakness, and therefore, even if Chiang were alive, he probably would not be able to return.[4]

A diametrically opposed view was held by Madame Chiang and H. H. Kung. They believed that since the Chang-Yang demand for a policy of war of resistance against Japan coincided with Chiang Kai-shek's long-cherished determination, it was simply a matter of time for the implementation of that policy. If the change in national policy had been the sole aim of the coup as the rebels claimed, there would be enough room for negotiation. Further, the Young Marshal in his telegrams had repeatedly guaranteed Chiang's safety. What had to be done was to find out the truth about the Generalissimo's situation before any punitive operation was undertaken.[5]

Madame Chiang fell into a fury with the Nanking generals, particularly Ho Ying-ch'in. First, she had to fight off the view that she was a woman who could not be expected to be reasonable under the circumstances. Then she had to persuade the hot-headed military leaders to postpone the planned attack on Sian until the full facts of the situation in Sian were known. Madame Chiang got her way not without great opposition, for one of the leaders said that "she is a woman pleading for the life of her husband."[6] But she made a vehement plea:

I am making this appeal to you, not as a woman thinking
of the safety of her husband, but as a citizen taking a
dispassionate and realistic attitude to secure the least
costly solution to a grave national problem. . . . But
what you are proposing today actually endangers the life
of the Generalissimo, and since in the mind of the
people, as well as in my own mind, the Generalissimo's
safety is inseparable from the continued unity, and even
existence, of the nation itself at this critical period of
our history, no effort should be spared to secure his
release by peaceful means. [7]

Her heroic stance and eloquence had won the day, and the march of
the Central Army to Sian was temporarily halted.

Typical of the reaction of the civilian leaders of the Nanking
government was a speech delivered at the weekly memorial service
on December 14 by Lin Shen, Chairman of the Republic of China.
Lin undertook a bitter attack on the Young Marshal. First, the
reported policy of the Young Marshal was a so-called union with the
Communists for the purpose of resisting the enemy. The policy
was childish because the purpose of resistance against the enemy
was survival and existence, whereas the result of union with the
Communists could only be extinction. Second, the Young Marshal
neither resisted the enemy during the September 18 Incident nor
fought against it under the direction of the Central Government, but
he wanted to resist the enemy five years after the loss of Manchuria, in the remote Northwest far from the enemy, and after his
revolt against the Central Government. Even a three-foot tall boy
would not fail to understand that what he preached had little to do
with his practice. Third, the policy of the suppression campaign
against the Communists was based upon the resolution adopted by
the KMT plenum, so that it would not undergo any change as a result of Chiang's temporary absence. [8]

Sharing the same rostrum with Lin Shen, Ch'ü Cheng, President of the Judiciary Yuan, challenged the Young Marshal's eight
demands set forth in the December 12 manifesto by pointing out that

in his telegram of treason, there is nothing to indicate
that he is prepared for resistance against the enemy.
First, he wants to reorganize the government and, sec-

ond, he wants to unite all parties and factions. It is obvious that his purpose is first, to overthrow the National Government and, second, to topple the Kuomintang. [9]

Probably the most intriguing reaction came from Feng Yü-hsiang, a well-known political enemy of Chiang, who was appointed Acting Chairman of the Military Affairs Council in the absence of Chiang. Feng sent a telegram to the Young Marshal, urging reconciliation. Apart from assuring the Young Marshal that "whatever opinions you may hold can be solved by your releasing Generalissimo Chiang who, as an open and frank revolutionary leader, would assuredly lend most favorable views to your suggestions," he offered himself and several of his friends to go to Sian and to be held as hostages for Chiang. Even to this day, Feng's overture is ridiculed as frivolous and insincere, consistent with his personality. [10]

Militarily, Nanking immediately mobilized its best troops for an expedition to Shensi and induced the defection of generals from the Chang-Yang camp. The Whampoa graduates, notably members of the first class, many of whom were division commanders of the Central Army, all flew into a fury and were the first to answer the call of a punitive expedition against Sian. Following the example of the thirty-eight ranking generals who sent a telegram to the Young Marshal on December 14 demanding the immediate release of Chiang, 275 young generals, all graduates of the Whampoa Military Academy of which Chiang had been the president since its founding, representing over 70,000 graduates and students, dispatched a telegram to the Young Marshal couched in most threatening language:

> If by chance you do not repent but cause harm to the Generalissimo, we, the alumni, swear that we shall deal with you with all our strength that is within us, and that we shall never live under the same sky and sun with you and with anyone related to you. This is our determination and there will be nothing to change it. [11]

Most interesting of all was the episode of Chiang's General Training Corps, then the best equipped and trained division in China, and commanded by General Kuei Yung-ch'ing. Kuei, without waiting for General Ho Ying-ch'in's order, began to move his troops from

Nanking to Tungkuan and to put them in the forefront to face the
Tungpei Army at Ch'ih-shui, where the only battle in the Sian Incident was fought but Kuei's army suffered a stunning defeat.[12] However, the increasing pressure from Nanking failed to intimidate the
Tungpei generals. Unlike some generals of Yang's 17th Route Army,
from beginning to end the Tungpei generals remained loyal to the
Young Marshal but hostile to Nanking, in spite of its repeated attempts at inducing their defection

Politically, the Central Government spared no time in winning
the support of individual military leaders, such as Liu Hsiang of
Szechwan, Sung Che-yüan of Hopeh, Han Fu-ch'ü of Shantung, Yen
Hsi-shan of Shansi, and Li Tsung-jen and Pai Ch'ung-hsi of Kwangsi.
All these semiwarlords publicly professed their continued loyalty to
the Central Government, but at best they sat on the fence watching
the outcome of the struggle between Nanking and Sian, while at
worst they connived with the Sian rebels to hasten Chiang's fall.
One typical appeal of the Central Government to the provincial militarists may be seen in H. H. Kung's message to Yen Hsi-shan,
which is given in part:

Arriving back at Nanking this morning, I received two
telegrams from Han Ch'ing [alias Chang Hsüeh-liang],
and have known the details of the incident. The whole
country is sympathetic to the policy of resistance
against Japan, a policy to which Generalissimo Chiang
and his colleagues in the Central Government all agree.
That we are united to fight the enemy in Suiyuan this
time is well known to all. While victory against the
enemy in eastern Suiyuan has been continuously reported an internal coup d'etat abruptly occurred. This
could not please the enemy more, for it would afford
the enemy opportunity to do damage to us. I beg you
to stand for justice and to lead the general public to
remove the great difficulty facing the nation. As an
individual, I know Han-ch'ing well. The coup was probably caused either by an emotional impulse or by his
subordinates who seized and forced him to advance radical policy. As Han Ch'ing always holds you in high
esteem, you can help him by showing your magnanimity
and personal friendship to save the present national
crisis.[13]

94

While the provincial warlords took a wait-and-see position on the one hand and Nanking mobilized its military machine for an all-out assault on Sian on the other, Madame Chiang and her relatives wasted no time in putting their personal diplomacy to work. On the very day Madame Chiang arrived back at Nanking, William Donald, formerly Chang Hsüeh-liang's adviser who had almost become Chang's mentor before he joined Chiang's camp in the fall of 1934, was on his way to Sian. The Young Marshal welcomed his coming to Sian. After only a day's sojourn Donald returned to Loyang, thus confirming Chiang's safety. There is no doubt that Donald was the most suitable person to make the trip. But others like T. V. Soong and Madame Chiang were equally willing to go to Sian and be given safe-conduct; so the difference in whether Donald or others went to Sian was not as great as people generally believe. In fact, the Young Marshal did invite Madame Chiang or H. H. Kung to come to Sian with the assurance of safety. [14]

Donald, the Herald of Peace

At the same time that the Sian rebels shocked the world with their telegram of eight demands, the Young Marshal sent personal telegrams to both Madame Chiang and H. H. Kung assuring the personal safety of the kidnapped Generalissimo. At the outset Kung, and also Madame Chiang, thought that the door to negotiations was open. The coming of Donald to Sian really set the stage for fruitful negotiations.

As late as October or November 1936, Donald had secret talks with the Young Marshal, in which the latter told the former about the futile efforts to persuade Chiang to accept a Communist overture of joining forces to fight the Japanese. Then Donald advised the Young Marshal to write out his complaint and to hand it to the Generalissimo which he did. [15] Because of his unshakable confidence in the Young Marshal, Donald never believed that Chiang's life was in danger, and he did not hesitate to offer to fly into Sian to find out the truth. Indeed there was no other person except Donald who commanded the full confidence of both the captor and the captive and whose presence at the most critical hours was looked upon by both as a friend in need.

Bearing letters from Madame Chiang to the Generalissimo and the Young Marshal respectively and accompanied by Colonel Huang

Jen-lin, who might serve as an interpreter, Donald reached Sian at
4 p.m. on December 14, and was immediately taken to Chiang.
With Donald present, the tension between Chiang and Chang eased
measurably. The first sign of a turn of events was Chiang's consent to move out of the Pacification Headquarters and settle in comfortable, secure quarters near the Young Marshal's. Once situated
in his new abode, Chiang apparently relaxed for the first time since
his captivity and began to discuss with Chang some national issues,
particularly the war of resistance against Japan. Evidently, some
discussion focusing on the rebels' eight demands emerged in spite
of Chiang's official denial. [16]

From the time that Chiang was detained, the Young Marshal
had never expected all eight demands to be met, but some of them
would have to be accepted before Chiang's release could be effected.
He explained repeatedly to Chiang that he was not alone in making
decisions and that he had to yield to the majority opinion of high-
ranking generals, particularly Yang Hu-ch'eng. The precarious situation that faced the Young Marshal was clearly comprehended by
Donald through many secret talks he had with the Young Marshal
since his arrival in Sian. Inasmuch as he wanted to save both the
captor and the captive, he approached Yang Hu-ch'eng and a few
high-ranking generals directly. With James C. Elder, a close
friend and personal treasurer of the Young Marshal, interpreting,
Donald admonished them for seizing Chiang, an act which would certainly have a bad effect on public opinion in China and throughout
the world. [17] There is no doubt that Donald personally advised the
Young Marshal to set Chiang free.

Late on December 14, Donald sent in the form of a telegram
the truth of Chiang's safety to the outside world. The next day, he
flew out of Sian to Loyang with James C. Elder. In Loyang, aside
from telephoning Madame Chiang, Donald released to the press the
following news according to a dispatch from Hallett Abend for the
New York Times:

> From the time of his seizure Saturday morning until
> Monday afternoon, Chiang Kai-shek kept his lips stub-
> bornly sealed, said Mr. Donald, and despite many
> visits and pleas by Chang Hsüeh-liang for discussion
> of the situation, the Generalissimo steadfastly refused
> to say one word to his captor.

When Mr. Donald visited the Generalissimo at his place
of detention, Chang Hsüeh-liang renewed his entreaties
that the Generalissimo break his silence and discuss the
impasse. Then for the first time the Generalissimo replied, declaring it was impossible for him to accept any
of Chang Hsüeh-liang's demands under existing conditions
and adding that even if the demands should prove to the
nation's best interests, they could be considered only by
the Central Government. [18]

The news of Chiang's safety brought back by Donald naturally
gladdened the heart of Madame Chiang, but she was not at all happy about Donald's comments on the incident which she regarded too
much in Chang Hsüeh-liang's favor. [19] Her confidence grew as her
view was vindicated. In spite of strong urging from Madame Chiang,
Donald did not return to Nanking but flew back to Sian as promised
the following day. However, Elder, the Britisher, flew on to Nanking. The presence of Elder at Nanking must have had a crucial
impact: the situation at Sian could be known to Madame Chiang and
Western diplomats, particularly the British Ambassador in Nanking,
whereas the reaction of the outside world to the Sian Incident would
be reported back to the Young Marshal. Immediately putting himself at the disposal of Madame Chiang, Elder must have strengthened
her determination to fight any plan for bombing or attacking Sian
which would jeopardize the life of the Generalissimo and lead to civil war. When Donald returned to Sian on the morning of December
16, he found that the Sian leaders were in a different mood. Their
immediate concern was to stop the Nanking attack before negotiations could even be started. [20]

Despite the good news of Chiang's safety, the Nanking government was in no mood to lessen its war efforts or to wait until the
situation cleared up a little more. The Central Political Council
with twenty-six members attending and with Sun Fo as chairman
met on the morning of December 16. [21] Three resolutions were
adopted at the meeting: (1) Ho Ying-ch'in was chosen as Commander-
in-Chief of the punitive forces; (2) the National Government presently issued a mandate of punitive expedition; and (3) Yü Yu-jen was
elected the "Envoy of Goodwill" to the military and people of the
Northwest. [22]

The punitive expedition against Sian was formally declared on
December 16, followed by the inauguration of Ho as its Commander-

in-Chief the next day. In turn, Ho appointed Liu Ch'ih Commanding-General of the Eastern Route Group Army and Ku Chu-t'ung Commanding-General of the Western Route Group Army. Mobilization for a full-scale war against the Sian rebels was well under way with eleven divisions converging at Tungkuan and with all the warplanes concentrated at Loyang for action.[23] It looked as if it needed a miracle to avert the impending war.

In the meantime, the goodwill mission also set out to work. Yü, a native of Shensi, had helped Yang's ascendancy, so that his mission had a special meaning and appeal. Before he left Nanking for Tungkuan on the 17th, he sent a telegram to Chang and Yang, reminding them that "although I will try my best to avoid the calamity of war, still it depends upon your changing of mind momentarily. . . . The safety and freedom of Generalissimo Chiang is the safety and freedom of yours and also of the Chinese people. Difficult as it may seem, the way to solution is easy and simple, but rather hinges upon your great wisdom and courage."[24] However, he had waited at Tungkuan until Chiang's release since he was not allowed to proceed to Sian.

Clearly, the military tension created by the punitive expedition of the Central Army worried the Sian leaders. Through the mediation of General Chiang Po-li, one-time President of the Paoting Military Academy, the Generalissimo agreed to send General Chiang Ting-wen back to Nanking with his personal message to Ho Ying-ch'in that if attacks and bombing were suspended for three days he would be able to return to Nanking by Saturday, December 19.[25]

The military posture of Nanking aroused not only the concern of the Sian leaders but also much resentment by the people of this ancient capital. On December 16, tens of thousands of people gathered in the park to listen to speeches given by Chang Hsüeh-liang, Yang Hu-ch'eng, and others. Having by no means changed his original stand, the Young Marshal had this to say:

In the past year I wrote and spoke to him often, arguing with him to give up a policy which he pursued in defiance of the will of the people. He rejected all my pleas. Recently, General Chiang arrested and imprisoned seven of our National Salvation leaders in Shanghai. . . . I said to General Chiang: "Your cruelty in dealing with the pa-

98

triotic movement of the people is exactly the same as
that of Yuan Shih-k'ai and Chang Tsung-ch'ang."

> Because of the December 9 student demonstration, I
> had a serious verbal clash with Generalissimo Chiang.
> He refused to turn our guns against the enemy but re-
> served them for use against our own people. . . . We
> are convinced that his determination and policy cannot
> be changed . . . and therefore I, together with General
> Yang Hu-ch'eng and other military leaders of the North-
> west, launched the December 12 coup. . . . I seek no
> gain, no territory for myself . . . instead I wish to
> stand with all our armed comrades at the front, fighting
> to the death against Japan.[26]

Chang's December 16th speech is extremely important in that he,
having read Chiang's diaries, did not repent as reported. Had he
changed his views on the Generalissimo, he would not have made
such remarks as to compare Chiang with the notorious Chang Tsung-
ch'ang. Nor did he drop any accusations levelled against Chiang.
Equally revealing is the fact that he was not the prime mover of
the coup but assumed the leadership of the movement.

The militant mood of the Young Marshal's December 16th
speech was caused in part by his anxiety about the military situation at the Tungkuan front created by the advance of the Central
Army, in part by the dissension within the Central Government and
the rise of a pro-Japanese faction led by Ho Ying-ch'in, and in part
by unequivocal support from the CCP based at Po-an, North Shensi.
To stave off the further advance of the Central Army, on December
18 the Young Marshal sent Ho Ying-ch'in a strongly worded telegram
saying that "the return of the Generalissimo has yet to be decided.
Your troops had better avoid military conflict for the time being.
My troops made no advance, but your troops have moved westward
into Tungkuan, while reckless bombing is going on. Who will resort to force? And who will start a civil war? Please order your
troops to move back east of Tungkuan while I halt mine. Conversely, as military men, we all understand the implications of the present military situation."[27] Had the situation gotten out of hand and
a military conflict become inevitable, the Tungpei Army alone, with
no help to be expected from the Hsipei Army, could not successfully
resist the Central Army. Yet with the full participation of the Red
Army, the military situation of Sian was not so desperate as the

Nanking generals envisioned at the time. It became increasingly clear that the CCP would play a greater role in the development of the Sian Incident, whether in a military showdown or in a nego- tiated peaceful settlement.

VII. THE CCP STANCE: A TRIUMPH OF REASON

The news of the Sian Incident greatly surprised the CCP leaders who had not been consulted beforehand.[1] To them, the news of Chiang's capture was too good to be true at first, but they soon were overwhelmed with joy as more telegrams flowed in from Sian to confirm the report. It is natural that some of them wished to see Chiang killed, while others remained composed and farsighted with the long-range goals in perspective.

The Young Marshal reported that Chou En-lai told him in Sian that the CCP leaders "were greatly surprised by the Sian Incident. They were divided into two groups: one more radical group, of which Yeh Chien-ying was one, held a view unfavorable to Chiang; the other group, to which Chou himself belonged, urged the necessity for a peaceful solution favorable to Chiang."[2] This report corroborates Chang Kuo-t'ao's account. In "A Letter to the People of the Nation" issued after his flight from Yenan to Hankow in April 1938, Chang commented on the instant reaction of the CCP leaders to the Sian Incident: "Right after the Sian Incident occurred, the CCP leaders at Yenan [sic] were inevitably excited and made some emotional remarks. At that time the most excited person was someone else but not I, an overt fact which cannot be denied. Later when a peaceful policy was adopted, other CCP leaders and I unanimously approved it."[3]

Who was the most excited person to whom Chang referred in his letter? It was none other than Mao Tse-tung. It is reported that Mao called a meeting of about 300 activists at 4 p.m. on December 13, at which he said, "Since April 12, 1927, Chiang has owed us a blood debt as high as a mountain. Now it is time to liquidate the blood debt. Chiang must be brought to Pao-an for a public trial by the people of the whole country."[4] But the rhetoric in a public speech should not be taken seriously, for Mao was the first to admit that the whole matter was out of his reach.

Chou En-lai's Mission to Sian

The matters decided in Mao Tse-tung's cave in the early afternoon of December 12 were revealed by Chang Kuo-t'ao twenty years after the event. Attending the meeting were probably Mao Tse-tung, Chou En-lai, Chu Teh, Chang Kuo-t'ao, Chin Pang-hsien, Chang Wen-t'ien, Wang Chia-hsiang, Kuan Hsiang-ying, and Jen Pi-shih, all members of the Politburo. The following actions were probably agreed upon: (1) a cable would be dispatched to Chang Hsüeh-liang, praising his action, and assuring him that the CCP would follow his lead in future actions; (2) Chou En-lai, Chin Pang-hsien, and Yeh Chien-ying would fly to Sian via Yenan as CCP representatives; (3) Peng Teh-huai and other generals would be instructed to move their troops to Yenan and its vicinity and to close ranks with friendly armies; (4) the CCP liaison office at Sian would be instructed to refrain from expressing any concrete views, except on the resistance to Japan, until the arrival of Chou En-lai's party; and (5) while in Sian, Chou would have to wait for the reply from Moscow before making any concrete statement. [5]

The departure of Chou's team for Sian was delayed. During the wait, Moscow's instructions arrived on the evening of the 13th. The long telegram from Moscow focused on three points: (1) the Sian Incident was regarded as a Japanese plot aimed at creating confusion and civil war in China; the Soviet Union would not be deceived in lending her support to Sian but rather explicitly would oppose it; (2) what China needed was a united national front, of which Chang Hsüeh-liang would never become the leader; conversely Chiang was probably the only person who had the quality to lead the nation in a war of resistance against Japan; and (3) the CCP should do its utmost to bring about a peaceful settlement and the release of Chiang, while using every opportunity to make approaches to him. [6]

It seems certain that the Moscow telegram was drafted by Stalin himself. Wang Ming, upon his return to China from Moscow in late 1937, told the CCP leaders that Stalin drafted that telegram, basing his information on the statement given by the Soviet foreign office in reply to the inquiries of foreign diplomats at Moscow. [7] Stalin's interpretation of the Sian Incident was fully reflected in an editorial in Izvestiia on December 14 with the heading "The Revolt of Chang Hsüeh-liang." The same view was upheld by Pravda the following day. Evidently Stalin interpreted the Sian event not lacking accurate information about the situation of China in general and the explosive situation of Sian in particular. Ample information must have siphoned to the Kremlin through at least three channels: the CCP representatives at Moscow, the Soviet embassy in China, and Chinese Nationalist and Western diplomats at Moscow. Besides, Marshal Chang had his own agent at Moscow; so did Sheng Shih-ts'ai, the strong man in Sinkiang. On the other hand, Moscow had its agents throughout Sinkiang and Outer Mongolia, who all watched the movement of the Chinese Communists with great concern.

Surely Edgar Snow had furnished the Tass Agency at Peking with the information concerning the fraternal relationship between the CCP and Chang Hsüeh-liang, which he gathered during his visit to the Chinese Soviet base in North Shensi only a few months before the Sian Incident. Snow further asserted that the Soviet military attaché and the Soviet Ambassador Bogomoloff were well aware of his reports which Snow firmly believed had reached Stalin. [8]

Further, the Kremlin must have been well informed of the rapprochement between the Red Army and the Tungpei Army that had been accomplished since the spring of 1936. Inasmuch as the Young Marshal and the CCP leaders had seriously toyed with the idea of setting up a northwestern anti-Japanese coalition government, a proposition well within the scope of the "united front" strategy designed by Moscow, the CCP must have reported to Stalin on the encouraging development and asked for his blessings [9]

It is reported that Mao Tse-tung then stated that "since Moscow has lent its support to China's resistance to Japan, it will also support an anti-Japanese political power in the Northwest. . . . As for Moscow's attitude towards Chang Hsüeh-liang and Yang Hu-ch'eng, it has never explicitly expressed its support for them, nor has it expressed its opposition to them either." [10] Mao believed that if a broadly based anti-Japanese regime in the Northwest were formed, Moscow could not help giving its support. [11]

But one wonders why the Moscow telegram entirely distorted the truth by alleging that the Sian Incident was a Japanese plot. It enraged to the utmost all the CCP leaders whose meticulous labor in forming a "united front" with the Young Marshal suddenly collapsed. It would be most embarrassing to Chou En-lai and his team who were entrusted with the task of explaining this about-face to the Young Marshal, whom they had tried their best to convince that Moscow's support would be forthcoming once the new situation was created. After all, every one of the CCP hierarchy had long since accepted the fact that Stalin's China policy always and everywhere was made first of all in the interests of the Soviet fatherland and that he never hesitated to sacrifice the CCP whenever the former's interests clashed with those of the latter. The Moscow instruction on the Sian Incident was merely another classic example of how Stalin conducted himself in the world Communist movement; it was probably the last instance in which Stalin exerted some great influence on the course of the Chinese Communist movement except for the Soviet intervention in Manchuria after the Allied victory in Japan in 1945.

Chou's party did not reach Sian until December 16 or 17. The date of his arrival at Sian is of paramount importance so far as the interpretation of the role of the CCP in the Sian Incident is concerned. [12] Chou's party of about twenty people was first to go to the airfield at Yenan where the Young Marshal's airplane had been dispatched for them. Upon their arrival at Sian, they were immediately taken to the Young Marshal's residence and warmly received by their host. [13]

To his great surprise, when Chou gradually revealed with apology and regret the Moscow position on the Sian Incident, the Young Marshal was somewhat disappointed but not upset. In the meantime, Chou assured the Young Marshal that under any circumstances the CCP would support and follow the Young Marshal for better or worse, swearing to keep the Yenan agreement. Having sensed that the Young Marshal was relaxed, Chou began to dexterously present the CCP view. Chou was of the opinion that to establish an independent government at Sian and to take some stern measures against Chiang was by no means a good course to follow, because such a development could only afford the best pretext to Chiang's disciples for launching a punitive war against Sian. Chou strongly believed that had the situation gotten out of hand, a prolonged civil war would have occurred, and its outcome would have been unpredictable. [14]

Approaching from the positive side, Chou held that what the Young Marshal and the CCP wanted was a nationwide anti-Japanese situation, certainly not a solidification of their hold on the Northwest.

Hence, they needed unity and cooperation rather than dissension and civil war. It was only logical that while they must make serious preparations for war, they should pursue, in great earnest, negotiations with Chiang for peace.[15]

Consistency in Policy

The CCP approach to the solution of the Sian Incident was underscored by the long-range guiding principle--the "united front" against Japan. The "united front" strategy had undergone a drastic alteration since the summer of 1936, when it was changed from the long-hold policy of "down with Chiang Kai-shek for resistance to Japan" to that of "support Chiang for resistance to Japan." The CCP leaders were fully convinced that Chiang alone could stop the "encircling" campaign against the Communists and lead the nation in a "united front" against Japan.

Less than two weeks before the outbreak of the Sian Incident, in a letter to Chiang Kai-shek, nineteen CCP leaders, mainly military and led by Mao Tse-tung, made a direct plea for the suspension of civil war in order to form a united front against Japan. The letter which undoubtedly reflected the genuine sentiment of the CCP leaders at the time is worth quoting here at length:

> Since last August 1935 the CCP, the Soviet, and the Red Army have repeatedly appealed to you to suspend civil war and form a united resistance to Japan. Since our policy was proclaimed, the whole country, people from all walks of life, and all parties and factions unanimously responded with favor, but you, regardless of the consequences, pursued the encircling campaign. . . . In the last few months when the critical situation had developed in eastern Suiyuan, we anticipated that you would change your policy by dispatching a large army to carry out the war of resistance. Unexpectedly you sent only eight regiments of T'ang En-po's army as a token force in support of the Suiyuan war. On the other hand, you concentrated 260 regiments of Hu Tsung-nan's and others' troops fiercely and irresistably to inundate Shensi and Kansu maintaining the posture that the anti-Japanese Soviet must be wiped out. . . . For the sake of self-defense, we were obliged to fight the battle of Ting-pien and Shan-ch'eng on November 21.

Whereas the people of the whole country were so enraged
by the Japanese invasion that they enthusiastically supported the soldiers in their resistance against the Japanese in Suiyuan, you concentrated all your forces to
engage in a civil war of self-destruction. But what is
the sentiment of the officers and soldiers of the armies
in the Northwest? In the front line, we are well aware
of it, as their feelings and those of ours coincide in an
earnest hope to stop the suicidal civil war but to march
immediately to the battlefield to fight the Japanese.
This is unequivocally demonstrated by the fact that even
your own crack troops could not avoid the terrible defeat at Shan-ch'eng; How could this have happened?
Not that they were incapable of fighting but that they
were unwilling to allow that Chinese fought against Chinese. The fate of the whole country rests with you
alone and hinges on this great decision, a word from
you. Should we stop civil war today, the Red Army and
your huge army of Communist suppression would march
together away from the self-destruction battlefield to the
front of resistance against Japan tomorrow. As a result,
the strength of our national force in Suiyuan will be
abruptly increased many times. Hence, a change of
heart within you will enable us to take our national revenge and to protect our territories as well as to recover our lost land, a result that will make you the glori-
ous anti-Japanese hero, for whom the smoke of burning
incense will not extinguish for generations to come.

We most sincerely beseech you once more that you make
a resolute decision to grant our request to undertake national salvation and transform our relationship from enemies into friends in order to fight the Japanese together.
It will not be merely our fortune but the only road open
to our country and people. The present issue is the
choice between resistance against Japan and surrender to
Japan. Vacillation will only lead astray--destroy the nation, make yourself a slave, and lose the confidence of
the whole people--that results in a curse on you for a
thousand years. Certainly we do not wish that the whole
country and our posterity unanimously say: "The man
who caused the extinction of China was none other than
Chiang Kai-shek."[16]

This lengthy letter unequivocally spelled out that civil war must be stopped because Chinese did not want to fight Chinese. With the suspension of civil war, the Red Army would join forces with the Central Army to fight the Japanese invader under the leadership of Chiang. And Chiang alone had the authority and prestige to stop civil war and lead the country in a war of resistance against Japan.

The CCP situation which had existed before December 12th remained unchanged, in spite of Chiang's captivity. The vacuum of power at Nanking created by Chiang's temporary absence could not, if ever, be filled by anyone, for neither Ho Ying-Ch'in at Nanking nor Chang Hsüeh-liang at Sian had the ability, prestige, and following that were attributed to Chiang's leadership.

Moreover, with Chiang temporarily removed from leadership, the danger of a civil war, greater than the one fought between Chiang and the Red Army for almost a decade, was looming ahead. Although the Communists must have felt greatly relieved by the Sian Incident from the peril of being destroyed by the Nationalists, yet only peace, not civil war, could facilitate the formation of the "united front" which would afford them a platform on the national level and an opportunity to reach the vast masses and most of all to have a respite from fighting. Still the CCP leaders must have been preoccupied with survival, though without losing sight of saving the nation from the Japanese aggression. To advocate war with Nanking might mean either to invite sufferings or to fall into the trap of the pro-Japanese faction then dominating the Nanking government. [17]

The general attitude of the CCP leaders toward the Sian Incident was further confirmed by P'eng Teh-huai in his interview with Helen Snow shortly after the Incident:

Our attitude toward Sian was this: to secure the first perspective--to stop civil war and organize a war against Japan--this is the general line. . . . If we do not hold a peace policy firmly and should have a little wavering, it would be very unfortunate for the Chinese nation, so the Sian event is a turning point of importance in whether this nation lives or dies. If war broke out, the unified three armies in the Northwest could not

annihilate Nanking in a short time and also the same is
true on the other side, so the war would be prolonged
and wide scale. If a civil war occurs, Japan will surely
destroy China.[18]

All those CCP leaders, such as P'eng Teh-huai, Lo Fu, K'ai
Feng, and even Mao Tse-tung, who publicly made their comments
on the Sian Incident shortly after the event, generally followed the
theme of "peace and unity" as the only way for China's survival
under the Japanese aggression. This feeling was embodied in the
CCP's belated public statement in the form of a circular telegram
not issued until December 19. Mao was not the sole author of the
statement as generally believed. Nor was it a result of a long
deliberation as reported by Edgar Snow. He wrote that "Chou En-
lai told Wang Ping-nan that 'we did not sleep for a week. . . . It
was the most difficult decision of our whole lives.'"[19] The document was rather a collective work with much input of opinions from
Chang Kuo-t'ao and Chang Wen-t'ien at Pao-an and Chou En-lai and
Po Ku at Sian. We should also bear in mind that Chang Kuo-t'ao
was still a strong force to be reckoned with, for his western army
was not defeated until January 1937. Further, Chang still had with
him a large force of 13,000 men stationed in North Shensi. During
the Sian Incident, he still played a leading role in the CCP decision-
making.[20]

The December 19 manifesto addressed to the leaders of both
Nanking and Sian opened with praise of the Young Marshal and Yang
Hu-ch'eng by stating, "Judging with all fairness, the Sian leaders
must be ranked among the great patriots and zealots whose policy
calls for immediate resistance to Japan. By contrast, the Nanking
leaders have lagged behind; however, with the exception of a few
pro-Japanese leaders, they are not unwilling to fight against Japan."[21]
As for the solution to the Incident, the CCP proposed four points to
the leaders of both sides:

1. Tungkuan should be the demarcation between troops
on both sides. While Nanking troops should not invade
Tungkuan, the Anti-Japanese Army of Sian will remain
within Shensi and Kansu, waiting for the outcome of
the peace conference;

2. Nanking should immediately call a national conference to comprise delegates of all parties, factions,

professions, and armies, in addition to those appointed
from Nanking and Sian. The CCP and the Soviet government will also send their delegates;

3. Prior to the peace conference, draft programs for
national salvation will be drawn up by all parties, factions, professions, and armies and the question of the
disposition of Mr. Chiang Kai-shek will also be discussed; but the fundamental program should be the unity
of the entire nation, opposition to all civil war, and
concerted resistance against Japan;

4. The conference is tentatively proposed to be at Nanking. [22]

In conclusion, the manifesto emphatically directed its appeal
to Nanking by stating that "all the above propositions are reasonable
and effective methods for solving the present exigency," and urging
that "the Nanking leaders decide the national policy without delay so
that the Japanese marauders will not take advantage of our present
chaos by invading our nation."[23]

The interpretation of this famous manifesto has aroused some
serious academic debates. Why did it take a full week for the CCP
leaders to produce a manifesto? It is generally assumed that the
CCP leadership awaited the telegraphic instruction from Moscow, a
view advanced by Edgar Snow and popular among Chinese and Western writers.[24] As already mentioned, Moscow's first instruction on
the Sian Incident reached Pao-an on December 13, and more instructions followed. Evidently the delay resulted from waiting for further
information from Chou En-lai's team. The delicate relations with
the Young Marshal and Yang Hu-ch'eng demanded careful handling.
The CCP would not do anything detrimental to the good will of Chang
and Yang it had so diligently fostered. Since the CCP leaders were
not consulted beforehand, the direction in which the Young Marshal
might turn remained unclear to them. For the moment, they did
not care whether or not Stalin, faraway at the Kremlin, agreed with
what they were doing, but they were deeply concerned with their own
survival and the immediate problem in which they were involved. It
was imperative that they first find out what was in the mind of the
Young Marshal before they could even act.

Another reason for the delay was due apparently to the military tension and uncertainty created by the Nanking punitive move, the incursion of the Central Army into Tungkuan, and the skirmish between the Tungpei Army and the Central Army at Hua-yin. Sian was vulnerable in the east, where the defense work near Hua-yin, improvised by the Tungpei troops commanded by General T'ang Chün-yao, could not withstand a major assault. Indeed, the Young Marshal even toyed with the idea of withdrawing to P'ing-liang in eastern Kansu, where the main force of the Tungpei Army was located.[25] Unless Chiang Ting-wen's mission were accomplished with Nanking's consent to the cessation of hostility for three days, the events at Sian might have taken a drastic turn.

It is highly doubtful that the Young Marshal had had a serious talk with Chou En-lai before he sent Chiang Ting-wen to Nanking at noon on December 17. For we know that the Young Marshal had a full day on December 16: he started the day with a visit to all the detained generals, followed by his appearance at the people's convention that morning, at which he delivered his first public speech on the Sian Incident (except for the short speech to the whole staff of his headquarters on the 13th and a radio speech on the 14th). On December 16, he visited his captive three times; one visit took place in the evening when he accompanied Chiang Po-li to request that the Generalissimo order Nanking to halt military operations for three days.[26] On the same day, Donald returned to Sian from Loyang. It is almost certain that Chou could hardly have had any lengthy talk with the Young Marshal to sound out his inclinations in the midst of all these happenings. Once this background is taken into account, it seems certain that even if he arrived at Sian on December 16, not the 17th, Chou could not have formulated his accurate assessment of the Sian situation until late in the evening of December 17 at the earliest. It follows that in all probability the CCP leaders did not deliberate on Chou's report and draft the manifesto before December 18.

The CCP December 19th manifesto has sometimes been construed as a compromising document.[27] Given the circumstances, the CCP stance could not be more positive. It unequivocally stood for a peaceful solution, a position consonant with that of Moscow. At the same time, the CCP stance also sharply differed from Moscow's pronouncements. Whereas Chang and Yang were depicted by Moscow as willing stooges of the Japanese imperialists in the plot to kidnap Chiang, the CCP in its manifesto praised them as great patriots and enthusiasts. While peace was their overriding policy for the Sian settlement, the CCP leaders would not have cared so much about what might have happened to Chiang personally as about their own relations with the Sian rebels, whose alliance had become their shield from Chiang's attack and which might have been greatly needed had Nanking resorted to force. In view of the conditions at Sian which were fluid and beyond their control, the CCP leaders could not make specific demands in the manifesto, and could only reinforce in the manifesto much that had been said in the December 12th manifesto of the Sian rebels.

Also contradictory to the Moscow instruction was the fact that the CCP did not seek Chiang's release; instead, "what to do with Chiang" would have to be decided by all those parties and groups concerned. Probably the CCP intentionally left the issue vague, but the term "disposition" (ch'u-chih) here does not convey the idea that the CCP might have sought Chiang's elimination as suggested by Edgar Snow and others.[28] Nevertheless, the word ch'u-chih does convey an unfavorable connotation: it refers to a problem that has to be resolved. In hindsight, Mao may have regretted his choice of word.[29]

Without concerning himself about the CCP proposal that a peace conference be convened to decide the future of Chiang, the Young Marshal suddenly set Chiang free and escorted him to Nanking. Upon learning of the news, Chou En-lai and Yeh Chien-ying rushed to the airfield, but it was too late to change the fait accompli.[30]

Approaching the situation from a pragmatic standpoint, the CCP in the December 19th manifesto, though in favor of the Sian rebels, did not offend Chiang and Nanking. Not only was Nanking chosen as the site of the peace conference but it suggested that the Nanking government convene the conference. It urged the Nanking leaders resolutely to decide national policy.

The stand taken by the CCP had some significant effect on the outcome of the Sian Incident. Although the arrival of Chou and his party did not change the course which the Young Marshal had decided to follow, Chou's presence strengthened his belief that China's hope lay in the united front against Japan. As a matter of fact, throughout the entire trying days of the Sian Incident, the Young

Marshal did not lose sight of the original goal of the coup--to transform the civil war into a war of resistance against Japan. One might argue that with the CCP standing for peace and with the promised support from Moscow vanishing, the Young Marshal was left no other choice but to pursue peaceful settlement. However, one can only say that the CCP became a stabilizing force in the course of negotiations for peaceful settlement.

VIII. REACTION OF THE OUTSIDE WORLD

From beginning to end, reactions of the outside world to the
Sian coup had considerable effect on the development of the Sian affair.   Unlike many warlords who had little understanding or concern
about foreign reactions, the Young Marshal had always been involved
in foreign affairs and had many Western acquaintances whose response
could not be ignored.   He was equally concerned with domestic reaction to the Sian coup: from the warlords he expected strong endorsement and concrete support; from other quarters he sought understanding and approval of his action; and from the students and leftist intellectuals with whom he had identified himself in the national salvation
movement he anticipated gaining a large following.

Warlords on the Fence

Among all the warlords Yen Hsi-shan appeared to be most important, and his support was not only desirable but even greatly anticipated as there was a tacit understanding between him and the
Young Marshal.   Immediately following the coup, the Young Marshal
dispatched Yen several telegrams seeking his advice and support, but
Yen's reply was long in coming.   It was not until December 14 that
Yen's ambiguous and deceptive telegraphic response reached Sian,
posing four questions to the Young Marshal:

(1) What is your plan for reconstruction afterward?
(2) Does your action increase the strength of war of
resistance or decrease it?   (3) Are you transforming
the civil war into a war against the enemy or an external war into a civil war?   (4) Could you guarantee
that the event will not lead to extremely cruel killing
in the country?[1]

The Young Marshal answered Yen's four questions point by
point.   First, he replied, his action was not against any one person
but against a policy.   If he were to deal with an individual it would
be difficult, but it would not be so difficult if he were to deal with
an affair.   Should the Generalissimo actively carry out the war of
resistance against Japan, he would still support him with absolute
sincerity, regardless of severe punishment which might result from

113

his wrongdoing. On the other hand, even if the Generalissimo still refused to lead the nation to resist Japan, his personal safety would be protected under any circumstances.

Secondly, whether the Incident would increase or decrease the strength of war of resistance would depend upon how this strength was to be used. If the Young Marshal's troops and people were truly awakened, a spirit of life-and-death struggle against the enemy would be generated and the increase of strength would be unlimited. His actions were intended to bring about a true awakening of the nation and to mobilize the whole nation in a war with Japan in which both the army and the people would take part, because depending solely upon obedient troops would not be sufficient.

Thirdly, the Young Marshal's intention was solely resistance against Japan without the slightest desire to create a civil war which, in fact, he would do his utmost to avoid. If the Central Government decided to dispatch its troops to fight the Japanese, he swore he would fulfill his promise by shouldering the task of fighting the Japanese in the forefront.

Fourthly, whether the Incident would lead to domestic killing or not would depend on the awakening of the masses. If the masses were awakened to face the external enemy, the internal fighting would naturally be avoided. Conversely, even if there were no domestic killing, it would still be impossible to save the nation from extermination. He observed that the army and the people had been awakened to such an extent that if the government ignored the people's opinion and oppressed them, it would not be able to survive. In a nutshell, the survival or destruction of the country had reached the crucial point. If the people wanted to deliver themselves from death, it seemed that they must take some extraordinary measure.[2]

With this telegraphed reply to Yen, the Young Marshal virtually discarded any hope of Yen's cooperation which he had cherished so much, even though he still kept contact with Yen by sending Li Chin-chou to Taiyuan. Had the situation become so critical that military conflict between Nanking and Sian was inevitable, the benevolent neutrality of Yen would have been greatly desired. In such an event the Young Marshal would need to transfer his 53rd Army under Wan Fu-lin's command from western Hopeh through Shansi--which would require Yen's permission--to Shensi.

Less involved in the Sian Incident, yet more influential on the national scene than Yen Hsi-shan, Liu Hsiang was the neighbor of the Sian rebels in the south. Liu, who had not been successful in his struggle against the penetration of the Central Government influence into Szechwan, was more than glad to learn that the Generalissimo was a captive at Sian. At first he tried to keep silent on the issue in public, while clandestinely he dispatched inflammatory messages to the Young Marshal praising his stand and probably assuming him that Szechwan would be used as the rear base of Shensi. Apparently Liu saw a chance of Chiang's downfall and a resurgence of his own supremacy in Szechwan.

Although there existed little contact between Liu Hsiang and the Young Marshal before the Incident, exchanges of letters and envoys began immediately after the Incident. Their respective envoys were very active in Sian and in Chengtu where Liu was staying. Liu was probably one of the last to wish for a peaceful settlement of the Incident, because he had already begun to take action against Nanking. He moved quickly to seize control of the Central Government institutions and armed forces, including the military police and the military academy. Further, he announced that he would henceforth personally direct the activities of the Kuomintang headquarters at Chengtu.[4] Po Ku, a Communist leader who came to Sian following the Incident, believed that had the Incident developed into a civil war Szechwan would certainly be on the side of the Sian rebels.[5] However, under the strong urging of the Nanking leaders, Liu did issue belatedly a circular telegram to the Young Marshal expressing his concern over the impending civil war and pleading for the release of Chiang. But in the same telegram, Liu supported the policy of the Sian rebels on resistance against Japan and salvation of the nation. The telegram was dispatched on December 19, 1936, by which time Chiang's safety was no longer a question and the peaceful settlement was in sight. It was reported that Liu flew into a fury and cursed the Young Marshal when he learned that Chiang had been released. Understandably he had earlier advised the Young Marshal to do away with Chiang.[6]

It was reasonable for the Sian rebels to expect cooperation from the Southwest, particularly from Kwantung and Kwangsi whose forces just four months before had been engaged in fighting against the Central Army. With the collapse of the Kwantung power, the Kwangsi leaders managed to maintain their semiindependent regime.

They especially vied for the goodwill of the Young Marshal and had their representative stationed at Sian. On the very day of the coup, the Kwangsi representative at Sian, Chung Yung-tan cabled Kweilin urging General Pai Ch'ung-hsi to fly to Sian for active participation in the future development. [7]

The initial response of the Kwangsi leaders to the Sian Incident was cautious. On the one hand, they tried to resurrect the old teamwork with Kwantung leaders during the Sian crisis by sending Governor Huang Hsü-ch'u to Canton, where he arrived on December 15; on the other hand, they made a lip-service reply to Dr. H. H. Kung's plea for national unity during the Sian crisis by stating their continuous support of the Central Government policy but suggesting a peaceful solution of the Incident. However, after a three-day meeting at Kweilin among the leaders, namely Li Tsung-jen, Pai Ch'ung-hsi, Li Chi-shen, and Huang Ch'i-hsiang, a "bombshell" manifesto was issued on December 17, demanding the reorganization of the Central Government into an anti-Japanese national salvation regime and denouncing armed suppression of the Sian rebels. It further declared that the Kwangsi provincial authorities were still firmly sticking to their anti-Japanese national salvation policy and that the Sian problem should be settled through political negotiations. [8]

Of all the Kwangsi leaders, Li Chi-shen, a long-time adversary of Chiang Kai-shek, was the most vociferous in his attack on the Central Government, even demanding the withdrawal of the order for a punitive expedition against the Sian rebels. [9] Apparently inspired by their leaders, the people of Kwangsi organized a "People's Salvation Association," consonant with a similar people's organization at Sian. In view of the favorable response from Kwangsi, the Young Marshal sent Chieh Ju-chuan to Kweilin as his personal envoy. [10]

Except for Kwantung, which was dominated by the pro-Nanking force, the whole Southwest was in opposition to Nanking. However, warlords in Kweichow and Yunnan, who may have seen the Sian coup as a golden opportunity to rid themselves of the Central Government influence in their region, played a relatively insignificant role in the national political scene. At least for the moment, the Young Marshal's attention was chiefly directed to the reaction of northern warlords, notably Sung Che-yüan of Hopeh and Han Fu-ch'ü of Shantung.

Sung Che-yüan, a protégé of the Christian General Feng Yü-hsiang, was the only force to be reckoned with in North China in the mid-1930s. As Chairman of the Hopeh-Chahar Political Council, Sung ran his quasi-buffer regime centering at Peking with the support of his 29th Army (of Hsi-feng-kou fame) with considerable independence. However, the very Council was a creation of circumstance brought about by Japanese aggression. The survival of Sung and his 29th Army depended on how well they could play their delicate role between Tokyo and Nanking, though their relations with Tokyo were far more important than those with Nanking. There were at least two minimum demands from Tokyo which must be satisfied by Sung: to suppress the anti-Japanese student movement and to prevent the spread of Communism mainly in Tientsin and Peking. On both counts Sung seemed to perform quite well. Yet Sung was not so servile to Nanking as to Tokyo. His relationship with Nanking was rather simple: as long as Sung continued his nominal allegiance to Nanking and did not become another Yin Ju-keng, Nanking would be satisfied. The Sian coup caught General Sung in a great dilemma: what the Sian rebels stood for as expressed in the December 12 manifesto was in sharp conflict with the two Japanese minimum demands. Throughout the entire Sian crisis, Ch'in Te-shun, Mayor of Peking and Sung's right-hand man, was obliged to make repeated assurances to Japan that the policy of the Council remained unchanged despite the Sian Incident--that is "it will continue to pursue a policy of promoting good relations with Japan and of suppressing Communist propaganda."[11]

On the other hand, General Sung had been on good terms with the Young Marshal and his generals, particularly Yu Hsüeh-chung. The 29th Army and the Tungpei Army had many things in common: they were all warlord armies; the rank and file of both armies came from northern China; both had fought Japan before and remained anti-Japanese; and both disliked Chiang Kai-shek. On the very day of the coup, the Young Marshal cabled General Sung stating, "With the Japanese aggression in North China unabated, we must unite all parties and factions in a war of resistance against Japan, if we want to survive and save our country at all. After my repeated pleas to Mr. Chiang had been ignored, I was obliged to detain him here in the hope that he may regret and change his mind. Concerning the current situation, I have eight demands which will be forwarded to you. After receiving this telegram, please come to Sian or send your plenipotentiary, so that we can discuss national affairs together."[12]

Sung's reply was not favorable, since he laid down two things pre-requisite for his coming to Sian: (a) the Young Marshal must sep-arate himself from the Communists, and (b) the safety of Chiang Kai-shek must be guaranteed.[13] Understandably, the Young Marshal did not even bother to answer Sung.

Under the strong urging of the Nanking leaders, Sung dis-patched a diplomatic message to the Central Government on Decem-ber 14 with his customary attack on the Communists. In regard to the Sian Incident, it spelled out that "the Central Government should quickly suppress the revolt, rescue the Generalissimo, and fully carry out the policy of anti-Communism."[14] Despite his official stand, Sung continued to show his goodwill toward the Young Mar-shal as borne out by his bestowal of flour to all families of the Tungpei Army then living at Peking.[15] On the Sian issue, Sung kept in touch with his former colleague, Han Fu-ch'ü, governor of Shantung, in order to present a common posture.

Han's first response to the appeal of the Nanking leaders was not as amiable as that of Sung. In his telegraphed message to H. H. Kung, Han wished that "leaders of the Central Government should immediately give serious deliberation and take decisive mea-sures to bring about the release of the Generalissimo, while leaving other political questions to be resolved later."[16] Unlike Sung, Han privately opened up direct contact with the Sian rebels, sending in-cendiary messages by promising that he would put himself in the service of the Young Marshal to lead the vanguard in marching to Nanking. In return for Han's support, General Yang Hu-ch'eng sent his personal envoy to Shantung.[17]

In spite of their official and outward posture, Sung and Han undoubtedly gave the Sian rebels strong support which culminated in their joint manifesto issued on December 23, which reads in part:

> Confronted with great difficulties arising from their pecu-liar local situation, provincial leaders would have differ-ent views. Whatever the differences, they should present their views to the Central Government and allow it to make overall decisions based upon majority opinion. At this exigent moment, it is absolutely necessary to avoid internal fighting and internecine destruction. The solu-tion to the immediate problem should be achieved in

accordance with three guiding principles: (a) avoidance
of the people's sufferings; (b) protection of the nation's
existence; and (c) safeguarding the life of the leader.[18]

In concluding their manifesto, Sung and Han made a startling proposal that "the Central Government should call a national conference to
be participated in by high officials of the Government and renowned
leaders outside the Government who would discuss and devise the
best means to save the nation," an idea very much consonant with
one of the eight demands set forth in the December 12 manifesto by
the Sian rebels.

Had Chiang's captivity been prolonged, further and more concrete
joint action from Sung and Han would have been expected. Moreover,
liaison work between Sung and Han in North China and Li and Pai in
the Southwest had been established,[19] and the formation of a counter-
force against Nanking was in the making. There also existed some
connection between Sian and Sinkiang. Had Sian become indefensible
in the face of the Central Army's attack, the Young Marshal might
have flown Chiang out of Sian and taken refuge in Sinkiang as Madame Chiang Kai-shek then conceived.[20]

The Young Marshal had good reason to expect support from
Sheng Shih-ts'ai, dictator of Sinkiang. Sheng, a native of Manchuria,
formerly a junior officer in the Tungpei Army, knew the Young Marshal personally. Secondly, Sheng's ascendancy in Sinkiang was, to
a large degree, the fruit of Moscow's doings; not only was the Soviet
economic aid directly involved but the Soviet Union even dispatched
the Red Army to help Sheng suppress the Moslem revolts on several
occasions. Economically and militarily, Sinkiang became a depen-
dency of the Soviet Union. Thirdly, consistent with his one-sided
leaning toward the Soviet Union, Sheng introduced socialism to Sinkiang by proclaiming the "Six Cardinal Policies."[21] Fourthly, just
as the "united front" against Japan was formed on the basis of Moscow's policy, so the proposed anti-Japanese coalition government in
the Northwest presumably had Stalin's blessings.[22]

Indeed Edgar Snow reported that he met a certain Mr. Li who
had just returned from Sinkiang where he served as "Chang Hsüeh-
liang's representative or liaison man with General Sheng Shih-ts'ai."
Mr. Li told Snow that "if the Sian incident had led to civil war, then
Sheng would certainly have backed Chang Hsüeh-liang."[23] Whether

or not the Sian Incident would develop into a civil war rested with Nanking. Clearly the Sian rebels had neither the intention nor the strength to fight a civil war.

Public Opinion

Traditionally the Chinese populace was silent on political matters, and no public opinion had ever been polled. However, in a broad sense, the "silent majority" had delegated their political opinions to the gentry or literati,[24] who, nurtured in Confucian precepts, were supposed to take upon themselves the responsibility of taking care of the people's interests. With the growth of the student population in the Republican era, the intelligentsia was broadened and no longer constituted a unique class to serve the ruling class on the one hand and to represent the people on the other. Consequently the students, though belonging to the intelligentsia, could not be identified with the ruling class as a thousand years before. One might still argue that the majority of the students came from the bourgeois or petit bourgeois, so they must have represented their class interests. Quite to the contrary, the students in thought and deed were close to the people and more often than not in opposition to the ruling class or the government. Moreover, the student group was most vocal and its voice became the closest thing to the opinion of the people.

Just as the Peking students took the leadership in the May Fourth Movement, so they again led the nation in the national salvation movement in the 1930s. To commemorate the anniversary of the December 9, 1935 student demonstration, the students in Peking delayed their planned demonstration until the 12th, a date coincident with the Sian coup. No less than 7,000 students took part in the demonstration, which was described as the most successful ever held in Peking, for the first time without being harassed by the police. Even the mayor of Peking, Ch'in Te-shun himself, addressed the demonstrators at Coal Hill just behind the Peking Palace; the students were satisfied with his long speech.

The students in the December 12 demonstration at Peking enunciated the same goals as they had a year ago except that they were more intensely angry at the new wave of suppression against the "united front." They demanded freedom of the united front movement, the release of the seven arrested leaders of the national salvation movement, and the cessation of the fratricidal ten years' civil war.

When the Sian coup was known to the Peking students on the same day of the demonstration, the Student Union Executive Committee published a six-point resolution:

1. Demanding in the name of the people that war be declared on Japan at once, to unite the country and prevent a period of disintegration and confusion.

2. Demanding the establishment of representative government.

3. Denouncing any form and kind of civil war on any pretext whatever.

4. Demanding that Chiang Kai-shek join with Chang Hsüeh-liang to fight Japan.

5. Demanding that Nanking receive all the anti-Japanese demands of Chang Hsüeh-liang and declare war as required.

6. Demanding that the Nanking Government and all parties and forces in China open an All-China National Defense Conference to resist Japan and save the country.[25]

Understandably, the stand taken by the Peking students was fully endorsed by students throughout North China, whose anti-Japanese sentiment was extremely strong, but not by the students in South China, where only the leftist students associated with the All-China Student Union and the Federation of the National Salvation Associations endorsed it.

Another important segment of the intelligentsia was the university faculty. The most celebrated liberal scholar, Dr. Hu Shih, who had just returned to China from the United States only twelve days before the outbreak of the Sian Incident, wrote his widely circulated Sunday editorial for Ta-kung-pao (Tientsin) on December 20, using the title "The Treason of Chang Hsüeh-liang." He made his ardent appeal to the intellectual youths to turn against the Young Marshal:

> There is no shadow of doubt that Chang Hsüeh-liang's
> deed is treason. . . . Most strangely, there is today
> a number of youths who are still in sympathy with him.
> If they do not intend to harm the nation, they must be
> ignorant. . . . They harbor suspicion of the leader of
> the Government for not being faithful to the nation . . .
> but the reason for tolerating all insults without standing
> up to fight for five years lies in the hopes that the coun-
> try can be unified, concerted action can be taken, and
> the power is strengthened--a point of view that has not
> been understood by the youths.[26]

In his editorial, Dr. Hu gave much space to discrediting the "united front" policy. First, the Communists, having embraced internation-alism, could not at the same time be patriotic; their outcry for a nationalist front was nothing but a strategy following the fiasco of armed rebellion. Second, their talk of resistance against Japan was nothing but a shameful deceit. No one who wanted to resist Japan could seize the supreme leader who was engaged in the war with Japan. Third, their deed lacked sympathy and support from the Soviet Union which had already publicly denounced the Sian coup.

The most vituperative attack on the Young Marshal came from the pen of a distinguished historian, Fu Szu-nien. In his "Discus-sion on the Rebellion of Bandit Chang," published in Chung-yang jih-pao [Central daily news] at Nanking on December 16, he strong-ly defended the stern measures adopted by the Nanking leaders. At-tacking the Young Marshal personally, Fu wrote:

> First, he is an hereditary bandit: that is why he acts
> in mind and deed much the same as a bandit. From
> youth he has been accustomed to this kind of practice;
> consequently he adopted it in killing his second father,[27]
> "suffering from his own failure at the Great Wall cam-
> paign," and now causing this great rebellion. Second,
> he is a person spoiled by his environment. He is very
> proud of being clever, but judging by his talk, he is a
> senior-middle-school student at the most; he cannot con-
> centrate for long on anything and the world of his mind

is entirely unrealistic. Third, fond of being flattered,
he has fostered the habit of considering himself above
everyone. In recent years he has become the object
of curses by the whole country and ridicule by the world.
Trying to get some relief from his chagrin, he was so
easily caught by the words of evil men and his own
imagination that he implemented his bandit measure.
Thus today's event was made possible [28]

Not so excited and biased as Dr. Hu Shih and Fu Szu-nien were
three Nanking university presidents and their faculty who issued a
circular telegram to the Young Marshal couched in quite different
language.[29] They posed the question to him: "How can you justify
using the pretext of saving the country to do that which will destroy
the country? . . . Yet we should not suspect you of guilt based on
our own narrow-minded thinking. . . . Though the Government has
declared severe disciplinary orders against you, room for negotiations is left open. For your own sake, you should escort Generalissimo Chiang out of danger, after which you will have the opportunity
of presenting your policy for adoption or rejection."[30]

Equally reasonable in its appeal to the Sian rebels was a statement from the All-China Press, evidently still the most important
group to influence public opinion in China in the 1930s. Newspapers
and news agencies from fourteen provinces and major cities including
Shanghai, Peking, Hankow, and Canton attached their names to this
statement on the current situation issued on December 16. In rather
vague language, the statement consisted of three major points:
(1) Under both internal and external threats, there is only one way
for China's survival, i.e., to maintain an immutable position of absolute independence and self-determination. No matter what doctrine,
it must be built upon the supreme foundation of the nation's survival.
(2) Chang Hsüeh-liang, by detaining Chiang Kai-shek, committed an
unforgivable mistake. We call upon the people of the whole country
to awaken his conscience to free the Generalissimo. (3) The solution must be simple and clear in accordance with the justice and law
of Chinese tradition as well as the spirit of Dr. Sun Yat-sen's teach-
ings.[31]

Ta-kung-pao, the leading newspaper in China under the editor-
ship of Chang Chi-luan, issued "An Open Letter to the Military Vo-
cation of Sian" on December 18, which was printed in large numbers

and dropped over Sian by airplane. The letter began with a deliberate admonition:

> The Sian Incident is not the work of one man; Chang
> Hsüeh-liang is as active as he is passive. . . . Please
> listen! Both the culprit and his accomplices are wrong,
> so wrong that it may cause the extinction of the country
> and yourselves. . . . Please behold the reaction of the
> whole country in the last few days. Who is not indig-
> nant! Not even one of those who are sincerely opposed
> to the Government . . . supports you. Also behold how
> the world is shocked! None of those countries who have
> sympathy for China are not seriously concerned about
> the situation.[32]

The letter went on to say that it was not too late to save the Sian situation from catastrophe, and Generalissimo Chiang alone could do it. The Sian rebels were urged to approach Chiang immediately and plead for his pardon. They could either set him free or restore him to authority even at Sian without demanding any terms, for his great personality was the best guarantee. Not only could he protect them from punishment but he certainly would adopt their policies, if they were beneficial to the country.

The open letter from Ta-kung-pao was doubtless read by many inside Sian, particularly the Young Marshal, but its effect on the development of the Sian event, if any, must have been minimal. Conversely, it would be wrong to assume that public opinion had no influence on the minds of the Sian rebels. In addition to domestic public opinion, reactions from abroad, especially the leading powers, certainly drew their great attention. After all, the Sian affair was as much a domestic issue as it was an external one.

Reactions of Great Powers

Foreign capitals received the news of the Sian Incident with dismay. Except for Japan who expressed some satisfaction over the event and may have anticipated great advantage for herself, the major powers thought that the event had dimmed the hope for China's progress and unity under Chiang's leadership and that China might again have fallen back into chaos. Significantly, China's two strong

neighbors, Soviet Russia and Japan, both of whom had special interest in China, denied their own involvement, but ostensibly accused
each other of having inspired the Sian rebels. Unlike her Nazi ally
Germany who was rather indifferent toward Asian affairs, Italy took
the same view as Japan, at least for the special reason that Galeazzo
Ciano, foreign minister and son-in-law of the Italian dictator, was
a personal friend of the Young Marshal and, therefore, showed some
genuine concern,

The three leading Western powers, England, France, and the
United States, particularly England, were sympathetic to the Nanking
government and willing to mediate between Nanking and Sian. Though
the resultant effect of their efforts cannot be exaggerated, suffice it
to say that their unfavorable reaction was brought to the attention of
the Young Marshal who had not anticipated such adverse response at
all, particularly from Moscow.

Only a week before Pravda still bitterly attacked Chiang Kai-
shek for his reported statement concerning the Japanese-German
agreement. With the outbreak of the Sian Incident, the same paper
praised Chiang for his efforts at unification as the best means of
resistance to Japan. In the meantime, it also declared that "the
Soviet Union remains true to its policy of strict non-intervention in
the internal affairs of Foreign Powers."[33]

A more comprehensive Soviet comment on the Sian event appeared in an editorial of Izvestiia on December 14. It directly attributed Chang Hsüeh-liang's coup d'état to a Japanese maneuver
designed to counteract the growing unification of China under the
Nanking government. However, it pointed out that Chang's troops
were genuinely anti-Japanese but Chang himself was acting under the
influence of "a notorious Japanese agent," Wang Ching-wei, with the
sole object of creating chaos favorable to Japan. Its main passage
reads:

> Chang Hsüeh-liang's revolt can break up the unity of
> Chinese anti-Japanese forces. One thing is evident:
> Whatever the slogans and demands which mask his
> real purpose, the revolt at this moment, according
> to the expression of one Chinese newspaper, is that
> 'the Japanese imperialist attacks against the sover-
> eignty of China have reached their highest point,'

the revolt which represents a danger not only for the
Nanking government but also for the entire Chinese
people.   One thing is more evident: although Chang
Hsüeh-liang waves the flag of struggle against Japan,
under the present circumstances his revolt objectively
is advantageous only to Japanese imperialism.   With
Nanking espousing the policy of resistance against
Japan, the only national front of struggle against Japan
is that which unites all those who will participate; it
is not a front against Nanking but a front united with
Nanking. [34]

In the opinion of the editor of Izvestiia, "the very best thing that
one can wish for China in connection with these latest events is rap-
id and peaceful liquidation of an act so obviously contrary to the interests of that great country. "

On December 15, Izvestiia published a long article on the Sian
Incident by M. Kantorovich, a journalist who specialized in Far
Eastern affairs.   First, he argued that the recent successful resistance to Japanese aggression in Suiyuan was the result of popular
anti-Japanese agitation rooted in the mass movement originating from
the student agitations in 1935 and 1936.   It now spread not only to
the working classes, the peasants and the intelligentsia, but also to
the army and governmental apparatus of the KMT itself.

Secondly, by gradual stages the mass movement turned against
the Nanking government, and finally Chiang Kai-shek himself was
faced with a serious political crisis--the choice either of aligning
himself with the resistance against Japanese aggression or joining
the anti-Communist camp of Japan and Germany.   Realizing that
further serious concessions to Japanese imperialism would be fatal
for Nanking, Chiang Kai-shek, if he was to avoid a catastrophe,
must immediately come to terms with the public opinion of the country.   In the last few months he had achieved a great deal inasmuch
as the repeated attempts of Japanese diplomats at squeezing new
concessions out of the Nanking government, particularly in regard
to North China and to the "common front against Communism, " were
of no avail.

Thirdly, this author confirmed that in the struggle against Japanese aggression, China had the advantage of certain international

support, particularly Great Britain who successfully helped China carry out its monetary reform, in spite of the most vehement Japanese opposition, and had recently encouraged anti-Japanese sentiments among the Chinese bourgeoisie.

In view of these conditions, the author reached the conclusion that "Chang Hsüeh-liang has chosen to rebel against the Nanking government, thus threatening the country with internecine war at a moment when Japanese imperialism was meeting with serious difficulties--at a moment when everything favored a successful resistance. His action constitutes a valuable gift to the Japanese usurpers."[35]

The gist of the December 14 and 15 editorials of the two Soviet newspapers was conveyed to Nanking by its ambassador to Moscow, Chiang T'ing-fu. In his interview with Ambassador Chiang, the Soviet Foreign Minister Maxim Litvinov strongly denied that Moscow had had any contact with Chang Hsüeh-liang since the latter was driven out of Manchuria. Asked whether the Soviet government could help to solve the Sian Incident, Litvinov answered that the only way was to let the CCP know the attitude of the Soviet government. [36]

Undoubtedly, the CCP leaders felt embarassed by the Moscow stance as reported by Edgar Snow, but it was even more embarassing to the CCP delegation to Sian headed by Chou En-lai who had to explain the about-face of the Soviet Union to the Young Marshal personally. Somewhat disappointed by the Soviet reaction, the Young Marshal was not so shocked as the CCP leaders first feared. For, it was clear to him that neither Soviet diplomatic support nor its military aid would directly affect his situation at Sian. He had extended material aid to the Red Army for over half a year, and even during the Sian Incident the CCP still pleaded with him to help the Fourth Front Army stranded in the western Kansu corridor. [37] Unless an anti-Japanese coalition government were set up in the Northwest, the Young Marshal would not be as much concerned about the Soviet attitude toward Sian as that of Japan.

Needless to say, the Japanese government denied any implication in the Sian coup. In fact, Japan made the countercharge that the coup was engineered by Moscow, as reported in the Italian and German presses. [38] But privately, the Japanese government had no suspicion of Soviet involvement as evidenced by the British Ambassador Sir R. Clive's telegraphed report from Tokyo on December 14, which reads:

> Japanese attitude is wait and see, combined with scarce-
> ly disguised feeling of satisfaction that the world must
> now realize that Chinese are hopeless, as Japanese al-
> ways knew.   Japanese have the utmost contempt for
> Chang Hsüeh-liang and the inevitable chaos which must
> ensue if Chiang Kai-shek disappears is not to their in-
> terest. Minister for Foreign Affairs said as much to
> me yesterday. He expressed no suspicion of Soviet con-
> nexion with coup d'état.[39] (Emphasis mine.)

Sir Clive's view of the Japanese attitude was also shared by the Chinese Ambassador to Japan, Hsü Shih-ying. Hsü reported that the Japanese Prime Minister and the Ministers of Foreign Affairs, Navy, and Army at a conference on December 16, reached an agree-ment that "any Japanese move during the Sian Incident would have tremendous impact on the Chinese situation and also cause great con-cern on the part of Western powers, so that it is necessary to have an attitude of watchful waiting for further development. In the mean-time all military inspection and gendarme units must be alerted to inhibit any impulsive action."[40]

The policy of Hirota Kōki, Prime Minister, was governed by one principle during the Sian Incident--had Japan overplayed its hand, the Nanking government would have compromised with Sian, thus tol-erating Communism. Ambassador Hsü, after his interview with Arita, the Japanese Foreign Minister, repeatedly reported back to Nanking that Japan had abandoned its China policy of military con-quest which could only drive China to Bolshevism. A new policy of friendship and positive economic cooperation was in the making.[41]

There was little doubt that Japan showed some sympathy for the Nanking government, then guided by Ho Ying-ch'in and Chang Ch'ün, both allegedly pro-Japanese. On the other hand, the Nanking government lost no time in approaching and urging Japan to act with restraint and prudence during China's crisis. To comply with Nan-king's wish, Japan halted its military operation in northern Suiyuan. Indeed, the Japanese collaborator Prince Teh, who revolted against Nanking and was defeated by the Chinese troops at Pai-ling-miao, declared his allegiance to Nanking.[42]

Japan's goodwill toward Nanking was also signaled by the return to Nanking of Ambassador Kawagoe and the resumption of negotiations which had been broken down since early December. During his first meeting with Chang Ch'ün on December 21, Kawagoe questioned the Nanking government stand concerning the Young Marshal's announced policy of resistance against Japan and cooperation with the Communists. The Chinese Foreign Minister replied that

> the Central Authorities have no intention whatever to
> effect a political compromise with the Young Marshal.
> He stressed that the Nanking government has already
> decided to punish the rebel leader and pointed out that
> military measures are being pushed through against
> the insurgents. He assured Kawagoe that Nanking for-
> eign policy will undergo no change at all as a result
> of the Sian rebellion.[43]

In meeting the press, Kawagoe stated that the Sino-Japanese negotiations were to be accelerated. Apparently, he did not anticipate Chiang's early release when he commented that T. V. Soong was making private efforts to bring about Chiang's release in his capacity as Chiang's relative. In his opinion, "In the event the Generalissimo is lost to Nanking, the Central Authorities seem to be considerably consolidated," and "China ought to be looked upon in a new light in view of such a fact."[44]

Kawagoe also met privately with Ho Ying-ch'in to sound out the intention and program of the Nanking government to cope with the Sian crisis. He was assured that the Central Government was determined to proceed with its announced policy of carrying out a punitive expedition. To the dismay of both Ho and Kawagoe, Chiang was released the next day after their meeting.[45]

Less attached to Chinese domestic politics than all the major powers, Fascist Italy was disappointed by the kidnapping of Chiang who had been on very good terms with Mussolini and tried to imitate him in many ways. Ciano, the Italian Foreign Minister, wired a strong message to his friend, the Young Marshal, urging him to free Chiang and warning him of the risk of any cooperation with Moscow. In the meantime, he also instructed the Italian Ambassador in China to communicate a similar message to the Young Marshal. Ciano maintained that the policy of seeking an agreement between Japan and China was the only wise course for China.[46]

On the Sian issue, Germany took a position close to that of England and the United States, although it did not join England and the United States in a mediation effort, an idea which was initiated by the British envoy to China, Sir H. Knatchbull-Hugessen. Great Britain had cogent reasons for making a positive effort toward helping the Nanking government bring about the release of Chiang. For one thing, both William Donald and James Elder were British in origin, the former being an Australian and the latter an Englishman. For another thing, Great Britain, more than any other Western country, had much at stake in China, and therefore was anxious to know that China could successfully resist further Japanese penetration, especially in South China where British interests were heavily invested. Despite the Japanese warning, Great Britain continued to grant large credit for trade with China, having aided the Chinese currency reform, and thereby strengthening both the position of China in relation to Japan and her own position in China.

When James Elder arrived at Nanking on the 15th of December, the British Ambassador immediately received him. Madame Chiang and Chang Ch'ün asked Elder to wire Chang Hsüeh-liang the views held by the foreign press concerning the Sian coup. Through Elder, Madame Chiang requested that the views of Sir Knatchbull-Hugessen be included in a telegram to the Young Marshal, a request to which he complied. The following message was drafted by Sir Knatchbull-Hugessen for Anthony Eden's approval:

> Without going into the underlying reasons which have prompted his action I cannot help feeling that nothing but harm can result. His action cannot fail to be interpreted in the outside world as one of treachery to his country, in fact a stab in the back, just at a moment when unity and progress seemed to be promised.
>
> It must be clear that negotiations or agreement with a man held in detention can be of no value whatever and if Chang Hsüeh-liang is confident of the justice of his cause, obviously he cannot be afraid of discussing it in an atmosphere of freedom. To refuse to do so is to condemn himself in advance. [47]

Sir Knatchbull-Hugessen's message to the Young Marshal was fully endorsed by Anthony Eden. Eden grasped the Chinese situation extremely well, and may have initiated the idea of good offices of the major powers. As a result, the British and American governments through their ambassadors in China offered their good offices in the hope that "they might be of assistance in carrying out any arrangements which may be reached by both parties." Joined by the French and Italian Ambassadors to Nanking, Nelson T. Johnson, the American Ambassador, and Sir Knatchbull-Hugessen formally proposed to H. H. Kung that their governments were prepared to take steps "to effect safe conduct of Generals Chang Hsüeh-liang and Yang Hu-cheng from, say, Tientsin to some point outside of Chinese soil."[48]

Obviously the good offices of the powers would not be needed so much as those of the Chinese warlords, Yen Hsi-shan, Sung Che-yüan, and Han Fu-ch'ü, but the reaction of the leading world powers must have had some effect on Chang's thinking. Donald reported that the Young Marshal seemed not to be greatly disturbed by the popular outcry throughout the country, although once he pointed to a newspaper and then turned to Donald and said: "Look what they are saying about me down there!"[49]

It was not difficult for the Young Marshal to see that his coup was improper, even though he still firmly believed that the underlying principle justified his action. Before long, he was convinced that he must liquidate the Sian Incident as quickly as possible; otherwise, once it were prolonged and expanded, it certainly would lead to a civil war greater than the one he tried to stop by launching the coup of December 12.

The Young Marshal
Chang Hsüeh-liang in 1925

The "Elderly" Marshal Chang Tso-lin
with Generals Yang Yü-t'ing and Sutton

Generalissimo Chiang Kai-shek
and the Young Marshal in 1933

Generalissimo Chiang and
the Young Marshal in 1936

General Wang I-che

Generalissimo Chiang, the Young Marshal,
and General Yang Hu-ch'eng and their
aides shortly before the Sian Incident

Peasant guards in armed
procession in Sian

Generalissimo Chiang and the
detained Nanking high officials
shortly after their release

IX. CHIANG'S RELEASE:
THE SUCCESS OF PERSONAL DIPLOMACY

In spite of pressure to bring about a quick release of Chiang--
public opinion and foreign diplomats condemning the rebels, warlords showing general apathy and lack of support for them and the
Nanking military ready to move in on them--serious negotiations
over some intricate, thorny issues had to be conducted in secret
and on a personal basis before an agreement could be reached.
Donald, who doubtless could understand the intentions of the Young
Marshal, lacked the authority, the language tool, and the trust of
the Chiangs to make a real deal with him.   However, he opened the
way for negotiations which were carried on first by T. V. Soong
and then by Madame Chiang.

The Duo-Negotiators

The three-day truce between Nanking and Sian slipped by almost without being noticed by the Generalissimo, who devoted himself to reading Mo-tzu.[1]   Other Nanking generals in captivity passed
away their time by playing Ma-jong or cards.   Probably the most
worried of these was the Young Marshal.   On the evening of December 19, the two men had an intriguing dialogue:

Young Marshal: Now we must wind up this matter as soon as possible.   You had better consider those demands
previously presented to you.   In order to facilitate
a settlement, please choose some of the demands
and promise to carry them out.   It is no longer
necessary to realize all the eight demands; only
four will be enough.

Generalissimo: Which four will be deleted?

Young Marshal: The last four can be dropped.

Generalissimo: As long as I am not free to return to Nanking,
not one of the demands can be realized; nor can
any of them be negotiated, whether they be eight
or four.[2]

135

At the height of tension, on December 17, the Young Marshal
sent Li Chin-chou, his secretary who had earlier undertaken two
missions to Yen Hsi-shen, again to Taiyuan.   Yen, since his December 14 telegraphed message to Chang raising four questions, had
posed as a true mediator, instead of a supporter of Sian as first
anticipated.   It appeared that he tried to dominate the mediation in
order to enhance his prestige.   He insisted that his two lieutenants,
Chao Tai-wen and Hsü Yung-ch'eng, both on good terms with the
Generalissimo and the Young Marshal, go to Sian only on one condi-
tion--that they have a direct interview with the Generalissimo.
While Yen was wavering, Li had to hurry back to Sian on the 19th,
planning to return to Taiyuan the following day.   On the morning of
December 20 before leaving, Li reported to the Young Marshal in
Donald's presence, when his mission was unexpectedly cancelled, in
spite of Yen's urging.   Then Li was convinced that the Young Marshal had made up his mind to send the Generalissimo back to Nanking, thus making Yen's mediation unnecessary.[3]

Li's observation was well-founded.   T. V. Soong arrived at
Sian that morning.   In company with Donald, the Young Marshal
took him to Chiang immediately.   Upon noticing T. V. Soong,
Chiang was so overwhelmed by emotion that he hardly uttered a
word.   Soong showed him a letter from his wife, the crucial passage of which reads: "If at the end of three days T. V. does not
return to Nanking, I must come to Sian to live or die with you."
Hardly finishing the letter, the Generalissimo burst into tears.
Then Soong with a gesture urged the Young Marshal and Donald to
leave.   It was the first time since his captivity that Chiang talked
with someone without being watched.[4]

At this juncture, Chiang handed over to Soong a copy of his
will which he had previously written and given to Colonel Huang
Jen-lin to take back to Nanking for Madame Chiang; he now realized
that Huang had not been allowed to return to Nanking.   The intimate
conversation between Chiang and Soong lasted about half an hour.
They discussed among other things two matters.   First Chiang told
Soong that Chang and Yang had changed their attitude towards him
after reading his diaries and other documents.   Second he explained
to Soong his military strategy for an invasion of Sian by the Central
Army and asked Soong to take the plan to Nanking military authorities.

Earlier, the Nanking leaders, particularly the military, had tried to block Soong's attempt to come to Sian, but to no avail. Soong outmaneuvered them by declaring that he was going as a private citizen. But they succeeded in persuading Madame Chiang not to fly to Sian with Soong. She compromised by saying, "If at the end of three days Soong does not return to Nanking, no more obstacles will be placed in the way of my flying to Sian."[5] In the meantime, the Young Marshal had wired her that "if fighting was not stopped, I was not to think of going to Sian since he could not provide protection."[6] Then Madame Chiang struck a bargain with the Nanking generals providing for the three-day truce to be prolonged for another three days. To the Sian rebels, the news of the truce which Soong brought to them must have been welcome. At least the Young Marshal must have felt temporarily relieved, for now there would be no immediate threat of attack on Sian and a plan for withdrawal to the west would not be necessary.

Both Soong and the Young Marshal came to see Chiang again that night. In his talk with Chiang, the Young Marshal said, "While Soong is here, it is better to discuss and decide to act on one or another alternative so that the present case can be quickly concluded."[7] As before, the Generalissimo without reservation rejected Chang's proposition by saying that "unless I am allowed to return to Nanking, nothing, however reasonable, can be negotiated."[8]

On the same day that Soong arrived at Sian, Donald flew out of Sian. His plane made a forced landing on the bank of the Yellow River near Loyang. He did not reach Nanking until Monday afternoon, December 21.[9] Coincidently, Soong also returned to Nanking about the same time. In receiving reporters on December 22, Donald was reported to have said,

> The outlook for early release of the Generalissimo is
> hopeful, but several formidable obstacles remain to be
> overcome. The attitude of General Yang Fu-cheng
> [sic], whose troops dominate Sian and therefore have
> Chiang Kai-shek at their mercy, is the big problem.
> . . . The problem of winning over General Yang and
> his men is a greater one than that of effecting a settle-
> ment with Chang Hsüeh-liang, for General Yang and
> his army hold more radical and uncompromising views.
> Further, General Yang's troops are ill-disciplined and
> undependable.[10]

Donald was fully convinced, as he pointed out to the reporters, that
the Young Marshal was sincere in his demands for a stronger national policy. But he hastened to add that he could moderate his
views. Probably crucial to the understanding of the Sian Incident,
Donald revealed the pure, patriotic intention of the Young Marshal
in staging the coup by quoting his words:

> When the Generalissimo returns to Nanking I shall go
> with him and am ready to stand trial before the people,
> if necessary, to justify what I have done. I feel sure,
> when my purposes are known, the people will be with
> me. [11]

However, the defense of the Young Marshal's patriotism was concluded with a note of warning or even threat. Donald asserted that
the Young Marshal "has definite plans to fly out of Sian with his
distinguished captive in the event of an attack." But for what destination? Yenan, P'ing-liang, or Tihua? With the three-day truce
prolonged, such contingency plans would become unnecessary; it was
the hour of negotiations.

Evidently Soong did not return to Nanking empty-handed. Originally he planned to stay at Sian for three days, but now he abruptly
returned to Nanking having stayed in Sian for barely a day. What
transpired between the two intimate friends on December 20 and 21
may not be too difficult to fathom. Although Soong was tight-lipped,
Donald unmistakably left a crucial hint to the reporters that

> After he had spent two days in attempts at personal medi-
> ation, Chiang Kai-shek and his captor arrived at an agree-
> ment in principle on many of the points at issue, al-
> though the Generalissimo warned Chang Hsüeh-liang that
> nothing in the way of a concrete settlement would be pos-
> sible while he remained a prisoner. [12]

But Donald denied that he knew what points had been agreed upon.
As Chiang mentioned, the Young Marshal voluntarily deleted the last
four of the eight demands. The third and fourth demands dealt with
the same problem, namely, the release of patriotic and political
prisoners. Furthermore, the third and fourth demands could be
well-covered by the first demands which called for "reorganizing
the Nanking government and admitting all parties to share the joint

responsibility of saving the nation." In fact, when Soong was still in Sian on December 20, Chang approached Chiang urging him to accept one or two demands so as to settle the Incident. In a nutshell, the negotiations concerning the Sian Incident centered around the first two demands covering two major issues: to establish a coalition government and to suspend the civil war.

In recounting the negotiations, Madame Chiang commented that "the situation at Sian was . . . that Mr. Donald had laid the foundation, T. V. had built the walls, and it would be I who would have to put on the roof."[13] On December 22, Madame Chiang, together with Soong, Donald, Chiang Ting-wen, and Tai Li, chief of Chiang's special secret service, made her historic trip to Sian. Stopping at Loyang for lunch, she noticed that the airfield was filled with bombers fully loaded for action. Before leaving, she took some precautionary measures by ordering the commanding officer that "no planes were to approach Sian till ordered to do so by the Generalissimo."[14]

Though having full confidence in the goodwill of the Young Marshal, Madame Chiang was not sure of other recalcitrant generals. Approaching Sian, she handed Donald a revolver and made him promise that "if troops got out of control and seized me he should without hesitation shoot me."[15] It was four o'clock when the plane landed. To her surprise, the Young Marshal warmly welcomed her as usual as if nothing had happened. After a cup of tea, she was led to Chiang's room. Seeing her, he exclaimed: "Why have you come? You have walked into a tiger's lair." But he quickly recovered from the surprise and was pleased with her presence saying that "although I urged you not to come in any circumstances to Sian, still I felt that I could not prevent it. I opened the Bible this morning and my eyes lit on the words: 'Jehovah will now do a new thing, and that is, He will make a woman protect a man.'"[16]

The coming of Madame Chiang to Sian doubtless expedited the negotiations for a peaceful settlement. First of all, she completely won over the Young Marshal to her side. She went so far as to say that "he was then classed as one of us, and the danger was constant that he and the rest of us would be arrested."[17] Possibly she had either exaggerated or misunderstood the real situation at Sian. It was also possible that the Young Marshal led her to believe that was the case. There is no denying that the relations between Chang and Yang as well as between the Tungpei and Hsipei Armies appeared more strained following Chiang's detention, for obvious reasons, such as the poor discipline of Yang's troops, defection of Feng Ch'in-tsai with one-third of Yang's force to the Central Army, the Young Marshal's domination of negotiations, and Yang's fear of being betrayed.

At any rate, suspicion and fear of Yang and his generals seemed inevitable. It has been reported that most of the Tungpei generals had some personal friendship with the detained Nanking generals. They and their wives and even the Young Marshal frequently visited the detained generals. In contrast, none of the Hsipei generals ever paid a personal visit to the Nanking generals under surveillance. [18]

Strikingly enough, at no time did the Young Marshal lose the control and loyalty of the Tungpei Army. The fact that, even after having been taken into captivity himself, he still sent orders to his subordinates at Sian attests to the truth that he was in absolute command of his troops while staying in Sian. Although Yang had complete control of the city of Sian with three or four regiments, the Young Marshal's well-equipped 6,000-man force was stationed just outside the city. Even within the city, his 400-man guard battalion was strong enough to withstand some attack until it was rescued by the Tungpei forces from the outside.

The presence of Madame Chiang certainly facilitated the negotiations, because she could speak for the Generalissimo with absolute credibility, which no one else could do. From now on, the negotiations definitely reached a new stage; the Generalissimo may have continued to refuse to make any commitment, but he virtually made his promise through his wife.

One of the most important factors that brought together the Young Marshal and the Chiangs was the Nanking pro-Japanese faction which had developed and gained strength at Nanking in the absence of Chiang. This faction was represented by two groups. The military group was headed by Ho Ying-ch'in, who was only next to Chiang in the Nanking military hierarchy, now acting in Chiang's place. The civilian group was dominated by Chang Ch'ün, Huang Fu, [19] and even T'ai Chi-t'ao. To be sure, all the four mentioned were Chiang's best friends in life. At no time did anyone of

them betray Chiang; on the contrary they were, in the main, patriotic and served Chiang extremely well. But they had one thing in
common; they were opposed to the Communists in the extreme.

As already pointed out, Nanking was split over the issue of
how to save the Generalissimo. The official policy was that law
and order must be maintained, the insurgents must be punished,
and a strong posture and punitive expedition were the best ways to
bring about Chiang's release. Diametrically opposed to the punitive
expedition and bombing of Sian which might cause the death of the
Generalissimo was the group of Chiang's relatives, namely Madame
Chiang, T. V. Soong, and H. H. Kung, who saw the door of negotiation open from the beginning and who wanted to avert the impending civil war and to save Chiang's life. Rumors had it that the
"punitive" group tried to get Chiang killed in the Sian Incident.[20]

The Nanking official policy on the Sian Incident was unquestionably influenced by the diplomatic pressure of Japan. The Sino-
Japanese negotiations which had virtually broken down were suddenly
revived with Chiang's captivity. Japan was probably the last country willing to see the Sian Incident settled peacefully. The Japanese
Ambassador to Nanking, Shigeru Kawagoe, under the instruction of
Foreign Minister Hachiro Arita, informed the Chinese Government
that "Japan could not remain unconcerned if Nanking concluded a
compromise with the rebels which included anything resembling a
policy of cooperation with the Communists against Japan."

It was primarily in response to the Japanese pressure that
Chang Ch'ün, Foreign Minister, made the statement, "The Central
authorities have no intention whatever to effect a political compromise with the Young Marshal. . . . Nanking foreign policy will
undergo no change at all as a result of the Sian rebellion."[21] As
late as December 24, Ho Ying-ch'in in his private talk with Kawagoe declared that "the Central Government is determined to proceed
with its announced policy of carrying out a punitive expedition."[22]

The pro-Japanese faction at Nanking may have found its leader
in Wang Ching-wei, had Chiang's detention at Sian been prolonged.
Wang was recuperating in Europe from an assassin's bullets inflicted
upon him at the KMT Fifth Congress in November 1935. Even now,
the case is still shrouded with mystery, but it did greatly strain the
Wang-Chiang relations which had been deteriorating since Chiang's

March twentieth coup d'état of 1926, by which Chiang wrested all the power from Wang and forced him into exile in Europe.

Upon learning of Chiang's kidnapping, Wang cut short his sojourn in Europe and made a hasty return to China. Before leaving Europe, he summoned to Genoa Wellington Koo, Kuo T'ai-ch'i, Ch'eng T'ien-fang, and Liu Wen-tao, ambassadors to France, England, Germany, and Italy respectively.[23] After the three-day conference, Wang released to the European press a brief statement deploring Chiang's misfortune, accusing the Sian rebels, and announcing his immediate return to China. What had transpired in the three-day conference was that Wang saw his opportunity of resuming the national leadership in the absence of Chiang whose quick release could not have been foreseen. Also decided at Genoa was Wang's plan to pursue the suppressing campaign against the Communists. According to Ch'eng T'ien-fang, Wang's view on the Communist issue was coincident with his view, but incompatible with that of Wellington Koo and Kuo T'ai-ch'i who believed:

> In view of her domestic situation, China cannot help being resolute in resisting Japan; in order to resist Japan, it is necessary to tolerate the Chinese Communists. In weighing the two, Japanese aggression causes greater harm to China, whereas the CCP does a lesser harm--it is better for China to stop the Communist-suppressing campaign and to devote all her power to fighting Japan.[24]

Unfortunately for Wang, when he was aboard the S. S. Potsdam bound for China on December 22,[25] Chiang's release was almost certain.

An Unwritten Agreement

Madame Chiang needed no rhetoric to win over the Young Marshal and to convince him that the Generalissimo must be freed without further delay. She reminded him that "you always told the Generalissimo that you looked upon him as a father and he took you at your word."[26] Indeed the Young Marshal said to her, and so she herself believed, that "if you had been in Sian, this situation would not have developed."[27] With this kind of friendliness and absolute

openness, nothing could stand in the way of a peaceful settlement.
First, the Sian Incident would not be allowed to develop into a civil
war between Nanking and Sian, which could result in a catastrophe
such as that which had affected Spain.   Further, such a civil war
would contradict the objective for which the coup was launched.

Secondly, it was only natural that all efforts be made to insure
that there would be no more civil war.   The "encircling" campaign
against the Communists was doubtless a civil war and as such must
be stopped.   It appeared certain that any negotiated settlement for
the Sian Incident would preclude the continuation of the "encircling"
campaign against the Communists.   After all the CCP now became
an integral part of the triune alliance; its own survival hinged upon
the suspension of the "encircling" campaign, to which end Chou En-
lai must have dedicated himself.

Negotiations were well under way on December 23.   The first
item on the agenda was, of course, the first demand put forth in
the December 12 manifesto.   Although the manifesto called for establishing a coalition government in which all parties and factions
should participate, the negotiations focused on the reorganization of
the present cabinet.   The new cabinet must be composed of men
whose anti-Japanese stance was unquestionable.   To the Sian leaders,
T. V. Soong would be the best choice to head the new cabinet, since
he had always supported a strong policy toward Japan and was even
more needed now because of his role in the negotiations.   The Sian
leaders believed that both the CC and the Whampoa factions were
primarily anti-Japanese. [28]   They proposed that the portfolio of minister of military affairs, a post then held by Ho Ying-ch'in who had
been labeled as pro-Japanese, should be given to Hu Tsung-nan, the
star student of Chiang Kai-shek, but Chiang considered Ch'en Ch'eng
a better choice, to which the Sian leaders had no objection.   As for
the minister of education, they suggested Ch'en Li-fu.   However,
the Sian leaders refused to recommend anyone from Sian to join the
war cabinet.   Throughout the negotiations, they repeatedly stressed
the fact that in launching the coup, they wanted neither money nor
territory but aimed only at pressuring the Generalissimo to change
his policy and to embark upon resistance against Japan. [29]

The change in policy from "achieving internal pacification first
before resistance to external aggression" did not meet with tremendous obstacles as might have been anticipated.   Undoubtedly, the

144

Sian coup had awakened Chiang to the seriousness of the anti-Japanese sentiment prevailing in the Tungpei and Hsipei Armies. On the other hand, he must have realized that, under the circumstances, pursuing his old policy had been impossible without precipitating the greatest civil war that China had ever seen since the founding of the Republic; the consequence could only lead to China's total submission to Japan, the kind of situation which no Chinese wished to happen.

Since the Sian rebels, as well as the CCP leaders, professed to support Chiang's leadership in a war of resistance against Japan, an undertaking which Chiang had planned anyway to carry out at a ripe time, he certainly had reviewed the issue and his timetable. In captivity he had had a chance to listen to views different from his own, to contemplate the problems of Chinese national revolution and the realization of Sun Yat-sen's Sun Min Chu I [Three principles of the people], and to envision his future leadership in China. He may have undergone a change of heart and been converted to the views of his captors. Moreover, he may have viewed the CCP in a new light. Though in desperation and out of necessity, the CCP's repeated overtures to the KMT, particularly Chiang himself, for suspending the civil war and forming a "united front" against Japan could not be construed as cynical and deceptive without good intent. The negotiations between Ch'en Li-fu and the CCP representative that had been initiated since May 1936 and the CCP stance on the Sian Incident may well have reflected a consistent, new policy which marked a departure from the old line calling for the overthrow of the KMT government, the establishment of the Soviets, and the confiscation of land. It is possible that Chiang now tended to accept the views of his captor that

> our attitude toward the Communists is different. While far from clearly understanding them, we believe that above all we are all Chinese. What has separated us is probably no more than a difference in point of view or a struggle for power. Though we are enemies today, we might become friends tomorrow when our goal would coincide with theirs.[30]

By contrasting the CCP's and the Sian rebels' support for his leadership in resisting Japan with the punitive expedition against Sian launched by the Nanking generals, Chiang should not have failed to see that the latter's approach would not only jeopardize his life but even throw the nation into the great catastrophe of a prolonged, unprecedented civil war. If Chiang did not think this way, Madame Chiang certainly did. She argued:

> Why was I fighting to prevent an attack on Sian? Not
> primarily to save the life of my husband, but because
> I foresaw the range of calamity that could come upon
> China as the result of any impulsive use of force [31]

Like his wife, Chiang must have reached the same conclusion that China could not afford a civil war greater than that which had been waged against the Reds, and that the Sian crisis must be resolved through peaceful means. As soon as he was convinced that there was no reason to doubt the sincerity of the CCP overture, Chiang apparently decided to resume the aborted talk between Ch'en Li-fu and the CCP representative by inviting Chou En-lai to Nanking.

With the first two major issues resolved, the rest, particularly the third, fourth, fifth, and sixth demands, which were concerned with people's liberal rights, became relatively easy matters. For, not only had the Nanking government not denied the rights of the people to organize, to associate, and to assemble, which were a part of Dr. Sun Yat-sen's doctrine, [32] it was supposed to advocate them. The seventh demand called for effectual realization of Dr. Sun Yat-sen's last testament. Among other things, Sun's will urged the earliest implementation of two things: the convening of the people's convention and the abolition of unequal treaties. [33] The "immediate convocation of a National Salvation Conference," i.e., the eighth demand, was certainly in line with Dr. Sun's will.

By December 23, the outstanding issue that remained insoluble was no longer the eight demands which had been accepted in principle by the Generalissimo, but a written pledge from him, a condition that he would not accept under the circumstances. The Young Marshal was persuaded to accept the fact that Chiang as the leader of the nation could not sign any terms under duress. Nor was the intent of the Young Marshal to humiliate the Generalissimo and to damage his prestige. Now he was fully satisfied with Chiang's verbal promise given in the presence of T. V. Soong and Madame Chiang as witnesses.

While negotiation for Chiang's ultimate release without signing any written terms was in progress, the truce between the Nanking and Sian armies became overdue. To forestall a resumption of hostilities on the part of the Central Army, Chiang sent General Chiang Ting-wen back to Loyang bearing a personal order from him. At Loyang Chiang telephoned H. H. Kung and Ho Ying-ch'in to report the progress of negotiations, and then he, with Chiang Chien-yin, flew to the Tungkuan front to restrain the pugnacious young generals of the Central Army. Chiang showed them the Generalissimo's own order requiring both the Tungpei and Central Armies to withdraw one thousand meters from the existing battle line. There were some misgivings on the part of the young generals, for they thought it was simply another maneuver of Sian to delay the Central Army's drive to Sian. They accepted the order only after being persuaded that even if it were a maneuver, they should obey in order to save the Generalissimo; and it would not be too late to attack later.[34]

Back at Sian, it proved to be no easy task for the Young Marshal to win over to his position his subordinates, particularly the young officers, let alone Yang Hu-ch'eng and his men. Since December 12, the Young Marshal had followed the practice of consultation with his subordinates on all important matters relating to the Incident, but he still was capable of exercising dictatorial power within the Tungpei Army. But he could not make any decision without the consent of Yang Hu-ch'eng and his men who were not only equally involved in the affair but even had a veto power over the release of Chiang because of their control of the city. T. V. Soong, sometimes accompanied by Madame Chiang, incessantly held conferences with one group after another, namely, the Tungpei generals, the Tungpei radical young officers, the Hsipei generals, and Yang Hu-ch'eng himself in the hopes of ironing out the delicate issue of Chiang's signature to any written promise. As late as two o'clock on the morning of December 24, no progress had been made, and the Young Marshal had to report to Madame Chiang that

> Yang and his men are not willing to release the Generalissimo. They say that since T. V. and Madame are friendly towards me, my head would be safe, but what about theirs? They now blame me for getting them into this affair, and say that since none of our conditions are granted they would be in a worse fix than ever if they now released the Generalissimo.[35]

Evidently, it was all a matter of saving their heads with which Yang and his generals were most concerned. Madame Chiang, T. V.

Soong, and the Young Marshal had made every effort to assure them
that the Generalissimo would recommend that they not be punished
and that the civil war would not be pursued to suppress them, but
to no avail.

To break the impasse, the Young Marshal sought the mediation
of Chou En-lai. Despite many years of hard life and isolation,
Chou still was a polished statesman when he was presented to Madame Chiang by the Young Marshal. The meeting lasted for two
hours; for the most part of the meeting, Chou did the talking. Madame Chiang was greatly impressed with Chou's grasp of national
issues, particularly that of the Northwest. She was further pleased
with Chou's repeated statements that "apart from the Generalissimo
there was no one capable of being the leader of the country at this
period of existence."[36] Chou also asserted to Madame Chiang that
"we do not say that the Generalissimo does not resist aggression,
but we say he does not resist definitely enough or sufficiently fast."[37]
He believed that the Sian coup was the result of accident; while assuring Madame Chiang that the Sian leaders held the Generalissimo
in the fullest respect he regretted that Chiang would not let them
talk on questions of policy. On the following day, December 25,
Madame Chiang received Chou again, at which time she said:

> I urged him to use his influence to convince various
> parties of the futility of opposing the Government. . . .
> As we were all Chinese we should not fight each other.
> Internal problems should be solved by political means
> and not by military force. That had been the policy of
> the Generalissimo, and was so even in the case of the
> Communists.[38]

As everyone knows, that had not been Chiang's policy with the Communists before his being detained in Sian. The above passages of
conversation between Madame Chiang and Chou may have been similar to the one between Chiang Kai-shek himself and Chou which took
place on December 24 or 25. According to one reliable account,
Chou in saluting Chiang still addressed him as "Commandant" (chiao-
chang), a title which Chou used to address him during the Whampoa
days. In their conversation, Chou did not touch upon any sensitive
topics which would offend Chiang except that he reiterated the CCP
wish to support Chiang as the leader of the nation to carry out resistance against Japan. He also assured Chiang that the CCP had

changed its policy in order that the nation could be united to repel aggression. Interestingly Chou's talk assumed a personal, informal mood as he reported to Chiang that Chiang Ching-kuo, the eldest son of the Generalissimo, was well-treated in the Soviet Union, and he promised to help bring about an early union between the father and the son. On the other hand, Chiang is reported to have greeted Chou with the words: "We must not have any more civil war."[39] Chiang also made some casual remarks that "all the time we've been fighting I often thought of you. I remembered even during war that you had worked well for me. I hope we can work together again."[40] At any rate, the Chiang-Chou talk struck a pleasant note conducive to more fruitful negotiations between the KMT and CCP in the future.

Christmas Day

Both the Generalissimo and Madame Chiang were professed Christians. Madame Chiang told the Young Marshal that the best Christmas present he could give them was the release of the Generalissimo from Sian. Failing to persuade Yang and his men, the Young Marshal answered Madame Chiang by saying, "We might have to fight and that will be very dangerous for you. I can smuggle the Generalissimo out. You and Donald fly off to Loyang. I'll have the Generalissimo disguised, get him out of the city by car, take him to where my troops are in barracks, and from there drive him by car to Loyang to meet you."[41] Soong had agreed to the plan as a last resort, but Madame Chiang strongly opposed it on the grounds that not only could the Generalissimo not stand the car journey, but that it was not the manner appropriate for his departure. However, she kept reminding the Young Marshal that an attack on Sian would inevitably be launched by Nanking should Sian fail to release the Generalissimo. In the meantime, H. H. Kung in his letter to the Young Marshal on December 22 wrote, "If you could escort the Generalissimo for a safe return around Christmas time, it would truly be the greatest gift bestowed by Santa Claus."[42]

For a while, the hope of the Generalissimo's release on Christmas day appeared very slim. Yang and his men insisted on a written pledge from Chiang, without which, they argued, Chiang would retaliate once he was released. At the conference, Chang and Yang were engaged in hot debate. Chang reminded Yang that

our original motive was to plead with the Generalissimo
to lead the nation in a war of resistance against Japan,
irrespective of consequences to ourselves. After reading his diaries, we know for certain that he is determined to resist Japan. Moreover, he has promised to
submit our proposals to the Central Government for consideration. As our goal has been attained, we should
not flinch at fear of losses and death [43]

To the Young Marshal, as long as the goal of resisting Japan was
attained, all other matters became less important and should not be
allowed to affect the primary goal. Further delay in the release of
Chiang would only lead the event in the wrong direction, contrary to
the intended goal. Apparently Chang and Yang began to lose patience
and exchanged harsh words with each other. At one point, Chang
threatened Yang and others that "if they did not 'finish with politics'
he would act 'as he saw fit.'"[44] It was Chou En-lai who rescued
the awkward situation by playing the role of intercessor between
Chang and Yang. That was one of the reasons why both the Young
Marshal and Donald confirmed that "Chou En-lai . . . was actually
the one man who enabled General Chiang to depart unharmed from
the 1936 Sian kidnapping."[45] It is beyond doubt that Chou, by suc-
cessively persuading Yang Hu-cheng to accept Chiang's verbal promise instead of a written statement, rendered a great service to
Chiang.

It was not until two o'clock in the afternoon that Yang agreed
to Chiang's release. Then Chiang invited Chang and Yang for a
brief farewell talk, which was released to the press under the title
"Admonition to Chang Hsüeh-liang and Yang Hu-cheng" at Loyang the
following morning. This important and controversial document has
often been regarded as a literary makeshift. This is untrue. The
document is genuine not only judging from its publication date but
also from its contents.[46] Probably Chiang did not speak in so many
words as taken down by Madame Chiang. The work was probably
revised and rewritten by the Generalissimo, for in tone as well as
in content it is in full accordance with the detailed description of
the Sian coup as embodied in his famous diaries. Its main points
are quoted here:

1. Because of your profound concern for the national
situation, today you are determined to send me back to

Nanking and no longer act excessively by compelling me to sign anything and to give orders. You also made no extraordinary demands. This is not only the golden opportunity of the Chinese people to turn peril into safety but also the manifestation of the superb culture and morality of the Chinese people.

2. Through the instigation of a reactionary group, you believed that I did not treat people fairly and that I am not faithful to the revolution. Now you have read my diaries for this whole year, public and private telegrams, documents, and drafts, in addition to my personal drafts of policies and methods on national construction, domestic and foreign affairs, military affairs, finance, and education which numbered over 100,000 words. After searching diligently, have you ever found a single word which is not good for the nation but showing only self-interest? Or is there a thread of insincerity and untruth so as to cheat myself and others? . . . If there is, now I am still in Sian, and you still could kill me.

3. The responsibility of this coup d'état naturally rests with you two, but I consider myself equally responsible for the fundamental causes that led up to the coup. I understood that you, under the spell of propaganda of the reactionary group, regarded my goodwill as being ill-intentioned. Fortunately you regretted what you did from the outset, having realized that not only did I harbor no ill-will toward you but I even took up the cudgel for you from time to time. . . . Your early awakening prevented the incident from expanding, for which the Central Authorities will be unusually magnanimous toward you. As your superior, I wish to bear the responsibility of the incident. You should be ready to abide by whatever decision the Central Government may make, but your subordinates need not have any fear for themselves.

4. For more than ten years, I have followed the motto: "words must be credible; action must be fruitful." Whatever is beneficial to the country and the people, I will do without any regard for my personal interests. Everything

that is beneficial to the nation and the people must be adopted or carried out.

The document prompted an immediate response from Mao Tsetung who styled it as "an interesting specimen among China's political documents."[47] The reason for its being "an interesting specimen" is its ambiguity and evasiveness. Mao's charge of ambiguity is definitely correct, but that was apparently intended. First, Mao's criticism is twofold: (a) the document failed to satisfy the demands of the Chinese people. "As a token of good faith he should have produced a better piece of writing, repenting his political past and setting a new course for the future."[48] (b) Chiang's repeated references to the "reactionary group" is deplorable. What Chiang termed "reactionary group," by which he apparently meant the Communists, Mao would call "revolutionary." Mao advised Chiang to revise his political dictionary by changing the word "reactionary" to "revolutionary" for better correspondence to the facts.

Secondly, Mao in his brief statement thrice repeated Chiang's words, "words must be credible; action must bear fruit," and challenged Chiang to uphold his words. In this he particularly referred to Chiang's release. Although Chiang did not sign the terms set forth by Chang and Yang, it was upon acceptance of these terms that he was set free. Specifically Mao listed the terms:

(1) To reorganize the Kuomintang and the National Government, expel the pro-Japanese group and admit anti-Japanese elements;

(2) To release the patriotic leaders in Shanghai and all other political prisoners, and guarantee the freedom and rights of the people;

(3) To end the policy of "suppressing the Communists" and enter into an alliance with the Red Army to resist Japan;

(4) To convene a national salvation conference, representing all parties, groups, sections of the population and armies, to decide on the policy of resisting Japan and saving the nation;

(5) To enter into cooperation with countries sympathetic to China's resistance to Japan; and

(6) To adopt other specific ways and means to save the nation.

Thirdly, Chiang was asked to remember that "in addition to Generals Chang and Yang, the two leaders of the Sian Incident, the mediation of the CCP really contributed to his safe departure from Sian."[49] Significantly, "throughout the incident . . . the CCP stood for a peaceful settlement, acting solely in the interests of national survival." From then on the question was whether Chiang would keep his pledge and fulfill all the terms he promised. Chiang would have to change his erroneous policies, "compromise in foreign affairs and civil war and oppression at home," and immediately unite all parties and groups in a front of resistance against Japan. Toward that end, the CCP had already given its support to the KMT and Chiang himself as early as August 1936.

Indeed Chiang left Sian with dignity. His party rushed to the airport where thousands of pupils were waiting, not to say farewell to Chiang, but supposedly to welcome General Fu Tso-i, the victor of Pailingmiao in Suiyuan.[50] While the party was aboard the airplane, the Young Marshal insisted on going to Nanking with Chiang. Chiang declined Chang's overture by saying that "if you leave, the Tungpei Army will be without a commander. Moreover, your going to Nanking at this time will also create an inconvenience," presumably on the part of Chiang.[51] However, Madame Chiang explained the reasons why Chang accompanied Chiang to Nanking:

> He was under obligation to go to Nanking. First, he had undertaken with his associates to take full responsibility for what had happened; and second, it was his duty to show that what had been done was not with mutinous intent, nor against the Generalissimo, his position, or power.[52]

In fact, she praised Chang's request to go to Nanking with Chiang as unprecedented in the annals of the Chinese Republic that "any high officer responsible for mutinous conduct had shown eagerness to proceed to the capital to be tried for his misdeeds. This explains why the Central Government was lenient to Han-ching, a fact which many foreigners could not understand."[53]

However, Chou En-lai considered Chang's trip to Nanking with Chiang very unwise, but it was too late to stop him at that time. Another CCP leader at Sian, Po Ku, viewed the Young Marshal's quixotic action as driven by a hero complex.[54] But Mao Tse-tung approached the matter quite differently. In his interview with Agnes Smedley on March 1, 1937, he said, "Had Chang Han-ch'ing not accompanied Chiang Kai-shek back to Nanking on December 25 and had the settlement of the Sian Incident not been made in accordance with Chiang Kai-shek's methods, peaceful settlement would not have been achieved."[55]

But how could the Young Marshal do otherwise? At a conference of the Tungpei Army shortly before Chiang's release, he announced his decision to accompany Chiang to Nanking, but all those present raised strong objections.[56] The crucial point was that he must honor his own words. On the very day of the coup, he told General Wan Yao-huang that once a portion of the eight demands was accepted, he would accompany Chiang back to Nanking. The following day in a public speech to the whole staff of the Northwestern Bandit-Suppressing Headquarters, he said the same thing. Then on the 14th, he reiterated it to the Generalissimo and Donald. Now the time had come for him to keep his promise, if for no other reason than that he expected Chiang to honor his. By surrendering himself to Nanking he took upon himself the entire responsibility of the Incident; in so doing he actually did a lasting service to the nation--he removed the danger of military confrontation between Nanking and Sian. More important still was his great service to Chiang whose damaged image as the leader could best be restored.

X. A SECOND COUP D'ÉTAT

Chiang Kai-shek made his heroic return to Nanking at noon, December 26. In addition to the two thousand or more dignitaries who met Chiang at the airport, there were about 400,000 people who had suspended their daily activities and thronged into the streets to watch their leader. Indeed Chiang's prestige had risen higher than ever before. The country was awakened to the fact that Chiang's leadership was needed in the face of Japanese aggression.

Aboard his own plane, the Young Marshal with T. V. Soong arrived at Nanking two hours after Chiang's arrival.[1] On the same day he submitted a letter to the Generalissimo, which read,

> I am by nature so uncultivated and rude that I have committed great crimes of violating discipline and of disrespect to you. With shame I have followed you to Nanking in order that I may sincerely accept your most severe punishment, thereby upholding discipline and to serve as a warning for the future. Whatever is good for the country, I wish to die for, even a thousand times without regret. Please do not take into consideration our personal relations. As I am not well-versed in writing, I cannot express myself fully other than presenting my humble feelings to you.[2]

The Young Marshal's repentence, gallantry, chivalry, loyalty, and dedication as demonstrated in his release of Chiang and his accompanying him to Nanking did not produce the result that was anticipated. He was court-martialed. During the mock trial, the Young Marshal lost his temper and shouted: "The only one of you all who is worth a damn is the Generalissimo! None of the rest of you would be any loss to China. If I am freed, I'll start a revolution!"[3] There was none of the forgiveness that Madame Chiang and H. H. Kung had promised.[4] On December 31 he was sentenced to ten years of imprisonment and denied all civil rights for five years. Upon receiving the petition from Chiang for clemency, the Central Government on January 4, 1937, declared that Chang's ten-year sentence was commuted to surveillance under the Military Council.[5]

As for Chang's accomplice in the coup, Yang Hu-ch'eng, the Central Government issued no punishment except that while he was allowed to keep his job, his official title was suspended. The aftermath of the coup involved personnel reshuffling at a minimum: Yang's right-hand man, Sun Wei-ju, was made governor of Shensi, while Yü Hsüeh-chung remained in his post as governor of Kansu without suspension of his official title. Furthermore, the Pacification Commissioner of Kansu, Chu Shao-liang, one of the detained generals at Sian, was replaced by a Tungpei military leader, Wang Shu-ch'ang. The Northwestern Bandit-Suppressing Headquarters was abolished, and in its place the Sian Headquarters of the Generalissimo was created with Ku Chu-t'ung as commissioner, to be in charge of the whole reconstruction work particularly in relation to the Red Army.[6] It appeared that the Central Government had done its best in the face-saving process; on the surface no one was terribly offended, nor did anyone except the Young Marshal lose power and prestige.

A Recalcitrant Sian

But the reconstruction work halted even before it started. The promised negotiated settlement which led to the release of Chiang suddenly became an illusion as a result of the detention of the Young Marshal and the criminal proceedings against him, as well as Chiang's retreat to his native place, Fenghua.[7]

Back in Sian, the Young Marshal's departure caused immediate concern within the Tungpei Army, particularly among its young officers. Before leaving, the Young Marshal issued a brief order to the Tungpei Army in which he delegated authority to Yang Hu-ch'eng and Yü Hsüeh-chung. Now from Loyang he cabled to Yang that arrangements should be made at once to fly the Nanking generals out of Sian. Yang paid a visit to the generals at noon on December 26, personally announcing Chang's cabled order. On the same evening, Yang invited all the Nanking generals, including the wives of Wan Yao-huang and Ch'en Chi-ch'eng, for a farewell banquet at his house, which was filled with laughter.

On the other hand, the issue of releasing the Nanking generals created some consternation among the Tungpei ranking officers. To the radical young officers, the detention of the Nanking generals as hostages was the best leverage to bring about the return of the Young Marshal. So, led by Sun Ming-chiu, the captor of Chiang at Hua-ch'ing-ch'ih and now commander of the special regiment, the radical young officers strongly opposed the release of the Nanking generals and insisted that as long as the Young Marshal was not allowed to return, they could not be released.[8] But Wang I-che, who presided over the conference since Yü Hsüeh-chung was away at Lanchow, fell into a fury. He is reported to have said, "Whoever refuses to obey the Young Marshal's order, I will kill him."[9] Consequently all the Nanking Generals left Sian on the 27th.

Evidently the Young Marshal did not anticipate that he would not be allowed to return to Sian, much less be put under house arrest at Fenghua. Upon leaving Sian with the Generalissimo, he ordered his aides to follow him to Nanking by commercial airline at the earliest date. However, Pao Wen-yueh, Li T'ien-ts'ai, Li Chin-chou, and Yang Huan-ts'ai did not reach Nanking until December 30. Unexpectedly, two of them were immediately put under house arrest at Tai Li's, while the other two were driven to flight.[10] Since neither the Young Marshal nor his four aides sent any news back to Sian, the insurgent city became restive and realized that something must have gone wrong with their men at Nanking. Although no serious clashes in the eastern front occurred, tension was mounting in the city of Sian. Regular air service was not resumed; railway traffic and even telegraphic service continued to be disrupted.

On the other hand, Sian showed a new spirit which had not been seen elsewhere in China at the time. Several hundred political prisoners--many Red Army captives but some patriotic students-- were freed. When James M. Bertram, a British journalist, and Miao Chien-ch'iu, the Young Marshal's counselor, arrived in Sian only three days after Chiang's return to Nanking, they realized that Sian had become a city of propaganda with the Communists dominating the newspaper and Agnes Smedley taking complete charge of the English radio broadcasts. Even the CCP news agency, Hung-chung She, came into the open in Sian. It was little wonder that rumors spread that the Reds would launch a coup on New Year's Day.[11]

To usher in the new year of 1937, Sian staged a huge celebration; hundreds of thousands of people crowded in the airfield to watch the exhibition of detained warplanes, which was followed by a military review of the Tungpei and Hsipei Armies. On the rostrum, General Yang Hu-ch'eng delivered a revolutionary speech, the crucial passages of which were recorded by James Bertram:

> These celebrations are very different from any that have been held in the past! For in the past, every year our country was torn by civil wars. Now our Generalissimo has accepted the demands of the people, and we will have no more civil war. The patriotic movement will be liberated, and all parties in the country will be united to resist Japanese aggression and win back our lost territories. . . . You, soldiers of our united armies, must clearly understand the meaning of our military review today. Formerly reviews were made for emperors, or for the highest commanders alone. But today you passed in review, not just before your commanders, but before the whole people of the Northwest, before your patriotic comrades in the national salvation movement. The masses of your own people wanted to see for themselves your anti-Japanese preparation and determination. [12]

This was unmistakably a "united front" message. Incongruously in concluding, Yang called upon all friends from provinces outside Sian to leave Sian in three days. In the next few days, the Sian press was inundated with circular telegrams demanding the return of the Young Marshal. At a press conference on January 4, the Anti-Japanese Allied Military Council declared that the Tungpei and Hsipei Armies could not be separated and that the solution of the Sian Incident proposed by the Central Government was unacceptable. [13] The next day, eight Sian generals led by Yang Hu-ch'eng lodged a protest against Nanking in a lengthy telegram to the nation. Its main passages are these:

> When Generalissimo Chiang was in Shensi, Hu Ch'eng and others, following the Young Marshal, presented eight demands for national salvation in the December 12 telegram. After repeated pleas, the Generalissimo accepted them and promised that he would carry them out after his return to Nanking. . . .
>
> All of us and our 200,000 troops are in one mind and one heart with the Young Marshal. All we ask is to

dedicate our lives to resisting Japan under the leadership
of the Generalissimo and to add a little to the strength
of our people in coping with the external aggression. . . .
After the Generalissimo reached Nanking, he ordered that
the Central Army withdraw east of Tungkuan. Further,
before leaving Shensi, he said: "While I am alive, there
shall be no more civil war." . . .

Not only has the Central Army not withdrawn east of
Tungkuan, but it has even pushed westward in great numbers. . . . This aroused a great public resentment and
raised doubt as to whether the Central Army intends pos-
itively to create a civil war or to use a blockade as a
passive means of pressuring us. . . . If then our earnest desire for internal peace and for external resistance
against Japan be of no avail, we would have no choice
but to rise to accept the challenge and to fight to the
death without regret. [14]

True to Yang's accusations, the Central Government did not
withdraw its forces west of Tungkuan as Chiang promised. Nor did
it show any sign of suspending civil war. On the contrary, it reiterated its policy of prosecuting the suppression campaign against
the Communists by mobilizing all its troops in Shensi and Kansu for
an "encircling" campaign to be commanded by Ch'en Ch'eng. [15]

To press their demands, Sian sent a three-man team to Nanking on January 5; Li Chih-kang represented Yang Hu-ch'eng, while
Yen Pao-hang and Mi Ch'un-lin represented the Tungpei Army.
Three days later, one hundred twenty-six senior officers of the two
armies signed a circular telegram expressing their full support for
the position taken by the eight generals in the January 5 telegram. [16]

On January 9, Sian staged the greatest popular demonstration
ever seen in the Northwest. About 100,000 soldiers and civilians
assembled first in the Park of the Revolution for a mass meeting
and then paraded in the streets with the Tungpei cavalry leading the
way, followed by the peasant guards, the anti-Japanese vanguards,
and students. The main theme of slogans for the day was the recovery of the lost "White Mountain" and the "Black River" that
symbolize Tungpei. [17] The Sian rebels seemed prepared for the
worst.

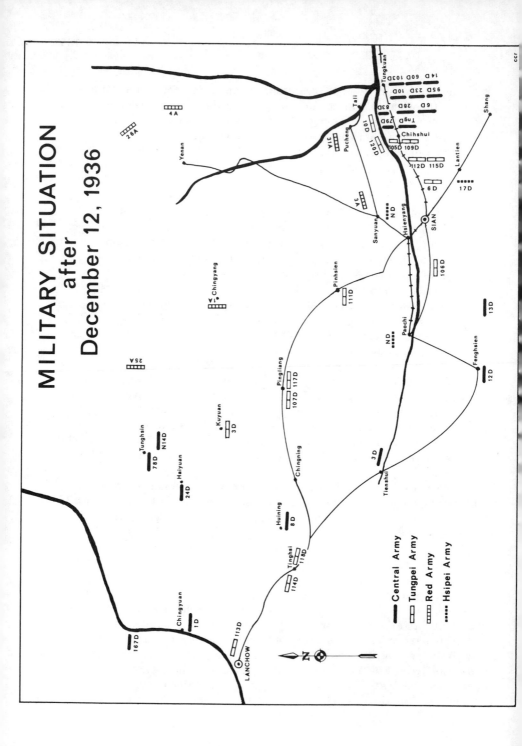

MILITARY SITUATION
after
December 12, 1936

Central Army
Tungpei Army
Red Army
Hsipei Army

A journalist who traveled from Lanchow to Loyang through Sian in early January reported that the insurgent city was making all preparations for a long siege. In crossing the front line at Wei-nan, he saw the Tungpei troops building massive defense works; he was checked six times before he left the Tungpei troops behind.[18]

The Rallying of Anti Communist Forces

On the other hand, the political arena at Nanking was very much dominated by the anti-Communist, if not pro-Japanese, leaders, with Chiang in temporary retirement and T. V. Soong virtually out of the government. At least for the time being, Nanking was not ready to tackle the question of policy change toward the Communists, let alone the reorganization of the government as agreed upon by the Chiangs, Soong, and the Young Marshal. In fact, there was a considerable backlash over the issue of Chinese Communists. Inside the Nanking government a strong opposition to the policy change from "internal pacification first before resistance against external aggression" to the suspension of civil war for a "united front" against Japan emerged. Most striking was the rightist view advanced by Wu T'ieh-ch'eng, Mayor of Shanghai:

> Now a small minority of intellectuals, willing to be used by the Communists, advocate the slogan of "popular front" which is regarded as the best theory for national salvation. Unfortunately, they failed to understand that the "popular front" is nothing more than a technical term employed in the change of strategy of the Third International. . . .

> That our leader wants "internal pacification before resistance to external aggression" is correct. We Chinese do not fight against Chinese. It follows that since the Communist is also Chinese, we should not fight against him but unite with him in fighting our external foes. This sounds rational. But the Communists in spite of being Chinese do not receive orders from Chinese but from the Third International. . . . It is therefore that our suppression of the Red Bandits is not fighting against Chinese, but rather fighting against the running dogs of the Red imperialist--Red traitors.

162

By the same token, now we are fighting against the ban-
dits in Suiyuan; we are not fighting against Chinese but
against the running dogs of the White imperialist--the
White traitors. [19]

Mayor Wu's view had wide support among the intellectual community. Many intellectual leaders tended unanimously to condemn
the "popular front" that was identified with the national "united front"
advocated by the CCP. The anti-Communist stand taken by Hu Shih
was echoed by such a leading historian as Fu Szu-nien. Fu went so
far as to term the "popular front" as "garbage front" whose constit-
uencies were made up of CCP-comprised Nationalists, elements of
the Fukien People's Government, feudalistic warlords and politicians,
and even disappointed writers. [20] Many intellectual groups including
all faculty of universities in Shanghai issued declarations denouncing
the position of Sian as the greatest obstacle to the nation's survival
and calling upon the Central Government to bring about unification
even if it meant resorting to force. [21] The opposition to the "united
front" found its natural leader in Wang Ching-wei, who in spite of
being somewhat embarrassed by Chiang's unexpected release, was
satisfied with the cordial welcome of the Nanking leaders to his return when he flew to Nanking in the early morning hours of January
18. [22]

On the very day of his arrival at Nanking, Wang enunciated his
anti-Communist ideology in a speech delivered at the weekly memorial service for Sun Yat-sen. Apparently having Japan in mind, he
first briefly dismissed the idea of a "common defense against Communism" by saying that the task of suppressing Communism in China
was well within the reach of her own power without recourse to external assistance. Then he dwelt at great length on refuting the
view of the "people's front for a common resistance to external aggression." First, it would be utterly impossible for China to apply
the "people's front." Using the French "people's front" as a case
in point, Wang argued that no parties in France either possessed
their own army or set up their own government; France had only
one national army under one national government. On the contrary,
the CCP had its own Red Army and set up a soviet government.
Under the circumstances, how could the "people's front" develop in
China?

Secondly, the correct policy of an-nei jang-wei should be maintained, not because the Chinese emphasized the internal foe more

than the external enemy but because achieving internal pacification
was the sine qua non for taking up resistance against external aggression. China's survival would depend upon victory or defeat in
her fight against the external enemy. But such an important undertaking could not even be considered until she was well-prepared and
had confidence in her own strength. Emphatically Wang reminded
his audience,

> During the Shanghai campaign when the Government trans-
> ferred its troops from Kiangsi to Shanghai, the Commu-
> nists immediately launched an attack on Kanchow. During
> the Ku-pei-kou campaign when the Government trans-
> ferred its troops from the Yangtze River, the Commu-
> nists seized Fu-chou and attacked Nanchang. From
> these lessons, we learned that without internal pacifica-
> tion, we cannot fight our external enemy. That is why
> we have been engaged in the bloody war in the last few
> years.[23]

Thirdly, the overture of the CCP for a common resistance
against external aggression could not be accepted on the grounds
that the CCP could not be trusted or believed. Wang cited a specific instance in which, during the First National Congress of the
KMT, the Communists made a solemn statement assuring that their
admission into the KMT was for the purpose of national revolution,
not for propagating Communism.[24] Later events proved that it was
not the KMT's mistake for believing the CCP but rather that the
latter broke its own promise. But could the CCP admit it?

> In their view the so-called keeping of one's agreement
> and promise represents only feudalistic morality and
> therefore is worth nothing. This being their view, what
> reason do we have for believing that their overture is
> real and will be kept?[25]

In conclusion, Wang made an emotional appeal by saying, "Let us
not allow the whole plan and measures for 'national salvation and
survival' to suffer from our own negligence. . . . We must lead
the whole country, to pursue the course of the 'Three Principles of
the People' and to build up our national strength for self-salvation
and independence."[26]

Four days later, Wang in his radio broadcast further expounded the theme of "How to Achieve National Salvation and Survival." The gist of his talk was that liquidation of domestic troubles and resistance to foreign aggression must go forward according to the original plan and schedule. This meant that the "suppression and encirclement" campaign against the Communists must be prosecuted, and the suspension of civil war was out of the question. Wang said that not only would the realization of Communism in China bring about national extinction but also China's close relations with the Communists, which would result in their dominating China's political policy, could create great turmoil, a situation which would again lead to extinction.[27]

Wang regretted that after Generalissimo Chiang's safe return to Nanking, some troops which had entrenched themselves in the Northwest disobeyed orders and even allowed themselves to be Bolshevized. He warned his countrymen,

> We shall never let ourselves be seduced by the Communists nor fall into their poisonous scheme of dividing us. . . . In order to carry out their poisonous scheme, the Communists tried to borrow our twin slogans, "Externally protecting our national territory" and "Internally uniting the masses." First, both the endangering of the life of the supreme military commander and the occupation and rule of a region are but the overt act of dissolving national territory instead of protecting it. While the Communists use the name of war of resistance, in reality they are dissolving the national territory. Next, the Communists set as their goal the class struggle which certainly could cause the dissolution of the united front of the people. Behold! While the whole country is united in resistance to aggression, the Communists, manipulating behind the scenes, cause the territory under the banner of the national revolutionary army to be dissolved, this being the best evidence of splitting the people's united front.[28]

Wang's anti-Communist stance coincided with the mounting tension in the Sian settlement, and afforded the focus of the surge of anti-Communist sentiment among the various groups in the Nanking government. The euphoria that was created by the release of Generalissimo Chiang had vanished. As each day passed, new obstacles were added to the old, unresolved issues, and the support for a punitive expedition against Sian gained new strength. The Central Army, which had withdrawn from the west of Tungkuan now returned and faced the rebel armies at Ch'ih-shui. For the moment it seemed that civil war was inevitable, unless some drastic measures were taken to stop it.

The Negotiation Impasse

The Nanking government, particularly Chiang Kai-shek, was confronted with a crucial dilemma of deciding between the release of the Young Marshal as demanded by Sian and a continuous drag on the political and military impasse. Following the release of the Nanking generals, Nanking's great concern was the return of 50 warplanes and some 500 air force personnel still held in Sian. They doubtless became a leverage of the Sian insurgents in their bargain for the release of the Young Marshal as well as for better terms in the final settlement. Having failed in obtaining the release of the warplanes and personnel, Ho Ying-ch'in was obliged to ask for the Young Marshal's help. Chang readily complied by writing a personal letter to Yang Hu-ch'eng and the Tungpei generals requesting the release of the warplanes and personnel. In the meantime a mission composed of Wang Hua-i and Wu Han-t'ao, two reputed Tungpei intellectuals, and Li Chin-chou, the Young Marshal's secretary who had been detained since his arrival at Nanking, was sent to Sian. While Li was glad to reach his family safely at Sian, the mission met with no immediate success.

There was little doubt that the Young Marshal still hoped to play a prominent role in the solution of the Sian issue when he accompanied the Generalissimo back to the capital. Naturally the Young Marshal may have regretted his coming to Nanking, as it was reported by Po Ku, a Communist leader who was with Chou En-lai at Sian at the time.[29] Nor did the Young Marshal anticipate the actions taken against him after his arrival at Nanking: his court-martial, sentence and pardon though under "strict surveillance." Had he foreseen all this, he would not have ordered his aides to follow him to Nanking. Not only were his aides not allowed to see him; they were all put under house arrest upon their arrival. Though he received the best treatment and enjoyed all comforts in the splendid residence of T. V. Soong, he was nevertheless virtually a prisoner. He was not allowed to receive callers, nor even to answer a telephone call. It was reported that he planned to go abroad, an idea with which he had toyed even before he took the command in the Northwest in 1935 and which may have reemerged in his mind in the time of despair. It was also reported that he intended to return to Sian in order to devise effective means for handling his troops in a manner which expressed his loyalty and sincerity to the Central Government.[30] Probably this idea was merely wishful thinking, for "under strict surveillance," he could neither go abroad nor return to Sian unless the Generalissimo changed his mind and granted him another pardon, which he has not done to this day.

Ironically, the loyalty of the Young Marshal remained unvacillating, at least on the surface. He undoubtedly thought his loss of freedom was temporary at the most; once the Sian issue was resolved, he certainly would be released. Until then all consideration must be made on the basis of national interest which he put above all personal interests, for to do otherwise could defeat the very purpose for which the coup was staged. Especially in expiation of his iniquity for having caused great trouble to the nation, he was resolute to do his utmost to cooperate with Chiang in solving the issue.

The Nanking leaders conducted the negotiations for the Sian settlement on several levels apparently with some contingency plans. With Chiang in retirement at Fenghua since January 2, Ho Ying-ch'in was in charge of general military affairs as he was during Chiang's captivity. To the public Ho was the man who handled the direct negotiations with the Sian representatives, namely Li Chih-kang, Mi Ch'un-lin, and Pao Wen-yueh (the first representing Yang Hu-ch'eng, the latter two representing the Tungpei Army). Another group active in the negotiations consisted of a few prominent political and military leaders of Tungpei, who once occupied lofty positions in the Nanking government. They were Wang Shu-ch'ang, Mo Te-hui, and Liu Che. Because of their long association with the Tungpei Army and their acquaintance with the Nanking leaders, their service was especially sought by Nanking on the one hand to mollify the Young Marshal and, on the other, to win the absolute trust of the Tungpei generals at Sian. The trio also became the spokesmen of the Tungpei community in the Peking-Tientsin area. It should be added that Nanking's outward respect for these men was also intended to win the support of the northern warlords, chiefly Sung Che-yüan, Han

Fu-ch'ü, and Yen Hsi-shan.   In other words, the Nanking leaders
tried to give the appearance that they did not dictate the terms of
the settlement.

In all public pronouncements, the Nanking leaders, particularly
Ho Ying-ch'in, assured the country that the Sian affair must be set-
tled by peaceful means in the spirit of magnanimity and benevolence
and that force would be used only as a last resort.   Despite all this,
Nanking lost no time in deploying its crack troops to converge on
Shensi with Chiang's two top lieutenants, Ku Chu-t'ung and Ch'en
Ch'eng, in command.

The Tungpei generals, and Yang Hu-ch'eng also, were not so
foolish as to have no misgivings about the good intentions of Nanking.
First, they seemed unanimous in their demand for the release of
the Young Marshal, whose detention was regarded as bad faith on
the part of Chiang and the Central Government.   This was the single
issue so important to them that they would not have hesitated to go
to war with Nanking; it was a test of their loyalty, not merely to
the Young Marshal but to the whole Tungpei military group.   Second,
the deployment of Nanking troops, the most conspicuous being the
Guard Division of Chiang commanded by General Kuei Yung-ch'ing,
could not go unnoticed by their watchful eyes.

Faced with real threat from the Central Army--whose all-out
offensive could have come at any time had the negotiations at Nanking suddenly broken down, or had the Nanking government wanted
to destroy the potential, disloyal, provincial, warlord armies once
for all, or had Chiang Kai-shek reversed his decision on the suspension of the campaign against the Communists--Sian had to prepare itself, in great haste, for several emergency measures.   The
Provisional Northwestern Allied Armies Military Council was virtually out of function in the absence of the Young Marshal.   The deputy chief of the Council Yang Hu-ch'eng, though preserving his nominal leadership of the Northwest, had no way to assume the direct
command of the Tungpei Army.   Yü Hsüeh-chung, to whom the Young
Marshal had delegated his authority upon leaving for Nanking as he
did in 1933 when he went abroad, and who had the prestige and experience in commanding the Tungpei Army, had returned to Lanchow
only a few days after the Sian coup.   To cope with the command
crisis, a Northwestern General Staff Group was organized with Ho
Chu-kuo as chief and Wang I-che as deputy.   The Group was also

168

to be responsible for coordination of the three Armies, the Tungpei
and Hsipei Armies and the Red Army.[31]

As the strongest of the three, the Tungpei Army was the natural, chief target of the Central Army's attack. A unique strategy
for its own defense, and therefore the defense of Sian, its political
center, was planned. A defense line, parallel to the Wei River and
the Lunghai Railway, stretched for three hundred miles from Ch'ih-
shui on the east and Lanchow on the west (see Map 3). Its main
forces concentrated on three strategic points: east of Sian on the
right bank of the Wei River; Hsienyang, northwest of Sian, on the
left bank of the Wei River; and Pingliang in east Kansu. The defense of the left bank of the Wei River in the east was chiefly left
to the Red Army. The north and south areas of Sian were garri-
soned by the Hsipei Army. It was expected that the Central Army's
major thrusts would come from two directions: from the front,
i.e., east of Sian, where massive governmental troops had poured
in through the bottleneck of Tungkuan, and from the northwest,
where a Nanking force of no less than 50,000 men commanded by
Hu Tsung-nan, Wang Chün, and Mao Ping-wen was maneuvering.[32]
Quite contrary to the common belief, in a military showdown Sian
was far from desperate; the terrain was very favorable for defense.
The chances for survival and the fighting of a protracted war were
too good to be overlooked. Further, under a joint attack by the
Tungpei Army and the Red Army, the situation of the Central Army
in east Kansu may have become precarious chiefly because of the
shortage of provisions and supplies unless the Central Army broke
through the Tungpei Army defense and reached the Lunghai Railway
in time.

War clouds loomed over Shensi. An eye-witness who traveled
through the Tungpei Army defense line reported that on the eastern
front four parallel lines of trenches and defense work had been built
and that the movement of troops was very busy. A temporary
bridge spanning the Wei River leading to San-yuan was erected for
military transportation. Political workers recruited mainly from
students and released prisoners were concentrated for training at
Ch'ung-an Temple; they undertook much of the propaganda work in
the Tungpei Army. Yang Hu-ch'eng's self-defense corps in many
counties near Sian suddenly emerged as a new force to buttress the
fighting strength of the Hsipei Army.

Inside the city of Sian, students and radical elements with marked differences in social background and political conviction all became active under the shield of the National Salvation Association and the aegis of the radical officers of the Tungpei Army, particularly Sun Ming-chiu. Sun, since his actions at Hua-ch'ing-ch'ih on December 12, had been promoted to commander of the special task regiment and served concurrently as chief of the office for police and soldier security. Beneath the level of a few top generals Sun was probably the most influential man inside Sian. Riding the tide of the mass movement, a committee of five members was set up to guide the masses, with Wang Ping-nan, Yang Hu-ch'eng's secretary and a Communist, as its leading spirit. It appeared that the masses might have become forged into a strong force had the quasi-independent political power of the Northwest been prolonged. In spirit and in action, Sian was put on a war footing and the worst was expected. The tension of war was also signaled by the visits of two officials of the American and British consulates, who had successfully withdrawn some fifty of their citizens from Shensi on January 18.[33]

To all appearances, the Northwest maintained the "united front" remarkably well. Behind the facade of unity, there were divergent groups with special interests and uncompromising political ideologies. So far their objectives coincided: they demanded the release of the Young Marshal, suspension of civil war, and resistance against Japan. The triune unity--the Tungpei, Hsipei, and Red Armies--could be preserved as long as their objectives remained unchanged and their interests did not clash. For the time being, they were determined to hold out until the final settlement which would be acceptable to all parties concerned.

After half a month of intensive negotiations, the two elderly Tungpei leaders, Mo Te-hui and Liu Che, left Nanking. Upon arriving at Peking on January 23, the two announced that they would not go to Nanking again in the near future. When asked about the outcome of the negotiations, they merely replied: "It is very complicated."[34]

More important than the role played by the two elderly Tungpei leaders, Li Chih-kang, Mi Ch'un-lin, and Pao Wen-yüeh flew back and forth between Sian and Nanking from January 6 to 20. When they left for Sian on January 20, their trip was described as

"the last peace mission. "[35] By all accounts, January 23 was
marked as the day when all hope for a peaceful settlement vanished.
It was then that the Central Government expressed the belief that a
peaceful solution had reached its final stage and that if Yang Hu-
ch'eng and his company still refused to repent, the Government
would have to take strong measures. On January 24, when Wang
Ching-wei flew to Fenghua to see Chiang Kai-shek, during which the
Sian issue must have been the central item on the agenda of their
talk, Ho Ying-ch'in enunciated at Nanking that "now the crucial point
is whether Yang Hu-ch'eng and others will be able to express genuine repentance. "[36]

But what led to the breakdown of negotiations? It was the single issue "that the Young Marshal should not be allowed to return
to Sian, " according to the mandate of the Generalissimo. [37]

The Tungkuan Conference and Its Aftermath

Failure to effect a political solution of the Sian affair meant
that negotiations for resolving military confrontation were to be
handled on the scene and, therefore, shifted from Nanking to Tungkuan. In the camp of General Ku Chu-t'ung, the newly appointed
Commissioner of the Generalissimo's Sian Headquarters, there was
a Tungpei man named Liu Chen-tung, formerly a brigade commander
of artillery in the Tungpei Army. Through this intermediary, Ku
Chu-t'ung and Ch'en Ch'eng had several telephone conversations with
the Tungpei generals, notably Liu To-ch'üan whose troops were facing the Central Army at Ch'ih-shui. As a result of these conversations on January 23, both sides agreed that they would refrain from
military clashes in order to gain time to iron out their problems.
The following day, Sian dispatched Mi Ch'un-lin and Hsieh K'o to
Tungkuan. Mi and Hsieh proceeded to Loyang to meet with Ku Chu-
t'ung for discussion on troop disengagements on January 25. Thus
they set the stage for the Tungkuan conference. [38]

When Mi and Hsieh returned to Tungkuan from Sian, they were
accompanied by General Ho Chu-kuo, the leading Tungpei general at
Sian. With the arrival of Ku Chu-t'ung, the Tungkuan conference
opened. The conference did not plan to touch upon the most thorny
issue--the return to Sian of the Young Marshal as a prerequisite to
any proceedings for the final settlement, a political issue outside the

purview of military questions. Another political issue--the question
of the CCP--which had not been brought into the open at the time,
was not to be discussed at the conference. Understandably, these
political issues, particularly the Communist issue, would be brought
up at the Third Plenum of the KMT Fifth Congress to be convened
on February 15.

As an initial step toward armistice, the Tungpei troops on the
eastern front were to be withdrawn to the left bank of the Wei River,
where they would await final assignment for their permanent station.
Secondly, one month's salary and food expenses were granted to the
Tungpei troops during their withdrawal. Thirdly, small units of the
Tungpei Army were permitted to be stationed along the Sian-Lanchow
highway and small units of the Hsipei Army were permitted to remain in Sian.[39]

Fruitful negotiations accomplished at Tungkuan revived much
optimism in certain quarters at Sian and Nanking. Ho Chu-kuo expressed his confidence in his leadership in the Tungpei Army and
announced that the Tungpei Army had withdrawn from the two flanks
of the eastern front before he left for Sian on January 29. In the
meantime, H. H. Kung publicly reported that "peaceful solution of
the Shensi-Kansu affair is in sight, while military confrontation can
be absolutely avoided."[40]

No sooner had the Tungpei generals at Sian become willing to
reach a temporary agreement with Nanking by accepting the terms
offered by Ku Chu-t'ung than they invited Yü Hsüeh-chung to Sian
for serious discussion. Yü arrived in Sian on the 31st and immediately entered into a series of conferences with the Tungpei generals,
Yang Hu-ch'eng, and Chou En-lai.

Yü, a native of Shantung and a former army commander under
Wu P'ei-fu, had joined Chang Hsüeh-liang's camp only after the total defeat of Wu in the fall of 1926. He had risen fast in the Tungpei Army and became the highest ranking general, second only to
the Young Marshal. Nurtured in the warlord tradition, Yü commanded great respect among the northern warlords like Sung Che-
yüan and Han Fu-ch'u. Having just flown his whole family in a
chartered commercial airplane out of Lanchow for Peking,[41] he certainly had little interest in the "united front," though remaining a
staunch nationalist and strongly anti-Japanese. Further, he had not

been involved in the new politics of recalcitrant Sian for the previous one and a half months.

In the Chinese press, Yü was more favorably treated than any other Sian leader at the time. In fact, many Nanking leaders personally urged him to save the situation by accepting the orders of the Central Government for settlement. So far Yü remained adamant and gave no sign that he would sever himself from the Tungpei Army and Sian.[42] Unquestionably this was due to his loyalty to the Young Marshal and the Tungpei group. His coming to Sian was of paramount importance in that he gave the Tungpei Army leadership at a time when it was badly needed.

Though the Tungkuan conference averted the impending war between Nanking and Sian, no viable solution to the Sian problems was yet to be found. While the peace settlement seemed within an easy reach, the outcry for recalcitrance still dominated the minds of the populace. On January 28, Sian witnessed a huge demonstration to commemorate the Chinese resistance to the Japanese invasion of Shanghai by the 19th Route Army.[43] There was no question that the masses were aroused by the Japanese aggression and that the spirit of the "united front" against Japan ran high.

Probably the scene of mass upheaval was pleasing to the eyes of Yang Hu-ch'eng, who may have seen real strength in the masses. He was by no means disappointed by the turn of events--the detention of the Young Marshal and the uncompromising demand for his release, Nanking's stonewall attitude toward Sian and its anti-Communist posture, and the progress of the three-in-one alliance--for he was suddenly raised to national prominence. An ambitious man, Yang, under the influence of his radical wife and some of his Communist entourage, may well have cherished aspirations to the leadership in the new Northwest. Now he had the following of the masses, the support of the CCP, and the possibility of winning the allegiance of the Tungpei Army. His case was rather simple: the longer the quasi-independence of the Northwest persisted, the more his new power would be consolidated. If a peace settlement came soon, however favorable, it would lead to his downfall as had been the case of the Young Marshal. Then his best hope would be a trip abroad, an action which later became a reality. Furthermore, being the weakest of the three in terms of military strength and the least dedicated to the cause of the "united front" against Japan, Yang must have accommodated himself to both of his partners to preserve his nominal leadership and the unnatural unity.

The stand of the Communists was quite different. To begin with, they had no real interest in allying themselves with any counter-revolutionaries, reactionaries, feudalistic warlords, and militarists, the very elements which they had tried so hard to overthrow. To them, Yang Hu-ch'eng, the Tungpei generals, and even the Young Marshal, were no better, if not worse, than Chiang Kai-shek. Their temporary union with the Tungpei and Hsipei Armies was a marriage of convenience, but they were the true beneficiaries of the alliance. Apparently the Communists enjoyed a good rest, recovery, and growth for the first time since they were driven out of Kiangsi two years earlier. Unexpectedly, many new opportunities were opened up to them: they were eager to become acquainted with important publications on the whole spectrum of cultural fields in China; they equipped themselves with needed supplies, particularly medicine; and they were provided with ample opportunity for mass work and propaganda among the soldiers and the people. [44]

Of the three groups, the CCP alone had definite, long-term goals which did not require immediate action in order to be successful. More important, the Communists had priorities. They certainly wanted to preserve the three-in-one alliance as long as they could, because its existence proved to be too advantageous to be given up for one with fewer opportunities. At the same time, they welcomed a peaceful settlement of the Sian affair provided that civil war was stopped. But they would not hesitate to fight on the side of the Tungpei and Hsipei Armies if Nanking decided to suppress the Sian insurgency by force. It is unreasonable to suggest that the CCP tried to reach an understanding with Nanking by forsaking the Tungpei and Hsipei Armies. By dint of its alliance with the Tungpei Army in particular, the CCP had the leverage to persuade Nanking or Chiang Kai-shek not to resume the "suppression and encirclement" campaign against the Communists. Were that alliance dissolved, the Tungpei Army would be reorganized into the Central Army, thereby losing its seemingly independent position; then the Red Army would have to stand on its own feet to deal with the Central Army, a situation the CCP must have tried to prevent from happening.

Also, there is no reason to assume that the CCP should not have negotiated with Nanking, independently of its two partners.

Since the CCP had already begun negotiations with Nanking before the Sian Incident and some basic terms had been laid out as reported by Chiang Kai-shek, it was only natural that the CCP proceeded with the negotiations with greater zeal.

At a time when the Tungpei generals were vacillating between insistence on their original demands and reasonable compromise for an early settlement, separate negotiations carried on by the CCP at Nanking readily afforded them a subterfuge to bring the negotiations at Tungkuan to fruition, while leaving the issue of the release of the Young Marshal and the Communist question to be resolved at the forthcoming Third Plenum of the KMT 5th Congress. A plausible account of the development was given by Miao Chien-ch'iu to Snow as follows:

> In the middle of January P'an Han-nien arrived in Sian from Nanking (as an emissary). We suspected him and arrested him as an "unknown." On him we found documents concerning direct Kuomintang-Communist negotiations concerning the formation of the Red district into a special area, payment of Red soldiers, existence of the Communist party, and so forth.[45]

Miao further commented that the Tungpei generals, notably Wang I-che, Ho Chu-kuo, and Yü Hsüeh-chung "had been pleased when they discovered that Chou was negotiating with Nanking. (It gave them an excuse for a break.)"[46]

But the Tungpei Army cracked from within. The young radical officers had thus far followed their generals since their interests did not clash. This young radical group, though not necessary to his power base, was heavily relied on by the Young Marshal in taking the drastic action on December 12. It was the same group which now wanted to stick to their original demands, the most important being the return of their leader. To them, a settlement without securing the release of the Young Marshal was no less than a betrayal of their leader and their own cause. While this group, an enlargement of the Alliance of Anti-Japanese Comrades that had existed before December 12, was composed of a number of middle-ranking military and civilian officers, no real leader had emerged. However, the trio of Miao Chien-ch'iu, Ying Te-t'ien, and Sun Ming-chiu, had become the most influential members by virtue of their

control of the communications center and command of the special
regiment at Sian, at the same time taking into account their personal ability, bent, and ambition.   James Bertram, who had been with
Miao on his journey from Shansi to Sian and remained in close contact with him throughout their sojourn at Sian, described their sentiment this way:

> The Tungpei "radicals"--the "Young Officer" group
> which included Sun Ming-chiu and others like my
> friend Miao--were the extreme wing; at this time
> they were demanding the immediate return of Chang
> Hsüeh-liang to Sian as a necessary preliminary for
> any settlement.   But what they wanted in any case
> was action; and if they could not get some positive
> anti-Japanese action out of Nanking, they were ready
> and even eager to fight for it.   There was a real
> split here between the young officers and the rank
> and file on the one side, and some of the older and
> more reactionary commanders on the other. [47]

The February Second Coup

On the morning of February 2, a manifesto issued by the Northwestern National Salvation Union, a mouthpiece of the CCP at Sian,
signaled that an agreement had been reached strongly opposing civil
war and "any efforts on the part of either side to gain special ad-
vantages in the settlement."[48]   In the meantime, about fifty officers
gathered for a conference at Sian.   Among those attending the conference many were important commanders, such as Pai Feng-hsiang,
commander of the 6th Cavalry Division, Kao Fu-yüan, a brigade commander of the 105th Division, K'ang Hung-t'ai and Ho K'uei, two of
Kao's regimental commanders, Wan Yi, regimental commander of
the 109th Division, Tu Wei-kang, commander of the engineering
corps, and Li Ch'ang-hsin, a ranking officer.[49]   As expected, there
were some Communists at the conference: for instance, Liu Lan-po,
brother of Liu To-ch'üan, Ma Shao-chou, Hsiang Nai-kuang, and
others.   Some of those anonymous Communists in the Tungpei Army
were Trotskyites whose activities were led by Chang Mu-t'ao.   In
fact, most of the Communists who worked in the Tungpei Army were
later labeled as Trotskyites by the CCP because of their failure to
follow the official line of the CCP and were not allowed to return to
the CCP fold.[50]

That which transpired at the conference must have been the reassertion of their goals. The peace terms which the generals regarded as the best and only course the Tungpei Army should take were viewed by the young radical officers as a betrayal of the Tungpei Army and the Young Marshal. Betrayers were no longer worthy of the Tungpei group and actually enemies of it. It followed that they must be eliminated as such. A blacklist of persons marked for death was drawn up. The listing probably included the following names: Ho Chu-kuo, Wang I-che, Miu Cheng-liu, Liu To-ch'üan, Mi Ch'un-lin, Pao Wen-yueh, Li Chin-chou, Hsü Fang, Chiang Pin, and Hsieh K'o.[51]

At noon on February 2, all gates of the city of Sian were closed and a wild search for the accused generals was under way. The first victim to fall was Wang I-che who was an invalid at home when the Tungpei Vanguards, led by Yü Wen-chün, rushed in and shot him in his bed.[52] Wang's chief aide-de-camp Sung Hsüeh-li was also killed. Hsü Fang, chief of the general staff department of the former Northwestern Bandit-Suppressing Headquarters, and Chiang Pin, chief of the communications department, were seized and killed. Chiang was charged with having held up messages between Sian and Nanking, Hsü with secret contact with Nanking.[53]

But the search for the chief target of the coup, Ho Chu-kuo, led the radical officers to the residence of Yang Hu-ch'eng, who alone was immune from any attack. Sun's men surrounded Yang's house in Hsin-ch'eng, where Yang's headquarters was also located; Yang refused to hand Ho over to the rebels. Sun and his men then approached Yü Hsüeh-chung and demanded that he issue an order to the Tungpei Army for an all-out attack on the Central Army, which Yü refused to do. Firing was heard for several hours and tension continued well into the early evening.[54]

Twenty miles away at Hsienyang, Liu To-ch'üan was informed of what had happened inside Sian. He immediately telephoned Yang Hu-ch'eng and confronted him with a strong protest on behalf of the Tungpei generals on the front and threatened that if Yang failed to protect the lives of Yü Hsüeh-chung and Ho Chu-kuo, he would turn back his troops and crush the whole city of Sian.[55] Contemporary accounts and later reminiscences all report that Yang Hu-ch'eng may have had some foreknowledge of the move of the young radical officers, but he did not make any effort to stop them, for he saw that

there were chances not only to incorporate some members of the
Tungpei Army into his army but also to improve his bargaining position with Nanking. [56]

At last Yang Hu-ch'eng managed to issue a warrant for the arrest of Sun Ming-chiu, Ying Te-t'ien, Miao Chien-ch'iu, and others,
after he had urged them to leave the city in order to avoid further
violence and embarrassment. The trio found time to load a number
of the special regiment soldiers in two trucks and to slip out of the
city in the dark, but not before they sacked the treasury department
of the Allied Armies Headquarters. They drove straight to the Red
Army stationed outside San yüan, where General P'eng Teh-huai received them warmly. [57]

Thus the Tungpei "left wing" collapsed, but the crisis of the
Tungpei Army was far from over. Yü Hsüeh-chung immediately
declared that he was sworn in as acting commissioner of the Lanchow Pacification Headquarters, a post to which Nanking had earlier
appointed Wang Shu-ch'ang. By assuming this office, Yü would have
the authority of commanding all the Tungpei troops as entrusted by
the Young Marshal. The three days following the February 2 coup
were full of alarms. "For the first time since December 12, there
was a feeling of real unrest within the walls of Sian. Martial law
had been proclaimed again, and after nine o'clock the streets were
deserted," witnessed Bertram. [58] First, there were many like-
minded young radical officers in the 105th Division, the most important outfit of the Tungpei Army that had to be reckoned with. Kao
Fu-yüan, then brigade commander of the 105th Division, who was
the first to help establish connections between the Tungpei and Red
Armies, was arrested and shot by order of Liu To-ch'üan. Several
regiment commanders, namely K'ang Hung-t'ai, Ho Kuei, and Wan
Yi, were arrested and thrown into prison only to be released a
month or two later. [59] These high-handed measures were not a
"white terror" as against the "red terror" staged by the February 2
rebels, not even aimed at silencing opposition to peaceful settlement,
but aimed at maintaining unity within the Tungpei Army.

Secondly, the February 2 coup had no great effect on the outcome of the Sian affair, the peaceful course of which had been set
at the Tungkuan conference. However, the coup did hasten that process. With the young radical officers eliminated or silenced, the
generals could be more resolute in settling quickly all the issues

with Nanking without worrying about the dissenting opinions of their young subordinates. In light of later developments, the coup did not weaken the Tungpei Army, though it did create some disruptions. On the contrary, it became the rallying point of the Tungpei Army which as a whole became more united, realizing the external threat and the internal dissension. Also the coup made Nanking more aware of the seriousness and complications of the Sian situation, so that it showed more willingness to settle the affair on Sian terms.

Thirdly, the CCP neither encouraged nor exploited the coup. It continued to hold steadily for peace. Snow's report is apparently correct that Chou En-lai, and the CCP, was more determined to fight jointly with the Tungpei Army against Nanking after the February 2 coup than before it.[60] As a matter of fact, Chou's approach could not be more reasonable. A separate peace by the CCP with Nanking would be as meaningless as it would be impractical. Although the Communist issue was a long-term, important one that concerned the Nanking government and Chiang Kai-shek more than any other provincial issue, the Sian affair still was a military issue that demanded an immediate solution. Failing a peaceful solution, it might have precipitated a civil war of enormous magnitude such as that which was being fought in Spain. Had that happened, not only would the Communist issue have remained unresolved, but also resistance against Japan would have become more remote. It was unmistakable to everyone that the Sian issue must be settled quickly and peacefully.

XI. THE CLOSE OF AN ERA

The February 2 coup was aimed at stopping the capitulation to
Nanking.   Once that failed, the working combination between the
Tungpei Army, Hsipei Army, and the Red Army which had never
been put to a test except in the conference room was no longer ob-
tained.   Each of the three parties moved fast to undo the others in
bidding to Nanking for peace terms.   Thus the Northwest defiance
to Nanking came to an end on the 4th, when Yang Hu-ch'eng and Yü
Hsüeh-chung jointly issued a four-point manifesto to review the February 2 coup and to announce their acceptance of Nanking's plan for
withdrawal of their troops.   To cushion the strong opinion of the
rank and file of the armies and the leftist elements among the
masses, the manifesto also stated that the Young Marshal be given
back his civil rights and that the mass movement and the National
Salvation Union be protected and supported by the Nanking government. [1]

All the Tungpei troops on the eastern front were withdrawn to
the left bank of the Wei River, while Yang Hu-ch'eng evacuated Sian
by moving his headquarters to San-yüan.   Sian welcomed the entry
of the Central Army on the 7th, which was followed by the arrival
of Ku Chu-t'ung, the new chief of the Northwest, on the 9th. [2]   Without bloodshed, Nanking reestablished her authority in the Northwest.

At Sian, Ku Chu-t'ung, together with Yang Hu-ch'eng and Yü
Hsüeh-chung worked out final arrangements for unresolved issues
before ushering in the new order.   The issue of the Hsipei Army,
the weakest of the three recalcitrant parties, was easily liquidated.
Sun Wei-ju, Yang's right-hand man, who had been appointed governor of Shensi, was formally sworn in.   Sun also took over the command of the 17th Route Army from Yang.   As it turned out, Yang
became the greatest loser.   He was allowed to go abroad, this time
visiting the Western nations as he had done about ten years ago
when he visited Japan--a typical way out for a fallen warlord in the
Republican era.

179

The Tungpei Army Disarmed

The Tungpei Army was not punished for its mutiny and persistent recalcitrance, nor was it reorganized and reduced in strength. Having withdrawn to the north of the Wei River,[3] it continued to be a formidable force and to be capable of joining forces with the Red Army. To handle this delicate situation, Chiang Kai-shek turned to the Young Marshal to finish the face-saving process which he had so quixotically started when he accompanied Chiang back to Nanking.

Nanking worked out two plans for the future of the Tungpei Army. Under the first plan, all the Tungpei troops were to be transferred to Kiangsu and Anhwei provinces. To take care of the unemployed civilian and military personnel of the Tungpei Army, the Kiangsu Pacification Commission was to be established and the Anhwei provincial government reorganized. Under the second plan, the Tungpei troops would concentrate on the Kansu-Shensi border with Yü Hsüeh-chung continuing to serve as governor of Kansu.

Yü immediately cabled the two plans to the Tungpei leaders then living in the Peking-Tientsin area. He asked them to send representatives to Nanking where they were to be joined by Ho Chu-kuo from Sian, and then together they were to proceed to Fenghua for consultation with the Young Marshal.

About a dozen or so Tungpei leaders met at Wang Shu-han's house in Tientsin and unanimously supported the first plan and rejected the second plan, i.e., that the Tungpei troops would concentrate on the Kansu-Shensi border, as hatching regionalism and warlordism. One of the participants Wan Fu-lin, Commander of the 53rd Army, expressed his views as follows:

> It is natural that if we still keep our old concept for the preservation of strength, the Tungpei troops should withdraw to the Kansu-Shensi border where they will be close to the power groups of the Northwest, not far even from the Communists. But how could we allow ourselves to commit this kind of mistake again! In order to help our national unification and progress, I am for plan one.[4]

The Tungpei leaders chose Wang Cho-yen and T'ien Yü-shih as their representatives, who at once journeyed south. Ho Chu-kuo

from Sian arrived at Nanking on February 14. He was immediately
received by the Generalissimo. Simultaneously with the arrival of
Ho's party at Fenghua, the Central Government proclaimed that
Chang Hsüeh-liang's civil rights which had been revoked for five
years be restored. [5]

The Young Marshal also favored the first plan. He wrote a
long letter to Yu Hsüeh-chung urging him to do his utmost to carry
out the order of the Central Government. He asked Wang Cho-yen
to accompany General Ho to Sian to convey his wishes to the officers
and the rank and file of the Tungpei Army. To mollify the Tungpei
Army further, Chiang Kai-shek allowed it to choose six generals to
fly to Fenghua for a visit with the Young Marshal. The party of
six generals arrived at Fenghua on February 25, and each of them
had an individual talk with the Young Marshal for no more than
twenty minutes. As one of them later reported, the scene of their
meeting with the Young Marshal was sad and full of emotion. There
was little that needed to be said: the six expressed their hopes for
his early return, and in turn he asked them to obey the orders of
the Central Government and to support Generalissimo Chiang, who
would lead them to fight the Japanese and to recover their homeland,
Tungpei. [6]

However, stopping at Shanghai on their return trip, the six
generals went to see T. V. Soong to express their deep concern
over the detention of the Young Marshal; they asked for his help in
bringing about Chang's early release, since Soong, like Madame
Chiang, was the mediator and guarantor of Chiang Kai-shek's release. Having received an audience with Chiang Kai-shek, the party returned to Sian without learning or accomplishing anything. But
the Sian affair, so far as the Tungpei Army was concerned, was
brought to a close with a happy ending. In the meantime, the Kiangsu Pacification Commission was officially inaugurated with Yü Hsüeh-
chung as commissioner, and the Anhwei provincial government was
reorganized with Liu Shang-ch'ing, an elderly Tungpei leader, as
governor. The Tungpei Army issued a manifesto to bid farewell to
the people of Shensi and Kansu on March 2 and began to move out
of the strategic Northwest. [7] The Tungpei Army was widely scattered
in the vast plain of central and eastern China and would soon lose
its special identity. In one sense, the conclusion of the Sian affair
marked not only the downfall of a warlord but also the disappearance
of a provincial army. But how could Nanking settle the issues with
the Communists?

The CCP Overture

It is undeniable that Chiang was released at Sian under the pledge of stopping civil war, which then meant the "suppression and encirclement" campaign against the Communists. As a national leader, Chiang must honor his promised word. It would have been very detrimental to his prestige and leadership in the eyes of the Chinese people, provincial warlords, mediators in the Sian negotiations, and the Sian rebels, had he changed his mind and revived his planned campaign against the Communists. Secondly, even if he did not mind breaking his promise, he would find himself faced not only with the Red Army, but also the Tungpei Army, with which the Central Army was unable to cope. In addition, such a horrible war would have pushed China back ten or twenty years in terms of progress, a step no Chinese would have liked to see happen. Third, the anti-Communist stand taken by Wang Ching-wei, to some extent, was also a camouflage for an anti-Chiang movement. Wang had good reason to expect that Chiang would give him back the presidency of the Executive Yüan, a post which he was forced to relinquish when he was wounded by an assassin's bullet a year and a half before.

It should be noted that the general public had undergone some change in its attitude towards the Communists whose persistence for a peaceful settlement of the Sian Incident won some support from the fair-minded leaders of the KMT and wide endorsement from intellectual quarters. The Communists and the Red Army men conducted themselves rather well in the areas of Sian and San-yüan where the people had contact with them for the first time. [8]

Despite the fact that the CCP made no special demands or conditions for the settlement of the Sian affair, it continued to urge Nanking to adopt the policy of "suspending civil war and forming a united front against Japan," the chief goal of the Sian coup; at the same time, the CCP missed no opportunity to cement the detente between the KMT and CCP by arranging details for their future relations. On his part, Chiang Kai-shek, considering that the national sentiment and political climate throughout the country in the post-Sian period made the prosecution of the anti-Communist campaign not only unfavorable but even unacceptable, saw a real chance to resolve the Communist issue through peaceful means.

On the eve of the opening of the Third Plenum of the KMT Fifth Congress which was convened for the sole purpose of solving the Sian affair and the Communist question, the CCP sent a telegram to the Plenum on February 10, laying down five points as national policy:

1. Suspension of civil war, concentration of national power, and unity in coping with external aggression.

2. Freedom of speech, assembly, and association, and the release of political prisoners.

3. Convocation of a conference of all parties, factions, professions, and armies; concentration of the talented of the whole country in a common cause of national salvation.

4. Quick completion of all preparations for a war of resistance against Japan.

5. Amelioration of the life of the people.

The telegram runs,

Should the Third Plenum resolutely decide to adopt the above as the national policy, the CCP, to show its sincerity in uniting the country against aggression, would give the Third Plenum the following pledges:

1. The Chinese Communist Party will stop its policy of armed uprisings throughout the country aimed at overthrowing the National Government.

2. The Soviet Government is to be renamed the Special Area Government of the Republic of China; the Red Army is to be renamed the National Revolutionary Army, directly under the guidance of the Central Government and of the National Military Council of Nanking.

3. Thorough democratic systems through general elections are to be carried out under the Special Area Government.

4. The policy of land confiscation is to cease and the Communist Program of the Anti-Japanese National United Front is to be resolutely enforced.[9]

The CCP telegram closed with a moving appeal to the Plenum, which could not have failed to impress and convince the KMT leaders at the Plenum that there were real changes in the CCP policy as well as in the minds of the Communists. The passage runs,

The daily pressing national urgency does not permit us to make further delay. The loyalty and sincerity of our party to our country can be testified before Heaven. You who have been dedicated to the country must grant the request of our party, so that a united front of our whole people against aggression and for national salvation can be realized. We are the posterity of Huang-ti [Yellow Emperor] and children of the Middle Kingdom. In the face of national exigency, we cannot but bury our individual, biased views for close cooperation; let us march together toward the great road of the last liberation of the Chinese people.[10]

The four CCP pledges represented drastic changes in principle, strategy, and practice; they were great concessions to the KMT, short only of total surrender. The changes ended an era of Soviet movement and armed struggle against the KMT and Chiang Kai-shek. In other words, the CCP utterly reversed its methods and gave up its ten-year struggle. A change in policy of such great magnitude in the history of the CCP could not go unchallenged and, therefore, adequate explanations from the CCP leadership must be called for. To allay the fear and doubt of the rank and file and to silence its opposition, the CCP leadership issued two documents in succession: "Outline of Propaganda and Explanation Concerning the Meaning of the Peaceful Settlement of the Sian Incident and the [CCP] Central's Telegram to the KMT Third Plenum," and "Questions and Answers Concerning the Party Central's Circular Telegram to the KMT Third Plenum," in early March 1937.[11]

The CCP admitted that it had made a great concession of principle to the KMT for the purpose of abolishing two opposing political regimes and facilitating the formation of a national united front against Japan. The concession was regarded as necessary in view of the difficulties of realizing a war of resistance against Japan; it was an integral part of the concrete measures for implementing the December 1935 resolution and that of September 1936.[12]

The abolition of the Soviet system in the Soviet area, which was replaced by a democratic system based upon general election, was not aimed at renouncing the political rights of workers and peasants, but rather at continuing the protection of such rights. Similarly, renaming the Red Army as the National Revolutionary Army was not aimed at forsaking the major components of workers and peasants of that army nor at renouncing CCP political and organizational leadership, but rather at continuing such leadership. Putting an end to the confiscation of landlords' property was not aimed at permitting the exploitation system to be resumed in the Soviet area, but rather at continuing the ownership of land by peasants.[13]

But the question remains: Did these changes--from a soviet system to a Special Area Government, from the Red Army to the National Revolutionary Army, and from the confiscation of landlords' property to the ending of such--constitute surrender?

The CCP leadership argued that the answer was no; concessions made to the KMT were necessary for the purpose of giving the Japanese imperialists a fatal blow, which was also a blow to the capitalistic system in the whole world. Like the renaming of the Red Army, the change from the Soviet system to the Special Area Government of the Chinese Republic would enhance CCP influence on the national leadership in the anti-Japanese movement. When the Red Army joined the Northwestern Anti-Japanese Allied Army, it exerted considerable influence on that army. By the same token, when the Red Army joined the National Revolutionary Army, it would be expected to exert similar influence on that body. Also, when the Red Army moved south during the Sian Incident, it failed to confiscate landlords' property.[14]

The KMT Third Plenum

Despite the great concessions of the CCP as embodied in its February 10 telegram to the KMT Third Plenum, the Communist issue ran into much opposition at the Plenum, which opened its week-long session on the 15th, with an attendance of about 200 members of the CEC of the KMT led by Wang Ching-wei and Chiang Kai-shek. Wang gave the opening address, expounding on the familiar theme of "National Salvation and Survival," a policy formulated at the Second Plenum in July 1936. With respect to the Communist question, Wang said, "After the Communists fled to the Northwest, their situation became increasingly critical, and their total destruction was in sight. Unexpectedly the Suiyuan war broke out, followed by the Sian Incident. . . . Fortunately Comrade Chiang Kai-shek returned safely. . . . But let our several years' national defense plan not be impeded and, more importantly, let our several years' work of suppressing the Communists not fall asunder in the last minute. The Communist issue is the immediate question pending our decision."[15]

Yet the cause of the "united front" was not without support. Interestingly the support did not necessarily originate from the KMT left wing as represented by Madame Sun Yat-sen and Christian General Feng Yü-hsiang, but from rightists like Sun Fo, the son of Dr. Sun Yat-sen, Chang Jen-chieh, the mentor of Chiang Kai-shek in the 1920s, and Liang Han-ch'ao. With Madame Sun heading the list, a joint proposal was submitted to the Plenum, calling for the reestablishment of the late party leader's policies. The proposal pointed out that the reorganization of the KMT in 1924 was accompanied by three policies--alliance with the Soviet Union, alliance with the Communists, and help for the workers and peasants--initiated by the late party leader Dr. Sun Yat-sen. A great deal of effort in rejuvenating the revolutionary party had been accomplished by these policies. Unfortunately, after the internal strife of 1927, the "united front" collapsed, thus completely nullifying the three policies. Referring to the CCP, the proposal stressed,

> In the past months we have received a number of letters and circular telegrams from the Chinese Communist Party to the CEC of the KMT, asking for Kuomintang-Communist cooperation presently to resist Japan. It proved that solidarity for struggle against the aggressor has become the unanimous demand of the people throughout the country which was further attested to by the Sian Incident. Since the Chinese Communist Party is also willing to give up the activities which are detrimental to the political power of our party and to support unity in order to resist Japan, it is all the more important that our party take the opportunity to reestablish the

three policies of the late Party Leader so as to save the party and the people from enslavement and to accomplish our revolutionary goals. [16]

In addition to strongly urging the adoption of the proposal, Madame Sun further laid stress on the application of the Min-sheng chu-i [Principle of people's livelihood] , the ending of the tutelage period, the abolition of censorship, the granting of freedom of speech, assembly, and organization, and the release of political prisoners, all of which would "give living reality to the late party leader's will for a democratic government." [17]

In concluding her speech, Madame Sun stated her regret that certain government officials had not been awakened to the fact that for the salvation of the country all civil war must cease. She said, "How ridiculous it is to hear today the antiquated theory that first we must suppress the Communists and then resist Japanese aggression!" [18]

Outside the Nanking circle, the powerful Kwangsi group led by Li Tsung-jen endorsed Madame Sun's ideas by formally introducing a resolution calling for freedom of speech and the press, protection of the patriotic movement, emancipation of the masses, and strengthening of the national salvation movement. Li's resolution, as Madame Sun's proposal, was shelved without action. [19]

However, on the issue of the convocation of the National People's Congress as repeatedly demanded by the Sian rebels and the Communists, the Plenum did take immediate action. It resolved that the Congress be convened on November 12, 1937, to enact the Constitution and to decide on its enforcement. [20]

At the fourth session of the Plenum, Chiang Kai-shek reported on the Sian Incident, accompanied by his resignation for the third time. As on two previous occasions, his resignation was unanimously declined. In the same connection, the Young Marshal's eight demands as embodied in the December 12th telegram were tabled without further discussion. [21]

The Plenum issued a declaration primarily based upon a draft prepared by the draft committee chaired by Wang Ching-wei. In foreign policy, the declaration reiterated the policy of the KMT Second

Plenum that China would not tolerate Japanese encroachment on her
territory and sovereignty, nor would the Central Government sign
any agreement with a foreign power which might result in infringe-
ment upon China's territory and sovereignty. With regard to Japan's
aggression, the declaration said that "China will strive for co-exis-
tence externally. Even if China is driven to armed resistance because of destruction and humiliation beyond the limits of forbearance,
she should be fighting only for defensive purposes, which should not
be mistaken for xenophobia."[22]

Domestically, the declaration stated that "the achievement of
internal unification through peaceful means has been the guiding principle of the party throughout recent years. . . . As for the Communist elements, in recent days they use the slogan of resistance
against foreign aggression to appeal for support. . . . In view of
their many feelings of guilt, it is impossible for us to believe in
their superficial promises. For the sake of our country and people,
how can our party bear the thought of allowing the sacrifice and hard
work of all our comrades in the armed forces and others engaged in
suppressing the Communists to fall short of completion? Whatever
methods we may use, we must depend on our own strength to root
out the Communist calamity in China."[23]

Before the Plenum adjourned, it adopted a resolution on the
Ken-chüeh ch'ih-huo an [Resolution on the eradication of the Red
Peril]. A great part of this important document was devoted to re-
viewing the history of the KMT-CCP relations; however, its crucial
passages stress the minimum, limited measures which read in full:

> 1.   In any country, there must be a unified system and
> a unified command, so that the effectiveness of command
> can be attained. There will never be the co-existence of
> two armies of diametrically opposed doctrines within one
> country. It is, therefore, our resolution that the so-
> called Red Army and all other camouflaged armed forces
> must be totally abolished.
>
> 2.   Unification of political power is the prerequisite for
> the unification of a nation. No country in the world tol-
> erates the co-existence of two political regimes. It is,
> therefore, our resolution that the so-called "Soviet Gov-
> ernment" and all other subversive organizations must be
> totally abolished.

3. The Propaganda of Bolshevization is incompatible
with the San-min chu-i [Three principles of the people]
which is dedicated to saving the country and its people.
Even to the life of our people and the social life of our
country, Bolshevization appears to be extremely absurd.
It is, therefore, our resolution that any propaganda of
Bolshevization must be stopped.

4. Class struggle is based upon the interest of one
class. Its method is to divide the whole society into
various, opposed classes and to stir up mutual killing
and hatred among them. As a result, policies of taking over the masses and armed uprisings must be used,
whereby unrest in society is created and the people are
greatly divided. It is, therefore, our resolution that
class struggle must be totally stopped. [24]

A comparison between the above four-point resolution and the
four pledges offered by the CCP in its February 10th telegram to
the KMT Third Plenum clearly indicates that the KMT resolution demanded much more than the CCP offered. The first two points of
the KMT resolution fully covered the second and third points of the
CCP pledges, i.e., the Soviet government was to be abolished and
the Red Army to be reorganized into the KMT army. Granted that
the abolition of landlords' property was a concession in Communist
ideology, the KMT still demanded a complete abolition of "class
struggle," a major doctrine of Communism. Even more concrete,
the third point of the KMT resolution prohibited the propaganda of
Communism. All together, the KMT resolution demanded nothing
less than a total surrender of the CCP and also aimed at stopping
the spread of Communism in China. It is evident from the title of
the resolution that the KMT Third Plenum had no intention of forming a "united front" with the CCP but instead intended to end Communism in China through peaceful means.

The KMT made no direct mention of the CCP five demands on
national policy which would be the quid pro quo for the implementation of the four-point pledge. However, on the day of the adjourn-
ment of the Plenum, February 23, Chiang Kai-shek in his press conference touched upon the CCP five demands, chiefly the second demand. He discussed three things:

190

1. Freedom of speech. With three exceptions to wit, propaganda of Bolshevism, disclosure of military and diplomatic secrecies, and fabricated rumors; freedom of speech always has been the policy of the Central Government and will continue to be.

2. Concentration of talents. The Central Government will make every effort to bring talented people, particularly the intellectuals, into the government for national construction, but cannot adopt the methods as advocated by the Communists and those of the so-called "people's front."

3. Release of political prisoners. At present, the so-called political prisoners are only Communists and reactionary elements who are against our country and destroy our society. Yet should they decide to repent, they could be freed on bond. Pardons can only be granted to those who are sincere in their repentance. An indiscriminate and wholesale pardon of political offenders will not be possible inasmuch as it is contradictory to laws of state and prejudicial to social stability. [25]

Like Wang Ching-wei, Chiang Kai-shek was determined to maintain a strong stand on the Communist issue, so far as their public pronouncements were concerned. Nor did he show any intention of forming a united front against Japan as demanded by the Sian rebels, but nevertheless, he did suspend civil war for the time being, if for no other reason than to honor his promise at Sian.

The Communists came a long way in their terms with Chiang, whom they had tried for ten years to overthrow since Chiang's April 12 coup to purge the Communists in 1927. However humiliating, the CCP was pleased with the outcome of the Sian affair, without which it would have to struggle merely for survival, let alone to repel the Japanese aggressor. On the other hand, Chiang, however reluctant he may have been, was equally satisfied with the settlement over the Communist issue, a real issue for which the Sian coup was launched. He resolved the Communist question through peaceful means, even though he may always have preferred force. He was confident in the settlement, as he had no fear of the Communists once the Tungpei Army was moved out of the Northwest and the Central Army moved in. Probably the Central Army was ready to deal with the Red Army at any time. Yet, as long as the CCP abided by the terms it offered to the KMT, Chiang saw no reason to suppress it.

Chiang emerged from the Sian Incident as the true leader of the Chinese people. The Sian Incident helped them to find their leader. It was unlikely that in the future any warlords from north to south China would dare to challenge Chiang as the Young Marshal did. Now with the Communists hailing him as the leader, Chiang's prestige was higher than it had ever been.

XII. CONCLUSION

With the completion of the Tungpei Army's transfer from the Northwest to the East, the departure abroad of Yang Hu-cheng from Sian, and the conclusion of the KMT-CCP talks, the Sian Incident came to a close at the end of April 1937. It had lasted four months from the December 12 coup to the April settlement. Yet the causes of the Incident could be traced far beyond December 1936. In the course of the prolonged negotiations for settlement, many unforeseen, intriguing developments had emerged. Only if we closely examine every aspect of the Sian affair can we understand it in entirety. And only if we are convinced through our own analyses of the cardinal issues that had become stumbling blocks in the negotiation process can we resolve the so-called mysteries with which the Sian Incident has been fraught. Only then may we adequately answer such questions as was the Sian coup inevitable?; were the negotiations bound to succeed?; did the Tungpei generals shift their allegiance?; was the KMT-CCP settlement a surrender on the part of the CCP or a formation of the second "united front" between them?; did the Sian coup succeed?; and what was the fate of the Young Marshal?

An Inevitable Course

In the age of warlordism, Chang Hsüeh-liang inherited and ruled the richest part of China, Manchuria, as his fief. He enjoyed all good things in life and experienced no hardships. Lacking any formal education except for military training, he fortunately was exposed to and interested in the Western way of life. But he was a young man of determination and intelligence. With one stroke he eliminated Yang Yü-t'ing and Ch'ang Yin-huai, who had allegedly connived with the Japanese to kill his father, thereby consolidating his rule. But his great difficulties were how to deal with his two strong neighbors, Japan and Russia. He did not allow himself to be induced and pressured by Japan to keep Manchuria independent; he joined the revolutionary south instead so as to achieve nominal unification with China. He was rewarded with the appointment of Vice Commander-in-Chief of the Chinese armed forces, for which he was called "Vice Commander." Without the support of Nanking, he went to war with Russia, trying to drive the Russian interest out of

193

the Chinese Eastern Railway. Though he did not win the undeclared war, he suffered no great loss.

Also he devoted himself to building his domain into a modern state. Schools were built and the Tungpei University, one of the finest at the time, was established with Chang as president. Trade and industry, especially an arsenal and a railway, were quickly developed. In addition to a well-equipped army, Manchuria had the best air force and navy in China. Naturally, this gigantic progress and success caused the Japanese to envy Chang and hasten their seizure of Manchuria.

With his star rising, the Young Marshal posed as arbitrator in the contest between Chiang Kai-shek and Yen Hsi-shan and Feng Yü-hsiang, a stand which influenced the outcome in favor of Chiang and for which Chiang had been grateful. During the few years between his joining the south at the end of 1928 and his being driven from his homeland in September 1931, the Young Marshal was the most popular and admired young man in China.

Then his fortune turned against him. When he led his huge army to North China to suppress Shih Yu-shan's rebellion, the Japanese struck at Mukden on September 18, 1931. On the advice of the Nanking government, the Young Marshal offered no resistance in order that China's case could be brought to the League of Nations. The failure of the League to take strong action against Japan encouraged her insatiable aggression in Manchuria. But the Young Marshal began to be stigmatized as the "nonresistant general."

The Mukden Incident was only a prelude to Japan's conquest of China. Japan extended the war to the Great Wall, where it met with strong resistance by the Tungpei Army and the celebrated 29th Army. Nevertheless the Young Marshal's further defeat in the war of the Great Wall made public opinion turn strongly against him. After a brief meeting with Chiang Kai-shek at Paoting, he voluntarily relinquished his command. After having been cured of his narcotic habit at Shanghai, he sailed for Europe accompanied by his Australian adviser William Donald. He saw much and immensely enjoyed his visits to Italy, Germany, and England. He was extremely impressed by the revival of Italy and Germany under Fascism. He planned to extend his European tour, only to be recalled by Chiang Kai-shek because of the outbreak of the Fukien Incident. Returning to China in January 1934, he immediately entered into the service of Chiang; he was appointed Deputy Commander-in-Chief of the O-Yü-Wan Bandit Suppression with his headquarters at Wuhan.

Now the Young Marshal became the champion of Chiang's leadership by building Chiang up in the image of Hitler or Mussolini. He presented himself as a new man of vision and energy with considerable charisma for leadership. Within a year Chiang had regained much of his lost prestige and the allegiance of the Tungpei troops and people. However, he had no enthusiasm for the suppression campaign against the Communists, which he viewed as a kind of civil war he had always abhorred for it could only exacerbate the sufferings of the people and weaken the country.

No sooner had the Communists ended their "Long March" in North Shensi than the Young Marshal with his army was transferred to the Northwest with Sian as his headquarters. In the initial encounter with the Red Army, his troops suffered two major defeats, in which two division commanders and several regiment commanders lost their lives, while the majority of the rank and file were taken prisoners. Using this victory as a vantage point, the CCP launched a propaganda campaign of the "united front" to both the prisoners of war and the Tungpei and Hsipei Armies. In contrast, Nanking greatly alienated the disheartened Young Marshal by refusing to replenish the annihilated two divisions and to grant handsome pensions to the families of those killed. To this day, some of the Tungpei generals still believe this was the turning point in the Young Marshal's relations with Chiang and his attitude toward the CCP.

The united front movement which was launched by the CCP August 1, 1935 manifesto gradually gathered momentum, as the Japanese aggression in North China grew apace. Japan's design to sever North China from the Nanking government had created a tide of student and national salvation movements throughout the country since the December 1935 student demonstrations. With the spread of student protest and demonstration, the national salvation movement took a nationwide form of organization. To still the surge of militant student and national salvation movements, Nanking took highhanded measures whenever possible.

At the height of national sentiment in the summer of 1936, the Liang-Kuang revolted against Nanking claiming the Central Government had failed to resist Japan. A civil war was prevented from developing but it made the general public more aware of the issue of Japanese aggression. Ironically, while patriotism was praised everywhere, nowhere was the national salvation movement patronized by the authorities except in the Northwest or Sian where the Young Marshal espoused the cause of the "united front" as the only way to resist Japan in order to recover the lost territory of Manchuria.

Through Wang I-che, Commander of the 67th Army, and the first high-ranking officer converted to the united front policy, the Young Marshal met with Chou En-lai at Yenan in May 1936. Out of this secret talk, the CCP changed its policy from "Down with Chiang Kai-shek for Resisting Japan" to "Support Chiang for Resisting Japan." From this time onward, the Young Marshal became active in favor of the united front. He gave active material aid to the Red Army; he openly protected the student and national salvation movements; he educated his troops in the united front ideology and guerrilla warfare; and he tried his utmost to persuade Chiang to change his unpopular and unpatriotic policy of "internal pacification before resistance to foreign aggression."

The CCP did not remain idle, leaving the matter to the Young Marshal alone, for it made repeated appeals to Chiang to stop civil war and to unite the whole country in resisting Japan. Not only was Chiang unmoved by the CCP appeal; he was even more resolute than before to end the matter once and for all. Chiang's stern attitude was also somewhat influenced by Japanese pressure.

Serious negotiations for resolving some outstanding issues over the Sino-Japanese relations were conducted at Nanking in the fall of 1936. But the exorbitant demands of Japan made concrete concessions by China unacceptable, and Chinese national sentiment would not tolerate further concessions, no matter how negligible. Chiang's Japanese policy was under attack by intellectual quarters, particularly by the Federation of the National Salvation Unions. As a result, six prominent intellectuals, popularly known as "the Six Gentlemen," were arrested in Shanghai. The Young Marshal viewed the arrest as an act of overt alienation of the people's trust. He appealed directly to Chiang for their release but to no avail.

More and more, Chiang's compromising posture toward Japan aroused the suspicion of the Young Marshal, while Chiang's determination to exterminate the Communists as indicated in his 50th birthday messages made his policy irreversible. The anti-Communist pact reached by Japan and Germany in late November 1936 was received in China with great dismay. It came at a time when the Chinese had successfully resisted Japanese aggression in Suiyuan, and the policy of the united front against Japan had a strong appeal. The Young Marshal had reason to assume that had Nanking joined the anti Communist camp of Japan and Germany, hope for the recovery of Manchuria would vanish forever, and the suppression campaign against the Reds would be prosecuted in earnest.

At Sian, the Young Marshal had openly encouraged and protected the national salvation movement since the fall of 1936. His championship of the cause of national salvation was no secret as borne out by his interview with Helen Snow on October 3. Like Chiang's anti-Communist policy, Chang's "united front" policy was equally irrevocable. His fervid appeal to Chiang for dispatching the Tungpei Army to the Suiyuan front to fight the Japanese was real and urgent. It appeared to be the only way to cut the Gordian knot to save himself from a breach of faith with his followers and the Communists as well as from precipitating a confrontation with Chiang.

Full of indignation, Chiang came to Sian in early December. Instead of probing the situation and mollifying Chang Hsüeh-liang and Yang Hu-ch'eng, he totally ignored their views and problems and even undermined their authority by directly summoning their subordinates for personal instruction. He confronted the Young Marshal with the choice of prosecution of the anti-Communist campaign or transfer of the Tungpei Army to eastern China. Still trying to weather the crisis to save himself and the country, Chang must have considered Yang Hu-ch'eng's suggestion--to detain Chiang--as his last resort. Both Chiang's wrath over the student demonstration of December 9 and his severe criticism of the Young Marshal afterwards convinced the latter to stage the coup d'état and to take Chiang into custody.

The Release of Chiang

From the time Chiang was seized to his release on Christmas Day, the Young Marshal in both his public pronouncements and in private talks stressed that he never meant to do any physical harm to Chiang. Further, he professed on the first day of Chiang's detention that he would escort Chiang to Nanking as soon as the latter accepted his major demands.

Apparently the Young Marshal's ambitious project for the coup ran into difficulty at the very beginning: the heavy toll of lives resulting from deaths incurred in seizing Chiang; disorder in Sian caused by the poor discipline of Yang Hu-ch'eng's troops; the failure of a unit of the Tungpei Army to stage a coup at Loyang; and the loss of Tungkuan to the Central Army as a result of Feng Ch'in-tsai's defection. Most of all, Chiang's adamant refusal to discuss the eight demands with the rebels, coupled with the strong stand taken by the Nanking war faction, discouraged the Young Marshal and disrupted his plans.

There had never been any definite plan for setting up a northwestern defense government as discussed among the three parties before the Sian coup. The Young Marshal did not bring up the subject after the coup in view of the adverse reactions from various power groups in China and from foreign capitals, particularly Moscow. However, a Northwestern Anti-Japanese Allied Army Military Council was inaugurated, serving as the highest organ to coordinate the work of the three constituents. After reading Chiang's diaries and other official documents seized at Hua-ch'ing-ch'ih, the Young Marshal and other Sian leaders dispelled all doubts in their minds that Chiang was not anti-Japanese. Then it was a matter of how to pressure him to assume the leadership of resistance against Japan-- the most important, if not the sole, objective of the Sian coup.

By the time William Donald arrived at Sian, the Sian Incident had definitely begun moving toward a peaceful solution, and the release of Chiang was almost certain. Chiang agreed to move to his new abode and began to discuss freely with the Young Marshal national policies with respect to possible war with Japan. All this happened before the arrival of Chou En-lai. The much publicized report that the CCP took a decisive stance in the release of Chiang could not have been further from the truth. Mao Tse-tung publicly admitted that the CCP, not having been consulted, was caught by surprise with the Sian coup. Moreover, the date of Chou's arrival at Sian could not have been earlier than December 16. Chou took no part in sending General Chiang Ting-wen back to Nanking to stop the plan by Nanking to bomb and attack Sian, which was arranged through General Chiang Po-li that day. Yet Chou certainly helped free Chiang. He played the role of diplomat rather than mediator. He agreed with the Young Marshal that Chiang was the only person capable of leading the country in the war of resistance against Japan. The CCP might have played a significant role, if a military conflict between Nanking and Sian had proven unavoidable, in which case the Red Army would have heavily supported the Tungpei Army in sustaining the burden of fighting.

Faced with the military pressure of the Central Army and with the threat of the ascendancy of the pro-Japanese faction at Nanking, the Young Marshal clearly sensed the need for an early release of Chiang. The longer Chiang was held at Sian, the more the pro-Japanese faction would consolidate its control of Nanking, and the less the chance of averting impending civil war. Still Chiang could not be released without commitment to the major demands put forth by the Sian rebels. T. V. Soong's visit to Sian not only convinced the Young Marshal that Chiang must be released but started negotiations on the terms of his release. It was Madame Chiang's trip to Sian that brought negotiations to an end. She rightly claimed that "the situation at Sian was . . . that Mr. Donald had laid the foundations, T. V. had built the walls, and it would be I who would have to put on the roof."[1]

There were two outstanding issues that were difficult to resolve: stopping the civil war and reorganizing the National Government. As far as the reorganization of the government was concerned, Chiang had no great objection to it, even though it would not be easy to accomplish. But the question of suspending civil war, i.e., suspending the suppression campaign against the Communists, involved a complete change in policy, which must have been the last thing he wished to do. During his detention, Chiang had done some deep contemplation and his thinking apparently had undergone some change especially on the issues of Japan and the Communists. There was no doubt that the CCP overtures to the KMT before the Sian Incident were made out of desperation; nevertheless, its concern for China's survival under Japanese aggression was beyond suspicion. When Chou approached Chiang at Sian, he reiterated the CCP support for Chiang without mentioning the demands of the Sian rebels. Like his wife, Chiang also may have thought, "As we are all Chinese, we should not fight each other."[2] Like the Young Marshal, Chiang may have thought that Chou, who had served him so well before, would serve him again in the common cause of national salvation. Also, Chiang, well-versed in Sun Tzu's "Arts of War," may have envisioned his chances of disarming a strong enemy without fighting.

One last obstacle had to be overcome before Chiang could be released. The rebel leaders, probably with the exception of the Young Marshal who was fully satisfied with Chiang's verbal promise as guaranteed by T. V. Soong and Madame Chiang, were opposed to the release of Chiang without a written assurance. They had good reason to fear that once Chiang was released, he would punish them. Yang Hu-ch'eng in particular, whose life and career were at stake, remained adamant, and his consent was absolutely necessary for he had full control of the city of Sian. It was then that Chou rendered a great service to Chiang; he successfully persuaded Yang to trust the leader to honor his words.

A Recalcitrant Sian

Chiang's departure from Sian accompanied by his captor did not result in a peaceful settlement of the Sian affair as anticipated. On the contrary, more difficult days were beginning. The general public was utterly incensed by the news that Chiang was freed upon acceptance of the demands of Sian. Riding the tide of anti-Japanese sentiment and victorious challenge to Nanking, Sian transformed itself into the new order of the "united front." Mass movements were unleashed, and Sian gave every sign of being prepared for resistance against Japan.

Also, the euphoria created by Chiang's return to Nanking was short-lived. The Young Marshal was tried and sentenced; his entourage was taken into custody at Nanking; and the Central Army advanced toward Sian. The rehabilitation plan was equally unacceptable. Ku Chu-t'ung was appointed to replace the Young Marshal in the Northwest. Yang Hu-ch'eng and Yü Hsüeh-chung were not punished but their power was greatly curtailed. The Tungpei and Hsipei Armies were assigned to scattered stations in remote areas. Further, it was announced that the suppression campaign against the Communists would be continued.

Sian received this bad news with considerable shock. Not only was this contradictory to the spirit of Chiang's release but it openly

violated the negotiated terms by which he was released. Yang Hu-
ch'eng, as titular head of the recalcitrant Northwest, backed up unanimously by the Tungpei generals, sent a defiant telegram to Nanking
on January 5, thus setting the stage for confrontation between Nanking and Sian and causing an impasse in the settlement for the next
two or three months. To cope with the urgent situation, Sian took
some drastic measures. The Tungpei Army was quickly concentrated
in the eastern front to block the advance of the Central Army. Yang's
self-defense corps in several counties adjacent to Sian were mobilized
and recruited into the newly expanded Hsipei Army. Students and
leftists of all political shades from liberals to Trotskyites were encouraged to take an active part in leading and educating the masses
in the national salvation movement. Newspapers and periodicals
served as effective propaganda machines to popularize the "united
front" against Japan and to rally the masses to the new order, while
radio broadcasts in Chinese and English propagated the "united front"
news for the consumption of the outside world. Close ties with the
CCP were established, and the Red Army was assigned the defense
of the left bank of the Wei River. Twenty miles north of Sian,
P'eng Teh-huai set up his headquarters; inside Sian Chou En-lai's
influence was visible and felt. As the Sian-Nanking relations further
deteriorated, the CCP posture became increasingly important and its
interests were ably represented by Chou at Sian and Nanking.

The union between the Tungpei and Hsipei Armies was expedi-
ent, as was their collaboration with the CCP. The dissension heretofore hidden gradually surfaced, as the future of the insurgent power
grew more and more uncertain. Yang Hu-ch'eng, entrenched inside
Sian and surrounded by leftist supporters, including the special regiment of the Tungpei Army commanded by Sun Ming-chiu, may have
seen his opportunity of rising to leadership in the Northwest. The
Tungpei generals at the front with their troops which undertook the
bulk of defense looked askance at the growing radical trend inside
Sian and at Yang's posture. At the outset, they were not enthusiastic about the "united front," especially about allying themselves with
the Communists. But they were resolutely anti-Japanese, and their
loyalty to the Young Marshal with whom they have worked for so
many years had not wavered.

Unmoved by the inducement of money or position, the Tungpei
generals demanded that the Young Marshal be allowed to return to
the Northwest before any settlement could be reached. Their insis-

tence on the release of the Young Marshal and Yang Hu-ch'eng's un-
ceasing demand for resistance against Japan so infuriated Chiang
that he was quoted as saying: "Any demands save the return of
Chang Hsüeh-liang to the Northwest can be accepted," and "If Yang
should persist in his stubborn attitude by January 24, the Central
Government would consider a peaceful settlement of the affair hope-
less."[3] Nanking then did two things to break the negotiation dead-
lock: Chang's return was to be a separate issue in negotiations and
the Communist question was to be resolved in the forthcoming KMT
Third Plenum. As a result, the Tungkuan conference convened only
to tackle the problem of local troop disengagement, leaving all political issues untouched.

The Tungkuan conference succeeded in avoiding a military confrontation between Nanking and Sian, but precipitated a revolt of the
young officers in the Tungpei Army. The Tungpei generals' willingness to reach a local armistice was interpreted by the radical officers as a betrayal of the Young Marshal for the sake of personal
gain. They staged a coup d'état at Sian on February 2, demanding
that the leading generals declare war against the Central Army.
They killed Wang I-che, the leading proponent for peace, and a few
other lesser generals who were charged with having connections in
Nanking. The coup was quickly suppressed with the arrest of several military commanders and the flight of the ringleaders.

The February 2 coup removed the obstacle for peaceful settlement, since it drove the radical elements from the Tungpei Army.
However, it did not break up the temporary union of the three armies, insofar as they continued to take concerted action in dealing
with Nanking. The Tungpei Army withdrew to the north of the Wei
River; Sian was evacuated by Yang Hu-ch'eng followed by the occu-
pation of the Central Army. At Sian, General Ku Chu-t'ung, on behalf of Generalissimo Chiang, carried on negotiations with the three
insurgent armies within the purview of military affairs.

The Capitulation of the CCP

While the negotiations on the transfer of the Tungpei Army
from the Northwest to the East continued to drag on, the KMT Third
Plenum opened on February 15, focusing its attention on the Communist question. The political climate in China and on the international

scene could not be more favorable for a settlement on the Communist question.

After the release of Chiang, Japan launched a new peace offensive toward Nanking by dispatching an economic mission to China. Japan viewed the possible rapprochement between the Soviet Union and China as a great threat to Japan and looked upon peaceful settlement of the Communist issue as a sign of the unification of China or the formation of a "united front" against Japan.

On the other hand, Stalin, capitalizing on his goodwill toward Chiang, allowed Chiang's son, Ching-kuo, to return to China after twelve years' sojourn in the Soviet Union. Fearful of Wang Ching-wei's return to power, which would swing China to the side of Germany and Japan, Stalin expedited his negotiations with Nanking. A modus vivendi between Nanking and Moscow was in sight. To reinforce his ties with Nanking, Stalin urged the CCP to seize the opportunity created by the Sian Incident to strike a deal with Nanking.

The Sian coup had disrupted Chiang's campaign plan against the Communists and created the atmosphere and situation in which a negotiated settlement could be reached. The CCP must have realized that the Sian Incident had saved the CCP from annihilation only temporarily, for with the Young Marshal now a prisoner and with the transfer of the Tungpei Army to the East, its position in dealing with the KMT had not been greatly improved except that public opinion was more in its favor and some recruitment and supplies were provided during the Sian insurgency.

Prodded by Stalin and realizing its own weak position, the CCP offered a four-point proposal to the KMT, the most humiliating terms in its party history. It agreed that the Soviet government be substituted by a regional, border government under Nanking; that the Red Army be organized into the national revolutionary army under Nanking; and that the confiscation of landlords' property be discontinued. Unexpectedly, even these genuine, humiliating concessions failed to mollify the Nanking leaders who demanded nothing short of complete surrender by the CCP. The KMT Third Plenum adopted the resolution entitled, "Eradication of the Red Peril" which counterproposed four points for CCP capitulation. It categorically demanded the abolition of the Red Army or any form of military force and of the Soviet regime and other organizations destructive to national unification, and discontinuation of Communist propaganda and fomentation of class struggle.

Ironically, both Chiang Kai-shek and Wang Ching-wei insisted on the acceptance of the four points as a quid pro quo for settlement with the CCP,[4] while utterly ignoring the CCP demand for the release of political prisoners and other matters. Far away in Moscow, Wang Ming, one of the top leaders of the CCP, commented on the KMT resolution:

> Instead of agreeing to collaborate with the Communist
> Party of China on the basis of a joint struggle against
> Japan, and for the salvation of the fatherland, the
> Plenary Session of the Kuomintang wrote about "the
> capitulation of the Communist Party."[5]

Indeed Chiang did not at all heed the continuous pleas of the CCP in its willingness "to struggle resolutely for the successful realization of the revolutionary San Min Chu I together with the KMT in the common struggle during the period of the Great Revolution in 1925-1927."[6] In the months ahead, Chiang continued to destroy Communist underground organs and to arrest Communists.[7]

However, there was one thing that Chiang could not do, at least for a while--that is to start a civil war anew to suppress the Communists. The Chinese people, probably with the exception of Chiang's own Central Army, would not tolerate that kind of war, let alone Madame Chiang and T. V. Soong, the two witnesses for his release. Even if he did, his chances of success would be much less than had been prior to the Sian Incident. Conversely, by allowing the Communists to maintain a separate existence in remote North Shensi, Chiang had achieved the desired unity, if not the unification, of China without resort to force. The Communists--shut off in the meager land of North Shensi, surrounded by hostile neighbors, the Moslems in the west, Yen Hsi-shan in the east, and the Central Army in the south--would no longer pose a threat to KMT power. Moreover, there still were other quasi-independent political powers existing in China: for instance, Sung Che-yüan and Yen Hsi-shan in North China and Li Tsung-jen and Liu Hsiang in South China, over whose armies and personnel Nanking had no control. These warlords, of course, were different from the Communists, especially in ideology. Apart from ideological differences, the psychological

barrier between the KMT and CCP created by ten years' fighting
would be difficult to overcome or forget. As a result, the settlement reached by them at the end of April was nothing more than a
temporary truce. [8] It was not until two months later when the Japanese attacked Loukouchiao (Marco Polo Bridge) on July 7, that both
sides publicly committed themselves to the "united front" against
Japan. [9]

The Fate of the Young Marshal

The suspension of civil war between the KMT and CCP from
December 12, 1936, to July 7, 1937, was the first fruit of the Sian
Incident. In a real sense, the pronounced aims of the Sian coup,
"to stop civil war and to form a united front against Japan," were
attained. Commenting on the Sian Incident in August 1937, James
Bertram gave the first authoritative account of the Incident:

> The coup d'état seemed to the outside world a failure;
> and in fact it succeeded. Chinese would no longer fight
> against Chinese. China had found a new unity; and so,
> before it should have time to form and strengthen itself,
> Japan turned swiftly and shrewdly to war on a large
> scale.

This new unity was led by none other than the man humiliated by the
Young Marshal. Inasmuch as the Sian Incident helped the Chinese
to unite and to find their leader, it raised Chiang's prestige to a
new high. Nelson T. Johnson assessed the rise of Chiang's leadership in the wake of his release:

> The idea has been fostered that Chiang's leadership is
> necessary to the nation's survival, his identification with
> that idea has been achieved concretely by action. . . .
> The majority of Chinese leaders have come to realize
> that China must become unified and show a united front
> against the common enemy. Chiang Kai-shek has dem-
> onstrated the possibility of unification despite old ha-
> treds and old feuds. He has become the symbol of this
> ideal of unity whose accomplishment is necessary if
> Japan is to be held off. [10]

The irony is that the man who made all this possible has not only spent the rest of his life in obscurity but also lost his freedom. The Young Marshal, though not necessarily a friend of the Generalissimo, had developed an intimate, personal relationship with him, a feat achieved by few people in China. Further, the Young Marshal became a close friend of the Soong family, particularly T. V. He had also helped Chiang stay in power on more occasions than one, for which Chiang had been grateful.

However, Chiang, like many heroes, religiously believed in hubris and nemesis and in reciprocity in personal dealings. Despite the fact that the Young Marshal had released him and accompanied him on his return to Nanking, Chiang apparently did not forgive him. For one thing, Chiang might have been killed at Hua-ch'ing-ch'ih, where wanton shooting occurred. Despite his claim to the contrary, Chiang was humiliated by his captor, and allowed to leave Sian only after having accepted the basic demands of the rebels. All this was probably hard for Chiang to take, for neither before the Sian Incident nor after it had he undergone a similar ordeal. But Chiang had even greater reason to be unrelenting; the Young Marshal had ruined his plans to exterminate the Communists. To this day, Nationalist writers consider the Sian Incident the root of the Communist takeover of China. It was easy for Chiang and others to forget that the Sian Incident had raised Chiang to the position of indispensable leader of China, united the whole country, and made the war of resistance against Japan possible, achievements that glorified Chiang's life and cemented his place in history.

The days during the liquidation of the Sian affair tested Chiang's forbearance. The circumstances did not permit him either to resume the suppression campaign against the Communists or to execute the Young Marshal.[11] Apart from public opinion, leading warlords like Li Tsung-jen and Sung Che-yüan all had enunciated opposition to civil war. The Tungpei Army, whose transfer was not complete until the end of April, still publicly supported the Young Marshal's policy, and its 120,000 men after reorganization were loyal to him.[12] The mutiny of the Tungpei Army or its joining forces with the Red Army or with any of the northern warlords' armies would not be too remote a possibility, if the delicate situation were not handled with care and dexterity.

Aside from Chiang's family and relatives, Madame Chiang, T. V. Soong, and H. H. Kung, who one by one had assured the Young Marshal of his personal safety, the British and American ambassadors in China, with the approval of their respective governments, offered their good offices for Chiang's release providing the Young Marshal assured safe conduct. Nor did the two countries forget about the fate of the Young Marshal later. Just before the British cancellation of a proposed loan to support China's war efforts in July 1938, Chiang invited the British Ambassador Clark Kerr for a talk and sought his advice. The latter stated that "if request was serious he would advise the Generalissimo to bring the Young Marshal out of retirement; call all the Soong family to Hankow; line them up there and present a solid front to Japan."[13] Chiang received the advice coldly.

Throughout the years, appeals for the release of the Young Marshal have never ceased, coming mostly from the Tungpei people, particularly his former subordinates, but only occasionally from the CCP. All appeals have been turned down indirectly under the pretext that the Chiang-Chang relationship has been comparable to that between father and son.[14] It is, however, unthinkable that Chiang has kept Chang for so long in the name of love rather than hate.

The perpetuation of the Young Marshal's confinement was probably not on Chiang's mind at the time of his release or even shortly afterward, for he did advise the Young Marshal not to accompany him on his return to Nanking. After his return, Chiang fell into a religious frame of mind. In his Good Friday message, Chiang referred to the Sian event, saying:

Following the settlement of the Sian affair, the rebels, knowing their unwise and treasonable actions, naturally were afraid. Remembering that Christ enjoined us to forgive those who sin against us until seventy times seven and upon their repentance I felt that they should be allowed to start life anew.[15]

Certainly the Young Marshal gave no sign of repentance shortly after the Sian Incident as evidenced by his pronouncement at the trial. But he probably did later, since he has devoted himself to the study of the history of the Ming dynasty for more than thirty years, a remarkable record of scholarly pursuit which has possibly substituted for his political ambition.

Yet, until the fall of Mainland China to the Communists, Chiang's fear of the Young Marshal's return to the political arena had remained unabated. Young and sentimental, he still represented a force to be reckoned with. More importantly, the course to which he, if released, may have turned--either support for Chiang or an alignment with the CCP--was unpredictable. Still more fortunate than his collaborator, Yang Hu-ch'eng, who was destined to pay for his sin against Chiang at Sian with his life,[16] the Young Marshal was transferred to the Island of Taiwan. It is understandable that he has not been granted full freedom in Taiwan. If allowed to leave Taiwan, he may choose to visit Peking where he will certainly be welcome or to write his memoirs to trace the unusual, eventful life, particularly the turbulent Sian Incident, which this volume has attempted to illuminate.

Chapter I

1. The true story of the split between Mao's and Chang's groups
    was revealed for the first time by Chang Kuo-t'ao himself.
    According to him, at Moukung, Szechwan, where the first
    Front Army from Kiangsi and the Fourth Front Army from
    northern Szechwan met in June 1935, Mao proposed that Ning-
    hsia, or North Shensi, be their future destination. Chang
    counterproposed that a Szechwan-Kansu-Hsikang base be built
    first; should they fall the first, it would not be too late to try
    the northward plan of Mao or a westward march toward Sin-
    kiang. In fact, Stalin approved both plans. See Chang Kuo-t'ao,
    "My Memoirs," Ming-pao yüeh-k'an [Ming-pao monthly] (here-
    after MPYK), no. 50 (February 1970), 85-86. (Chang's memoirs
    were published consecutively in MPYK, nos. 3-62, March 1966-
    February 1971, but later were put into book form. An English
    translation of the book in two volumes was published by the
    Kansas University Press in 1971 and 1973.) Other important
    sources that corroborate Chang's account are found in Kuo Hua-
    lun, Chung-Kung shih-lun [Analytical history of the Chinese
    Communist Party] (Taipei, 1969), III, 57-60; Ts'ai Hsiao-ch'ien,
    "Reminiscences of the Red Army's Westward Flight," Chung-
    kung yen-chiu [Studies on Chinese Communism], no. 46
    (October 1970), 118.

2. Chiang Kai-shek, Si-an pan-yüeh chi [A fortnight at Sian], in
    Chiang Tsung-t'ung chi [Collected works of President Chiang]
    (hereafter CTTC) (2nd ed., Taipei, 1961), II, 2421. ("A Fort-
    night at Sian" was first published in book form in both Chinese
    and English.)

3. John Gunther, Inside Asia (New York, 1939), p. 223.

4. Much of the information concerning Chang's early life was
    provided by General Miu Cheng-liu, a Chief lieutenant of Chang.
    Also see Wang Cho-yen, Chang Hsüeh-liang tao ti shih ko tsen-
    yang jen [What kind of person is Chang Hsüeh-liang?] (Peking,
    n.d., but apparently written in 1937), p. 3.

Chapter I Notes

5. Chang, "Confession of the Sian Incident," (hereafter "Confession") MPYK, no. 33 (September 1968), 50.

6. The main force of the Tungpei Army was then in the hands of Chang Hsüeh-liang and Kuo Sung-ling, both representing a new faction against a pro-Japanese faction led by Yang Yü-t'ing and Chiang Teng-hsüan. The failure of Kuo was due not so much to Japanese intervention as to Kuo's own indecision. While wavering, Kuo was betrayed by his subordinates. See H. C. Chapman, The Chinese Revolution of 1926-1927 (London, 1928); Ts'ao Te-hsüan, "Chang Tso-lin As I Know Him," Ch'uan-chi wen-hsüeh [Biographical literature] (hereafter CCWH), V, 6 (December 1964), 24-28.

7. Chang, "Confession," p. 50.

8. Akira Iriye, "Chang Hsüeh-liang and the Japanese," Journal of Asian Studies, XX, 1 (November 1960), 33-43; Earl Albert Selle, Donald of China (New York, 1948), 258-59; Chiang, II, 2427. Since this new appointment, the Young Marshal has also been known as "Vice Commander."

9. Wang, p. 9. For an extensive study, see Wang Chi, "The Young Marshal Chang Hsüeh-liang, 1928-1931" (unpublished Ph.D. thesis at Georgetown University, 1969).

10. See O. Edmund Clubb, China and Russia: The "Great Game" (New York, 1971), chap. 18; Wang T'ieh-han, "A Brief History of the Tungpei Army, II," CCWH, no. 109 (June 1961), 37.

11. Among the many good works on the Mukden Incident, two books should be consulted: Sadako N. Ogata, Defiance in Manchuria (Berkeley, Calif., 1964); Liang Ching-tun, The Conspiracy of the Mukden Incident, September 18, 1931 (New York, 1970). For an eyewitness account of the Incident, see Wang T'ieh-han, "Resistance in the Non-resistance Policy, I, II," Chung-yang jih-pao [Central daily news] (Taipei), January 9, 11, 1964.

12. Selle, p. 291; Wang Cho-yen, p. 12.

Chapter I Notes

13. Selle, p. 291; Wang Cho-yen, p. 12.

14. Selle, p. 285; Wang Cho-yen, p. 15.

15. China Weekly Review (hereafter CWR) (Shanghai), LXVII, 7 (January 13, 1934).

16. Chang, "Confession," p. 50.

17. Liu Chien-ch'ün, Yin-ho i-wang [Reminiscences from Yin-ho] (Taipei, 1966), pp. 233-34; Li Chin-chou, "An Eyewitness Account of the Sian Incident," CCWII, no. 115 (December 1971), 5.

18. For a recent discussion on the subject, see Lloyd E. Eastman, "Fascism in Kuomintang China: The Blue Shirts," The China Quarterly, no. 49 (January/March 1972); Yü kuo-hsün, "Reminiscences of Liu Chien-ch'ün and An Explanation of the 'Blue Shirt Club,'" CCWH, no. 124 (September 1972), 17-21.

19. Chang, "Confession," p. 50; Wang Cho-yen, p. 16.

20. See Li Yün-han, "The So-Called Ho-Umetsu Agreement," CCWH, no. 126 (November 1972), 75-81.

21. Wang was the President of the Executive Yüan and concurrently the Minister of Foreign Affairs, and Chiang Kai-shek was the Chairman of the Central Military Council, which was organized in the spring of 1932.

22. Wang Cho-yen, p. 16.

23. For narratives on the collapse of CCP organs in the KMT-held areas, see U. T. Hsu, Invisible Conflict (Hong Kong, 1958); Yang Tzu-lieh, Chang Kuo-t'ao fu-jen hui-i lu [Memoirs of Mrs. Chang Kuo-t'ao] (Hong Kong, 1970); Yueh Sheng, Sun Yat-sen University in Moscow and the Chinese Revolution (Lawrence, Kansas, 1971), chap. 16, 17.

212

Chapter I Notes

24. Before the "Long March" set out from Kiangsi in October 1934, there were four major Soviet bases, namely the Kiangsi, western Hupeh-Hunan, Hupeh-Honan-Anhwei (already reduced to guerilla bases after the Fourth Front Army left for northern Szechwan), and northern Szechwan areas.

25. Ch'in Te-shun, "North Chahar Incident and Others," CCWH, no. 9 (February 1963); Li Yün-han, "Sung Che-yüan Before and After the Establishment of the Hopei-Chahar Political Council," CCWH, no. 110 (July 1971).

26. The full text of the Hirota "Three Principles" may be found in the Institute of International Affairs, Survey of International Affairs, 1933-1937 (London, 1939), pp. 632-38. A summary of of the three principles is given in O. Edmund Clubb, Twentieth Century China (3rd ed., New York, 1967), p. 486.

27. Li Yün-han, loc. cit., p. 55; Li T'ien-lin, "A Portrait of a Prominent Figure of North China, Hsiao Chen-ying," CCWH, no. 116 (January 1972), 21-27; Clubb, Twentieth Century China, p. 203.

28. Pao Tsun-p'eng, Chung-kuo chin-tai ch'ing-nien yün-tung shih [A history of youth movement in modern China] (Taipei, 1953), p. 96.

29. For a recent pro-KMT view of Chinese policy toward Japan, see Joseph W. Ballantine, "International Background: China's Intense Relations with the Powers," in Hsüeh Kuang-ch'ien (ed.), Chien-ku chien-kuo ti shih nien ("Strenuous Ten Years of Nation Building") (Taipei, 1971). The quotation is taken from Chiang, CTTC, I, 921.

30. John Israel, Student Nationalism in China, 1927-1937 (Stanford, Calif., 1966), pp. 114-18.

31. Israel, p. 119; Pao, pp. 96-97.

32. Israel, p. 124; Pao, pp. 98.

Chapter I Notes

33. The present writer attended Chung-shan Middle School in Peking and personally participated in the events of December 16.

34. Tung-fang tsa-chih [Eastern miscellany], XXX, 1, 2 (January and February 1936); Pao, pp. 98-99.

35. See note 34.

36. Pao, p. 102; Israel, pp. 134-36.

37. Nym Wales, Notes on the Chinese Student Movement, 1935-1936 (Stanford, 1959), pp. 37-46. Communist sources claim that Liu Shao-ch'i was then at Peking directing the student movement. See Hu Hua (ed.), Chung-kuo hsin min-chu chu-i ko-ming shih [A history of Chinese new democratic revolution] (rev. ed., Peking, 1952), p. 166; Mao Tse-tung, Selected Works (Peking, 1965), III, 202-203. Evidently Liu Shao-ch'i was not at Peking in 1935. For a discussion on Liu's whereabouts in 1935, see Kuo, III, 113, 129n.

38. Jessie G. Lutz, "December 9, 1935 Student Nationalism and the Chinese Christian Colleges," Journal of Asian Studies, XXVI, 4 (August 1967), 640.

39. Israel, pp. 144, 146.

40. Lawrence K. Rosinger, China's Wartime Politics, 1937-1944 (Princeton, 1944), p. 90; Wang Chien-min, Chung-kuo Kung-ch'an-tang shih-kao [Draft history of the Chinese Communist Party] (Taipei, 1965), III, 76.

41. For instance, with Mesdames Sun and Liao heading the list of 1,779 persons, the preparatory committee of the Chinese People's Armed Self-Defense formulated and issued the "Basic Platform for the Chinese People's War against Japan" in September 1934. See Hung-se Chung-hua [Red China], no. 236 (September 21, 1934) in Ch'en Ch'eng Collection (hereafter CCC) on microfilm.

214

Chapter I Notes

42. Lu Hsun, popularly known as the "Gorky of China," was a devoted Marxist and, therefore, opposed the shift of party line by uniting with its former class enemy and renegades. See Tsi-an Hsia, The Gate of Darkness: Studies on the Leftist Literary Movement in China (Seattle, 1968), p. 129.

43. The translation is taken from Wen Han Kiang, The Ideological Background of the Chinese Student Movement (New York, 1948), pp. 115-16; cf. Hsia, p. 131n.

44. Rosinger, pp. 90-91.

45. Hu Han-min, "The Rise and Fall of the Party and Military Powers and Remedies for the Future," San-min chu-i yüeh-k'an [Three principles of the people monthly], I, 6 (June 15, 1933), 21; Hu Han-min, Hu Han-min hsien-sheng cheng-lun hsüan pien [Selected political writings of Mr. Hu Han-min] (Canton, 1934), p. 626.

46. Wang Chien-min, III, 75.

47. Mao Tse-tung and others, China: The March Toward Unity (New York, 1937), pp. 60-61.

48. Ibid.

49. Ibid., pp. 70, 72.

50. Ibid., p. 82.

Chapter II Notes

1. Hung-se Chung-hua, no. 149 (February 14, 1934).

2. Hung-se Chung-hua, no. 221 (August 1, 1934).

3. The "Five Great Programs" is found in CCC, reel VII and the "Six Great Programs" in reel XVI.

Chapter II Notes

4. The Chinese text of the Manifesto can be found in K'ang-Jih
    min-tsu t'ung-i ch'an-hsien chih-nan [Guide to resistance against
    Japan and people's united front], vol. I, in Yushodo Microfilm
    Materials on the Communist Party of China (hereafter Yushodo)
    (Tokyo, 1969), reel XIII; Yü Ch'i (ed.), Shih-lun hsüan-chi
    [Selected writings on current affairs] (Shanghai, 1937). A
    reprint is made in Kuo, III, 88-88, Wang Chien-min, III, 42-45;
    Hu Hua (ed.), Chung-kuo hsin min-chu chu-i ko-ming shih ts'an-
    k'an tzu-liao [Source materials on the history of Chinese new
    democratic revolution] (Shanghai, 1951), pp. 263-268. The
    English text of the Manifesto can be found in The Communist
    International, XIII, special number (February 1936), 218-224;
    also Rosinger, pp. 63-69. For a discussion of the Manifesto,
    see James C. Thomson, Jr., "Communist Policy and the
    United Front in China," Papers on China, XI (1957), 105-112.

5. Kuo, III, chap. 26; Ts'ai, no. 46 (October 1970); Chang Kuo-
    t'ao, no. 52 (April 1970); Liu Po-ch'eng, "Reminiscences of
    the Long March," in Hsing-huo liao yüan [A spark will start
    a prairie fire] (Peking, 1962), II, 9-12.

6. The December 25, 1935 Resolution is reprinted in Wang Chien-
    min, III, 49-53 (with some omissions). The full text is found
    in K'ang-Jih min-tsu t'ung-i ch'an-hsien chih-nan, vol. I; Yü
    Ch'i, pp. 211-31.

7. Kuo, III, 114; Wang Chien-min, III, 53-54; Hu Hua, Chung-kuo
    hsin min-chu chu-i ko-ming shih, p. 177.

8. Yen then believed that "'private property' is a time bomb mined
    for the present society." To stem the tide of Communism, he
    devised the program of "the village ownership of land," accord-
    ing to which the village administration issued noninterest public
    bonds with which to purchase all the land in the village for
    distribution among the villagers. The program was compared
    to Communism by some liberal writers, but discredited as
    being the "landlord line" by the CCP. The most informative
    discussion is found in Li Fei, "The So-Called Village Owner-
    ship," Hsin wen-hua [New culture], initial issue (February 1,
    1936), 13-15. Also see Committee of Compilation for Com-

Chapter II Notes

8.   memorating Mr. Yen Hsi-shan, Yen Po-chuan hsien-sheng chi-nien chi [Collection of writings in commemoration of Mr. Yen Hsi-shan] (Taipei, 1963), pp. 16-17.

9.   Kuo, III, 114; Otsuka Reizō, Shina kyōsantō shi [History of the CCP] (Tokyo, 1940), I, 204-208.

10. Wang Chien-min, III, 57; Kuo, III, 115.

11. Chiang Kai-shek, Soviet Russia in China (New York, 1957), p. 75.   Chiang reports that Chou En-lai was at Shanghai taking charge of the negotiations.   It is unlikely that Chou had ever been at Shanghai in 1936.   See Kuo, III, 168, 198; Edgar Snow, Red Star Over China (Black Cat Ed., New York, 1961), pp. 24, 46.

12. Chien Yu-wen, "Reminiscences on Joining the Army in North-west," CCWH, no. 121 (July 1972), 20; Meng Po-ch'ien, Tsou hsiang jen-tao [March toward humanity] (Hong Kong, 1953), pp. 55-59.

13. Li Chin-chou, no. 116 (January 1972), 15; Wu Chih, "The Tendency of Thought of the Shensi Youths during the Previous Period of Over Ten Years," Kuo-wen chou-pao [National news weekly] (hereafter KWCP), XIV, 1 (January 1, 1937).

14. Chang, "Confession," p. 50.

15. CWR, LXXVIII, 8 (October 24, 1936), 271; Nym Wales, p. 73.

16. Wang Cho-yen, p. 16.

17. Ibid., p. 18.

18. Chang, "Confession," p. 50.

19. Li Chin-chou, no. 115 (December 1971), 7; Nym Wales, "My Yenan Notebooks" (unpublished ms., 1961), p. 118.

20. Snow, Red Star Over China, pp. 22-23; Wang Cho-yen, p. 17.

Chapter II Notes

21. Kuo, III, 168-69.

22. Chang, "Confession," p. 50.

23. Ts'ai Hsiao-ch'ien, "Reminiscences of the Kiangsu Soviet," Chung-kung yen-chiu, no. 28 (April 1969), 106; Kuo, III, 168.

24. Ho Kan-chih, Chung-kuo hsien-tai ko-ming yün-tung shih [A history of modern Chinese revolution] (Hong Kong, 1958), pp. 193 94.

25. Chang, "Confession," p. 51.

26. One of the students then arrested was Ch'ü Hsiu-hsi, who later received his Ph.D. at the University of Colorado.

27. Wang Cho-yen, p. 18; Chang, "Confession," p. 51.

28. Chang thought that Liu Ting was an ex-Communist. Helen Snow met Liu at Sian both before and after the Sian Incident. Liu taught at the Anti-Japanese University at Yenan in 1937. That Liu was a ranking Communist was also confirmed by Edgar Snow. See Chang, "Confession," p. 51; Nym Wales, "My Yenan Notebooks," pp. 39, 192; Edgar Snow, Random Notes on Red China, 1936-1945 (hereafter Random Notes) (Cambridge, Mass., 1957), p. 8.

29. Chang, "Confession," p. 51.

30. Chang, "Confession," p. 51; Li Chin-chou, loc. cit., p. 7; L. F. Yao (ed.), Si-an shih-pien chen shih [Precious history of the Sian Incident] (hereafter Chen shih), Hong Kong, 1967, vol. II, pp. 7-9.

31. Li Chin-chou, loc. cit., pp. 6-7; Lu Pi, Lun Chang Hsüeh-liang [Evaluation of Chang Hsüeh-liang] (Hong Kong, 1948), p. 20.

32. This information is based upon the writer's interview with Ma Shao-chou in Taipei on September 3, 1971. It corroborates the

Chapter II Notes

32. account given by Shu Liu, "Chang Hsüeh-liang and 'Confession of the Sian Incident,'" MPYK, no. 33 (September 1968), 47.

33. Ma Shao-chou interview, September 3, 1971; Li Chin-chou, loc. cit. Hsiang Nai-kuang had an interview with the writer in Taipei on July 10, 1971.

34. Chang, "Confession," p. 51; James M. Bertram, The Story of the Sian Mutiny (New York, 1938), p. 106.

35. Chang, "Confession," p. 51. Li K'o-nung was a secret service man of the CCP. During the second Sino-Japanese War, he was stationed at Kweilin, Kwangsi. After the Communist victory in China, he served as deputy minister of foreign affairs and deputy general chief of staff and died in 1962. See Kuo, III, 198n.

36. Chu Teh and others, Ti pa-lu chün [The eighth route army] (Hankow, 1937), p. 34, in Yushodo, reel VII; Ch'ang Chiang (Fan Ch'ang-chiang), "Trip to North Shensi," in Huang Feng (ed.), Ch'ang-cheng shih-tai [During the Long March] (Hankow, 1938), p. 95, in Yushodo, reel VII. The same account is also given by Edgar Snow, but he mistranslates "supporting Chiang" as "using Chiang" because "support" and "use" have similar sounds in Chinese. See Snow, Random Notes, p. 6.

37. Chang, "Confession," p. 51.

38. Ibid.

39. Chu Teh, p. 34; Ch'ang Chiang, p. 95; Chiang, Soviet Russia in China, p. 74.

40. Chu Teh, pp. 37-38; Snow, Red Star Over China, p. 27.

Chapter III Notes

1. The school was located at Wang-ch'ü, a historical scenic spot, seven or eight miles south of Sian. Ho Ching-hua has revealed

Chapter III Notes

1. some valuable information about the school. See Ho, Shuang shih-erh yü min-tsu ko-ming [Double twelfth and the national revolution] (Hong Kong, 1941), pp. 6-7; Li Chin-chou, no. 116 (January 1972), 16; Bertram, p. 108.

2. Hu Hua, Chung-kuo hsin min-chu chu-i ko-ming shih, pp. 176-77. Wang Kuan-ying, Chiang Tsung T'ung yü chung kuo [President Chiang and China] (Taipei, 1966), pp. 58-59.

3. The speech published under the Chinese title Chung-kuo ch'u lu wei yu k'ang-Jih (n.p., June 1936), is also included in Chang Hsüeh-liang chiang-yen chi [Collected speeches of Chang Hsüeh-liang] (n.p., Preface dated November 11, 1936).

4. See Chung-kuo ch'u-lu wei yu k'ang-Jih, pp. 11, 21.

5. Ibid., p. 47.

6. Ibid., pp. 27, 31.

7. Ibid., pp. 33-34.

8. Ibid., pp. 43-46. This part is also related to another lecture of his under the title "Theory and Practice of Resistance against Japan."

9. Ibid., p. 51.

10. Li Chin-chou, no. 115 (December 1971), 7.

11. Military History Bureau, Chiao-fei chan shih [A history of military actions against the Communist rebellion during 1930-1945] (Taipei, 1967), vol. VI, table 69.

12. Miu's interview with the writer on August 10, 1971, and Tung's on August 12, 1971.

13. Li Chin-chou, loc. cit.

14. "The New Appointment of Chiang Kai-shek," San-min chu-i

220

Chapter III Notes

14. yüeh-k'an, VI, 4 (October 15, 1935), 4; cf. Mu Ching-yun "Calamities of Szechwan Brought About by Chiang Kai-shek," Chin-tai shih-liao [Materials of modern history] (Peking, 1962), vol. VI, pp. 85-87.

15. William Teeling, "Will South China Go Communist or Fascist?" Asia (July 1936); Dryden Linsley Phelps, "Chiang Kai-shek Cleans Up in Szechwan," Asia (July 1936); "Suppress the Communists," San-min chu-i yüeh-k'an, V, 5 (May 15, 1935), 1-2.

16. "The Policy of Indulgence to the Communists and Its Crisis," San-min chu-i yüeh-k'an, IV, 6 (December 15, 1934), 3.

17. Allen S. Whiting and Sheng Shih-ts'ai, Sinkiang: Pawn or Pivot? (Ann Arbor, 1958), pp. 159ff.; Sheng Shih-ts'ai, "From Nanking to Sinkiang," CCWH, no. 99 (August 1970), 93; Chang Ta-chün, Shih-shih nien tun-luan Sin-chiang [Forty years of chaos of Sinkiang] (Hong Kong, 1956), pp. 75-78; Norman D. Hanwell, "The Course is Set in China," Asia (February 1937); The Japan Times, November 9, 1936.

18. Chiang, CTTC, I, 920-21.

19. Chang, "Confession," p. 50; Selle, p. 280.

20. Chang, "Confession," p. 50.

21. Chang, Chung-kuo ch'u-lu wei yu k'ang-Jih, p. 12; Committee of Compilation for Commemorating Mr. Yen Hsi-shan, pp. 16-17.

22. Committee of Compilation for Commemorating Mr. Yen Hsi-shan, p. 17; Donald G. Gillin, Warlord Yen Hsi-shan, 1911-1949 (Princeton, 1967), p. 217.

23. Li Chin-chou, no. 116 (January 1972), 14.

24. According to Li Chin-chou (no. 116, January 1972, 17), Chang and Yen did make a joint recommendation to Chiang that evening. Chiang repeatedly explained his policy to Chang and Yen by

Chapter III Notes

24. saying that the Communist power was waning like a falling arrow; it would not have been difficult to give a coup de grace to it, thereby rooting out any future trouble. However, Chang and Yen were only silenced when Chiang flew into a rage. Li's account is rejected because it contradicts not only Chang's "Confession" (p. 50), but also his speech given on December 13, 1936 (loc. cit., p. 8).

25. Chang, "Confession," p. 50; The Japan Times, November 3, 1936.

26. Li Chin-chou, loc. cit.; "Yen Hsi-shan's Telegram to Chang Hsüeh-liang," KWCP, XIII, 50 (December 21, 1936).

Chapter IV Notes

1. Yao, Chen shih, II, 11, 13; Li Chin-chou, no. 116 (January 1972), 15; Kuo Tzu-chün's interview with the writer on July 20, 1971.

2. Chang, "Confession," p. 52.

3. Snow, Random Notes, p. 4; Li Chin-chou, loc. cit.

4. Sun Ming-chiu, Wo huo cho liao Chiang Chieh-shih [I caught Chiang Kai-shek alive] (Hong Kong, 1950), p. 6; Bertram, p. 108; Ma Shao-chou's interview with the writer on September 3, 1971.

5. Li Chin-chou, no. 116 (January 1972), 15; Chang, "Confession," p. 52.

6. Li Chin-chou, no. 116 (January 1972), 16; Chang, "Confession," p. 52; Sun Ming-chiu, p. 6.

7. Hsü Pin-wen, "Reminiscence of the National Salvation Movement in the Northwest," Chieh-fang jih-pao [Liberation daily news] (Sian), December 20, 1936, as reprinted in Wang Chien-min, III, 85-86; Nym Wales, Notes on the Chinese Student Movement, pp. 1-3; CWR, LXXVIII, 8 (October 24, 1936), 271-72.

222

Chapter IV Notes

8. The eighth meeting between Chang and Kawagoe was held on December 3, 1935. See Hollington K. Tong, Chiang Kai-shek-- Soldier and Statesman (Shanghai, 1937), II, 418-422, 444; Hugh Borton, Japan's Modern Century (2nd ed., New York, 1970), p. 390; The Japan Times, December 4, 1936.

9. Chang Hsüeh-liang, "Chairman Chang's Speech at the People's Rally, December 16, 1936" (hereafter "December 16, 1936 Speech") in K'ang-Jih chiu-wang yen-lun chi, p. 27; Wang Chien-min, III, 80.

10. Li Chin-chou, no. 115 (December 1971), 6; Kuo Cheng-k'ai, "History is Not Written with Lies," Je-feng [Hot wind], no. 34 (February 1, 1955); Ta-ti Press (ed.), Si-an shih-pien san i [Three memoirs on the Sian Incident] (Macao, 1962), p. 68.

11. Fang Shu-chung, "The Causes and Results of the Sian Incident," in the Historical Archives Commission of the Kuomintang, no. 480/11; Liu Chien-ch'ün, 240.

12. CWR, LXXVIII, 8 (October 24, 1936), 271-72.

13. Chang Hsüeh-liang, "Speech to All the Staff of the General Headquarters on December 13, 1936") in K'ang-Jih chiu-wang yen-lun chi, p. 13.

14. Yao, Chen shih, II, 86; H. H. Kung, "Memoirs of the Sian Incident," in Kung Yung-chih hsien-sheng chiang-yen chi [Collected speeches of Mr. Kung Yung-chih] (Taipei, 1960), II, 699-70.

15. Chang, "Confession," p. 50; Lu Pi, p. 26.

16. Yao, Chen shih, II, 22-24; Li Chin-chou, no. 116 (January 1972), 16.

17. See note 16. Also Liu Chien-ch'un, p. 240; Kuo Cheng-k'ai, "Background of the Sian Incident," Je-feng, no. 31 (December 16, 1954).

Chapter IV Notes

18. The First Division, to which many of the radical officers were attached and which was to be dispatched to Manchuria, staged a coup d'état at Tokyo on February 26, 1936, by occupying key government buildings and murdering former Prime Minister Saito, General Watanabe, and Finance Minister Takahashi. Primarily owing to the strong stand of the Emperor Showa, the rebels, having occupied the city for three days surrendered For Miao's speech, see Li Chin-chou, no. 116 (January 1972), 16; Bertram, p. 37; Edgar Snow, Random Notes, p. 6.

19. Snow, Random Notes, p. 5.

20. Chang, "Confession," p. 52.

21. Ibid.

22. Ho, p. 7.

23. Chang, Chang Hsüeh-liang chiang-yen chi, p. 3.

24. The seven were Shen Chun-ju, Chang Nai-ch'i, Tsou T'ao-fen, Wang Chao-shih, Li Kung-pu, Sha Ch'ien-li, and Shih Liang (who was a famous woman lawyer and immediately released). The six others known as the "six gentlemen" after the six martyrs of the 1898 coup d'état were imprisoned and released only after the second Sino-Japanese war broke out. See T'an Ling, (ed.), Kuo-Kung ho-tso k'ang-Jih wen-hsien [Documents on Kuomintang-Communist collaboration and resistance against Japan], in Yushodo, reel XIV; Wang Chien-min, III, 70-73, 80; K'ang-Jih chiu-wang yen-lun chi, pp. 8-9, 16.

25. Thomas M. Williamsen, "The Development of German-Chinese Military Relations, 1928-1936," (unpublished Master's Thesis at Duke University, 1967), p. 109; Fu Pao-chen, "Biographies of German Military Advisors in China, 1928-1938, (II)," CCWH, no. 140 (January 1974), 90-97.

26. Shira A. Scheindlin, "The Political Career of Chang Hsüeh-liang, 1928-1963," (unpublished Master's Thesis at Columbia University, 1969), pp. 57-58; T. A. Bisson, Japan in China

224

Chapter IV Notes

26. (New York, 1938), pp. 162-63; Ho, pp. 7-8.

27. General Wan Yao-huang's interview with the writer on September 6, 1971; The Japan Times, December 1 and 4, 1936.

28. Chang, "December 13, 1936 Speech," pp. 8-9.

29. The Japan Times, December 4, 1936; Ta-kung pao (Tientsin), December 4, 1936.

30. The Japan Times, December 7, 1936; CWR, LXXIX, 2 (December 12, 1936), 53.

31. The Japan Times, December 9, 1936; CWR, LXXIX, 2 (December 12, 1936), 53.

32. The Japan Times, December 10, 1936.

33. The Japan Times, November 11, 1936.

34. Tong, p. 542; The Japan Times, November 9, 1936.

35. Chang Kuo-t'ao, no. 54 (June 1970), 91-92; Lu Pi, p. 27.

36. Kuo Cheng-k'ai, Je-feng, no. 40 (May 1, 1955); Bertram, p. 110.

37. The Japan Times, December 3, 1936; Liu Chien-ch'un, p. 241.

38. Tong, II, 456; H. H. Kung, II, 703; Chiang, CTTC, II, 2421.

39. Kung, II, 703.

40. Chiang, Soviet Russia in China, p. 76.

41. Ibid.

42. Chiang, CTTC, II, 2421; Chang, "Confession," p. 52; Lu Pi, p. 27; Ho, p. 8.

Chapter IV Notes

43. Chiang, CTTC, II, 2421.

44. Chang, "Confession," pp. 50-51; Li Chin-chou, no. 115 (December 1971), 7.

45. Li Chin-chou, no. 116 (January 1972), 17; Van Slyke, p. 72; Shen Po-shun, "Reminioconoco of December Twelfth," in Hu Hua, Chung-kuo hsin min-chu chu-i ko-ming shih ts'an-k'ao tzu-liao, p. 347.

46. The confusion of Chiang Ting-wen's appointment was accounted for by Madame Mayling Soong Chiang in a footnote to her Sian: A Coup d'État (Shanghai, 1937), p. 22. It is also mentioned in Bertram, p. 115; Van Slyke, p. 74; and U.S. Department of State, Foreign Relations of the United States, IV (1936), 416. This account was mistaken in that no one except Chiang Kai-shek has ever held such a lofty position in the O-Yü-Wan (Hupeh, Honan, and Anhwei) or Hsipei (Northwest) Bandit-Suppression Headquarters. Chiang Ting-wen's status in the Central Army was subordinate to that of Ho Ying-ch'in and Ku Chu-t'ung, let alone of the Young Marshal. That his appointment was not intended to replace the Young Marshal's is confirmed by Li Chin-chou and Mao Ching-hsiang (interview with the writer on April 3, 1974). For his appointment, see Wan Yao-huang (one of the Nanking generals detained in Sian), "Diaries on the Long Journey of Pursuing Campaigns," Hu-pei wen-hsien [Documentary literature of Hupeh], no. 29 (December 1973), 74.

47. Chang, "December 13, 1936 Speech," pp. 6-7.

48. Ibid., cf. Chang, "Confession," p. 51.

49. Chang, "December 13, 1936 Speech," p. 10; Chiang, CTTC, II, 2424.

50. Chang, "December 13, 1936 Speech," p. 10.

51. Chang, "Confession," p. 52; Chiang, Soviet Russia in China, p. 75.

Chapter IV Notes

52. Chang, "December 13, 1936 Speech," pp. 9-11; "December 16, 1936 Speech," p. 28.

53. Chang, "December 16, 1936 Speech," p. 26; CWR, LXXIX, 4 (December 26, 1936), 142.

54. Chiang, CTTC, II, 2424.

55. Chang, "December 16, 1936 Speech," p. 28.

Chapter V Notes

1. Ma's telegram to Kung Hsiang-hsi on December 9, 1936, as reprinted in Kung, II, 685.

2. Chiang, CTTC, II, 2422; Li Chin-chou, no. 117 (February 1972), 10-11; Wan Yao-huang's interview with the writer on September 7, 1971.

3. See Table 1 (infra, p. 95), which is based upon Li Chin-chou, no. 115 (December 1971), 6; Yao, Chen shih, I, 1; Chiao-fei chan-shih, VI, Table 69; Wang T'ieh-han, p. 37.

4. Sun Ming-chiu, p. 11; Li Chin-chou, p. 11; Ho, p. 8.

5. Li Chin-chou, p. 11; Lu Pi, pp. 30-31.

6. Sun, pp. 11-12; Yao, Chen shih, I, 17-30; Chiang, CTTC, II, 2422.

7. See note 6.

8. Sun, p. 11; Yao, Chen shih, I, 32-33.

9. Sun, p. 12; Yao, I, 33-34.

10. Chiang, CTTC, II, 2423; Li Chin-chou, no. 117 (February 1972), 11.

7. 227

Chapter V Notes

11. Agnes Smedley, Battle Hymn of China (New York, 1943), pp.
140-44; Ta-kung pao (Shanghai), December 13, 1936; Wan Yao-
huang, p. 74.

12. Li T'ien-chih, "One Month in Sian," KWCP, XIV, 6 (February
1, 1937); "Records of One Month in Sian," Ta-kung pao
(Shanghai), January 13, 1937. These two articles are almost
identical, apparently written by the same author, but the first
article is more complete. See also Li Chin-chou, no. 117
(February 1972), 11-12.

13. See note 12.

14. "Major Events of the Week," KWCP, XIII, 50 (December 21,
1936), 2; Chang Chün, "Chu Shao-chou's Great Skill to Save
the Situation," Tzu-yu pao [Liberty news] (Hong Kong),
September 21, 1968; Chu Shu-shou, "An Account of the Sian
Incident as Involving Loyang," CCWH, no. 121 (June 1972),
17-23.

15. See note 14.

16. See note 14.

17. Pai Yung-feng, Lan-chou shih-pien chi liao [A brief account of
the Lanchow incident]; "List of Martyrs of the Kansu Pacifica-
tion Headquarters during the Sian Incident," both in the Histor-
ical Archives Commission of the KMT, no. 480/10. Also
T'ien Chiung-chin, "Reminiscences of Working in My Native
Place," Chung-yang jih-pao, December 7, 1963; "A Student's
Report on the Situation in Kansu and Shensi," Shen pao [The
Shanghai newspaper], February 1, 1937.

18. For the original text, see K'ang-Jih chiu-wang yen-lun chi,
pp. 1-4; Chiang, CTTC, II, 2426. For an English translation,
see CWR, LXXIX, 2 (December 19, 1936, 148; Rosinger, pp.
94-95.

19. As late as May 1937, Chiang had not recovered from injuries
sustained from his fall at Sian. See U.S. Department of State,
Nelson T. Johnson's Letter to the Department of State, May
11, 1937, ref. no. 893.00/14126.

Chapter V Notes

20. Chiang, CTTC, II, 2423.

21. Ho Ching-hua, Chang's aide, reported that on the morning of
     December 12th, when Chiang was taken into custody, opinions
     ran wild. Some people proposed that Chiang be turned over to
     the people's convention for trial. Others held that Chiang's
     guilts be immediately proclaimed, followed by his execution.
     Still others suggested that Chang should replace Chiang and
     set up a national defense government. To all these suggestions,
     the Young Marshal replied: "Let us clearly understand what
     is our aim in detaining Generalissimo Chiang: It is for the
     sake of stopping civil war, of changing our national policy,
     and of uniting all the strength of our country to support Gen-
     eralissimo Chiang to lead us in the war of resistance" (Ho,
     op. cit., pp. 8-9). Ho later was appointed commander of the
     special regiment to replace Sun Ming-chiu who fled after the
     February 2nd coup (see Shen-pao, February 14, 1937). In
     fact, Chiang himself overheard people talking about bringing
     him to a people's trial (CTTC, II, 2425). Hu Shih, in "The
     Treason of Chang Hsüeh-liang," Ta-kung pao, December 20,
     1936, confirmed that one of the slogans advanced in Sian was
     "Support Chang Hsüeh-liang and down with Chiang Kai-shek."

22. Chiang, CTTC, II, 2424.

23. Shao gave the advice out of fear for his personal safety. See
     Li Chin-chou, no. 117 (February 1972), 12.

24. The well-publicized book by Chiang, Si-an pan-yüeh chi [A
     fortnight in Sian] (Nanking, 1937), was actually written by Ch'en
     Pu-lei, Chiang's reputed secretary. It was first distributed to
     those who attended the KMT Third Plenum in the middle of
     February 1937. See Ch'en, "Memoirs of Ch'en Pu-lei, II,"
     Ch'uan-chi wen-hsueh, V, 2 (August 1964), 53.

25. Wan Yao-huang, p. 75; also Wan's interview with the writer on
     September 7, 1971.

26. Kung, II, 660.

Chapter V Notes

27. K'ang-Jih chiu-wang yen-lun chi, p. 12.

28. Ibid., pp. 15-21.

29. Chiang, CTTC, II, 2425.

30. Ibid., 2427.

31. Ibid.

32. Yao, Chen shih, II, 31-32; cf., The Japan Times, June 28, 1936.

33. Chang, "Confession," p. 53.

34. Ibid., p. 52.

35. Li Chin-chou, no. 117 (February 1972), 11-12; Ho, pp. 9-11. Twenty-one of Chiang's officers and soldiers were killed. The names of the officers as later announced at the memorial meeting held at Nanking on February 23, 1937, included: Chiang Hsiao-hsien, Yang Chen-ya, Hsiao Nai-hua, Chiang Jui-ch'ang, Chiang K'un, Mao Yu-li, T'ang Ken-liang, Chang Hua, and Hung Chia-yung (see Shen-pao, February 24, 1937).

36. Kung, II, 670-80.

37. See Map 3.

38. Chang, "Confession," p. 53.

Chapter VI Notes

1. Kung, II, 658-59; Hallett E. Abend, My Life in China, 1926-1941 (New York, 1943), p. 233.

2. "Major Events of the Week," KWCP, XIII, 50 (December 21, 1936), 2; Kung, II, 661-62.

230

Chapter VI Notes

3. See note 2.

4. Kung, II, 662-63; Mayling Soong Chiang, Sian: A Coup d'État (Shanghai, 1937), pp. 4-5.

5. See note 4.

6. Mayling Chiang, p. 10.

7. Ibid., pp. 10-11.

8. I Ming (ed.), Si-an shih-pien shih-liao [Historical materials of the Sian Incident] (Taipei, n.d., but apparently published in 1973), pp. 35-36.

9. Ibid., pp. 32-33.

10. "Major Events of the Week," KWCP, XIII, 50 (December 21, 1936), 3.

11. This list was headed by Hu Tsung-nan, Huang Chieh, Li Mo-an, Sun Yuan-liang, Li Yen-nien, Yü Chi-shih, Wang Ching-chiu, Kuan Lin-cheng, Kuei Yung-ch'ing, Tseng Wan-chung, and Sung Hsi-lien whose names were also attached to the telegram of the 38 ranking generals (see I Ming, pp. 78-81).

12. Yang Ping-wen, "A Brief Account of the Punitive War of General Training Division against the Rebels during the Sian Incident," April 29, 1953, in Historical Archives Commission of the KMT, no. 480/31; Yao, Chen shih, I, 47-48.

13. Kung, II, 667.

14. Mayling Chiang, p. 14; Kung, II, 663.

15. Selle, p. 327.

16. Chiang, CTTC, II, 2426; New York Times, December 16, 1936, p. 1; Shen-pao, December 17, 1936.

Chapter VI Notes

17. Selle, p. 326; Chiang, CTTC, II, 2426.

18. New York Times, December 16, 1936, p. 16.

19. Mayling Chiang, p. 17.

20. Great Britain, Public Record Office, Chang Hsiieh liang Rebellion, ref no. F7014/166/10; Mayling Chiang, p. 16.

21. The twenty-six members were: Sun Fo, Lin Shen, Wu Ching-heng, Feng Yü-hsiang, Ting Wei-ton, Yeh Ch'u-ch'ang, Yü Yu-jen, Kung Hsiang-hsi, Chu P'ei-te, Tai Ch'uan-hsien, Wang Ch'ung-hui, Ch'en Li-fu, Ch'en Kuo-fu, Ch'ü Cheng, Ch'eng Ch'ien, Ch'en Pi-chün (Madame Wang Ching-wei), Ch'en Kung-po, Ma Ch'ao-chün, Chang Chi, Ho Ying-ch'in, Wang Po-ch'un, Niu Yung-chien, Li Wen-fan, Liang Han-ts'ao, Wang Lu-i, and T'an Chen. Of the 26 members, six were unquestionably Chiang's men: Wu Ching-heng, Kung Hsiang-hsi, Tai Ch'uan-hsien, Ch'en Kuo-fu, Ch'en Li-fu, and Liang Han-ch'ao. See "Major Events of the Week," KWCP, XIV, 1 (January 1, 1937), 1-2.

22. "Major Events of the Week," KWCP, XIV, 1 (January 1, 1937), 1-2; Shen-pao, December 17, 1936.

23. Shen-pao, December 19, 1937; Kung, II, 679-80.

24. "Major Events of the Week," KWCP, XIV, 1 (January 1, 1937), 2-3; I Ming, p. 9.

25. Chiang, CTTC, II, 2428; Chiang Po-li's interview with Lung Yü-chün, a reporter of Hsin-wen pao [News report], December 27, 1936, in Historical Archives Commission of the KMT, no. 480/9; Yao, Chen shih, I, 67-72.

26. K'ang-Jih chiu-wang yen-lun chi, pp. 27-28. A slightly different English translation is given in Bertram, p. 130.

27. Kung, II, 682-83.

Chapter VII Notes

1. Chang, "Confession," p. 52; Chang Kuo-t'ao, no. 55 (July 1970), 86; Mao Tse-tung and Agnes Smedley, "The Sino-Japanese Question and the Sian Incident," the Mao-Smedley talk on March 1, 1937, p. 10, in Yushodo, reel XIII.

2. Chang, "Confession," p. 52.

3. Chang Kuo-t'ao, no. 62 (February 1971), 89; Wang Chien-min, III, 124.

4. Kuo, III, 169-70; Nym Wales, "My Yenan Notebooks," p. 74; Snow, Random Notes, p. 2.

5. Chang Kuo-t'ao, no. 55 (July 1970), 86; Kuo, III, 170.

6. According to Hsiang Nai-kuang, the Comintern telegraphic instruction to the CCP during the Sian Incident ran as follows:

> (1) Insist on peace and unity in order to gain a preliminary success in unity and resistance against foreign aggression, and try every way possible to avoid civil war; (2) under the rising tide of national patriotism if the CCP continually holds the line of "class struggle," it will be difficult to escape from a fate of destruction. It is, therefore, necessary to use the camouflage of "national united front" so as to attain survival and development; and (3) gain a respite first and then proceed with a nationwide movement of Bolshevization based upon definite plans; and employ the tactics of "Destroying fortress from within" to bring about infiltration on a large scale and to accumulate the capital for an all-out insurgence.

See "Chinese Communist Strategy of Negotiations and Historical Lessons," Chung-yang jih-pao [Central daily news] (Taipei), July 21, 1972.

7. Chang, p. 87. Snow reported (loc. cit.), "Madame Sun Yat-sen forwarded the telegram from Stalin to Mao. . . . It was appar-

Chapter VII Notes

7. ently the first direct communication of the kind sent from Moscow for some time." Stalin may have telegraphed Madam Sun, but the direct communication between Moscow and the CCP had been established with the return of Lin Yü-ying (alias Chang Hao) in December 1935.

8. Snow, p. 3.

9. Chang Kuo-t'ao, no. 53 (May 1970), 90.

10. Chang, no. 55 (July 1970), 85.

11. Ibid.

12. All Communist sources confirm that Chou En-lai arrived in Sian on December 16 or 17. See Lung Fei-hu, Ken sui Chou fu-chu-hsi shih-i nien [Following Vice-Chairman Chou for eleven years] (Peking, 1960), pp. 3-6; Huang Feng, p. 96; Chu Teh, p. 36. Both Chiang Kai-shek (Soviet Russia in China, p. 78) and Chang Hsüeh-liang ("Confession," p. 53) have confirmed that Chang invited Chou to come to Sian after December 15. Kuo Hua-lun (III, 169) gives Chou's arrival as the 17th, whereas Agnes Smedley (Battle Hymn of China, pp. 146-47) gives it as the 13th (but said to Helen Snow that Chou arrived on the 19th ["My Yenan Notebooks," p. 74]).

13. Lung, p. 5.

14. Chang, no. 55 (July 1970), 87.

15. Ibid.; Ch'ang Chiang (Fan Ch'ang-chiang), "A Journey to North Shensi," in Huang Feng, pp. 96-97.

16. The December 1, 1936 letter of the CCP is reprinted in Wang Chien-mien, III, 65-66. An incorrect and partial translation is given in China: The March toward Unity, pp. 119-121.

17. The earliest, and probably the best, exposition of the CCP position on the Sian Incident by the CCP leaders is K'ai Feng's "Discussions on the Various Problems of the Anti-Japanese

Chapter VII Notes

17. National United Front" published on January 28, 1937, when the
Sian affair was far from settled. Mao Tse-tung gave his view
on the Sian Incident and its settlement in an interview with Agnes
Smedley on March 1, 1937, which was published under the title,
"The Sino-Japanese Question and the Sian Incident." Both articles were reprinted in Lun k'ang-Jih min-tsu t'ung-i chan-hsien
chu wen-t'i [Discussion on problems of the national united front
in resistance against Japan], in Yushodo, reel XIII.

18. Nym Wales, p. 29.

19. Snow, Random Notes, p. 3.

20. Chang Kuo-t'ao, no. 55 (July 1970), 87-88; Ma Pu-ch'ing, "The
Annihilation Battle of the Western River Corridor," Chin-jih
ta-lu [Mainland China today], no. 146 (October 1961), 20-22.

21. See Wang Chien-min, 101-102; Kuo, III, 201; T'an Ling, pp. 74-75
An English translation is given in China: The March toward
Unity, pp. 122-23.

22. See note 21.

23. See note 21.

24. In Snow's view (Random Notes, pp. 1-14), the drastic change
in CCP policy toward Chiang from eliminating him to releasing
him was the result of Stalin's instruction. Japanese Ishikawa
Tadao opposes Snow's view in Chugoku Kyosanto shi kenkyu
[Studies on the history of the Chinese Communist Party] (Tokyo,
1960), pp. 217-43. According to Ishikawa, the CCP simply
followed the line of "united front" as laid down by the Comintern. For a full discussion of both views, see Lucien Bianco,
"La Crise de Sian" (unpublished Ph.D. thesis at Sorbonne,
University of Paris, 1969), pp. 51-58.

25. Wan Yao-huang, "Diaries of the Sian Incident," Hu-pei wen-hsien,
no. 30 (January 10, 1974), 18; Mayling Chiang, p. 20; New York
Times, December 22, 1936, p. 1.

Chapter VII Notes

26. Wan, p. 17; Chiang, CTTC, II, 2427.

27. Lyman P. Van Slyke, p. 83.

28. Snow, Random Notes, p. 2; Chiang Kuo-t'ao, no. 55 (July 1970), 86.

29. Chang Kuo-t'ao, pp. 86-87.

30. This information provided by Kuo Hua-lun (III, 170, 199n), whose sources included Chou En-lai, Yeh Chien-ying, and Li K'o-nung, is supported by Snow (Random Notes, p. 14).

Chapter VIII Notes

1. "Major Events of the Week," KWCP, XIII, 50 (December 21, 1936), 3; Kung, II, 696-97; Teng Ch'i, "Yen Po-chuan and the Sian Incident," CCWII, IX, 5 (November 1966).

2. Kung, II, 696-97.

3. According to Li Chin-chou, preparations for transferring the 53rd Army via Shansi were actually made (no. 117, February 1972, 13). Wan did make contact with Yen by sending his aide to Taiyuan. See Shen-pao, December 22, 1936.

4. Robert A. Kapp, "Provincial Independence vs. National Rule: A Case Study of Szechwan in the 1920's and 1930's," Journal of Asian Studies, XXX, 3 (May 1971), 546; Phelps, pp. 440-41; Li Chin-chou, loc. cit.

5. Nym Wales, p. 41.

6. Li Chin-chou, loc. cit.; Kapp, loc. cit.

7. Kung, II, 685-86; Li Chin-chou, no. 115 (December 1971), 7.

8. Kung, II, 686; The Japan Times, December 20, 1936.

Chapter VIII Notes

9. Kung, II, 696-97; CWR, LXXIX, 3 (December 19, 1936), 84; The Japan Times, December 20, 1936.

10. Kung, II, 692-93; Li Chin-chou, no. 117 (February 1972), 14.

11. The Japan Times, December 17, 20, and 24, 1936; Ch'in Te-shun, "Reminiscences on the Period of the Hopeh-Chahar Political Council," CCWH, II, 1 (January 1963), 21-22.

12. Ch'in Te-shun, p. 22.

13. Ibid.

14. Ibid.; Kung, II, 688-89.

15. Lu Pi, p. 37.

16. Kung, II, 686-87.

17. Li Chin-chou, no. 117 (February 1972), 13-14.

18. Kung, II, 689-90; The Japan Times, December 26, 1936.

19. Kung, II, 690-91.

20. Mayling Chiang, p. 23.

21. Kuang Lu, "Sinkiang Question," Sin-chiang yen-chiu [Studies of Sinkiang] (Taipei: Society for History and Language Studies of Chinese Border Regions, 1964), p. 427; Chang Ta-chün, "Sinkiang Since the Founding of the Republic," Sin-chiang yen-chiu, 122-23; Whiting, p. 165.

22. Chang Kuo-t'ao, no. 53 (May 1970), 90; Wang Ming, "The Struggle for the Anti-Imperialist United Front and the Immediate Tasks of the Communist Party of China," Communist International, XIII, special issue (February 1936), 115-16.

23. Snow, Random Notes, p. 11.

Chapter VIII Notes

24. The overwhelming majority of Chinese have been illiterate until recently and therefore could not understand the complicated governmental affairs which were left entirely to the intelligentsia. Since writing--the only medium through which public opinion could be disseminated--was denied to the common man, only intellectuals dominated public opinion.

25. CWR, LXXIX, 4 (December 26, 1936), 143.

26. Ta-kung pao, December 20, 1936; "The Forum of Current Affairs," KWCP, XIV, 1 (January 1, 1937), 7.

27. The Chinese original is "Ya-fu" which may be translated as "second father" or "next to father." This obviously alludes to his execution of Yang Yü-t'ing, a right-hand man of Chang Tso-lin. The original "Tzu-chui ch'ang-ch'eng" is rendered here as "suffering from his own failure at the Great Wall campaign."

28. Chung-yang jih-pao, December 16, 1936; reprinted in I Ming, pp. 185-89.

29. The three university presidents were Lo Chia-lun of the Central University, Ch'en Yü-kuang of the University of Nanking, and Wu I-fang of the Ginling Girls' College. The last two institutions were funded by American churches.

30. I Ming, pp. 131-32.

31. Ibid., pp. 153-58.

32. Ta-kung pao was simultaneously published in both Shanghai and Tientsin with a slight difference in national news reports. The open letter can be found in KMCP, XIV, 1 (January 1, 1937). In his letter to the Young Marshal, T. V. Soong enclosed a copy of the open letter. See U.S. Department of State, Foreign Relations of the United States (hereafter Foreign Relations), IV (1936), 443.

33. Pravda, December 14, 1936, as quoted in Lord Chilston's (the British Ambassador to Moscow) reports from Moscow, in

Chapter VIII Notes

33. Public Record Office, ref. no. F7688/166/10. Apparently a
     similar view was followed by writers for Communist Interna-
     tional and International Press Correspondence (hereafter Inprecor).

34. This is based upon a French translation by Lucien Bianco, pp.
     322-23. Other Soviet pronouncements on the Sian Incident made
     available by Bianco include: "The Chinese Revolution Continues
     and Will Win," Inprecor, December 19, 1936; "New Disruption
     of an Anti-Japanese Struggle," Inprecor, December 19, 1936;
     and "The Chinese People Will Not Be Delivered to Japan,"
     Inprecor, January 2, 1937. The French Communist view is
     found in Marcel Cachin, "National Insurrection in China,"
     l'Humanite, December 14, 1936, and Marius Magnien, "Chang
     Hsüeh-liang, the Instrument of Japan," l'Humanite, December
     16, 1936, as reprinted in Bianco, pp. 325-27.

35. A six-page summary of Kantorovich's article together with
     Ambassador Lord Chilston's letter to the British Foreign
     Minister, Anthony Eden, on December 15 is found in Public
     Record Office, ref. no. F7807/166/10.

36. Kung, II, 672-74. Indeed, Molotov in his conversation with
     General Hurley in Moscow claimed that "due to the political
     and moral support of the Soviet government, Chiang had been
     allowed to return to the seat of his government and the revo-
     lutionary leader Chang Hsüeh-liang had been arrested." See
     Department of State, United States Relations with China (Wash-
     ington, 1949), p. 72; Snow, Random Notes, p. 4.

37. This was the bulk of the Fourth Front Army which was annihi-
     lated by Muslim troops led by Ma Pu-fang. A remnant of 800
     men led by Hsü Hsiang-chien reached Sinkiang. The collapse
     of this western army made Chang Kuo-t'ao's downfall inevitable.

38. The Japan Times, December 17, 1936; Foreign Relations, IV
     (1936), 432-33; Ch'eng T'ien-fang, "The Sian Incident," CCWH,
     V, 1 (July 1964), 36, note 1; "Japanese Press Urges War with
     China," CWR, LXXIX, 3 (December 19, 1936), 77-78.

39. Public Record Office, ref. no. F7687/166/10.

Chapter VIII Notes

40. CWR, LXXIX, 4 (December 26, 1936), 118; Kung, II, 672-73.

41. Kung, II, 673-74; "Major Events of the Week," KWCP, XIV, 1 (January 1, 1937), 5.

42. Kung, II, 693; "Major Events of the Week," KWCP, XIV, 2 (January 1, 1937), 57, OWR, LXXIX, 4 (December 26, 1936), 118.

43. The Japan Times, December 23, 1936; CWR, LXXIX, 4 (December 26, 1936), 118.

44. The Japan Times, December 23, 1936.

45. The Japan Times, December 26, 1936.

46. Ciano's telegram to the Young Marshal, dated December 21, 1936, ran: "You are my friend. If you join the Communists, you will be my enemy. China cannot exist without Chiang Kai-shek." See CWR, LXXIX, 4 (December 26, 1936), 118; I Ming, p. 263.

47. Public Record Office, ref. no. F7688/166/10. Sir Knatchbull-Hugessen does not mention the episode in his Diplomat in Peace and War (London, 1949).

48. Foreign Relations, IV (1936), 434, 438-39; vol. III (1937), 12.

49. New York Times, December 22, 1936, p. 16.

Chapter IX Notes

1. Chiang, CTTC, II, 2428; Wan Yao-huang, loc. cit. Mo-tzu is a philosophy book named after its author (c. 470-391 B.C.)

2. Chiang, CTTC, II, 2428.

3. The Japan Times, December 22, 1936; Li Chin-chou, no. 117 (February 1972), 14.

Chapter IX Notes

4. Chiang, loc. cit.

5. Mayling Chiang, p. 24.

6. Ibid., p. 25.

7. Chiang, CTTC, II, 2428.

8. Ibid.

9. Madame Chiang was confused on the date of Donald's departure from Sian (p. 25).

10. New York Times, December 22, 1936, p. 1.

11. Ibid., p. 16; Mayling Chiang, p. 16.

12. New York Times, December 22, 1936, p. 16; Li Chin-chou, no. 117 (February 1972), 12.

13. Mayling Chiang, p. 25.

14. Ibid., p. 27.

15. Ibid.

16. Ibid., p. 30.

17. Mayling Chiang, p. 38.

18. Wan Yao-huang, loc. cit., p. 19.

19. Huang died on December 6, 1936. Another well-known pro-Japanese leader, Yang Yung-t'ai, then Governor of Hupeh, was assassinated on October 25, 1936.

20. Mao Tse-tung, Selected Works of Mao Tse-tung (Peking, 1965), I, 257; Selle, p. 325.

21. The Japan Times, December 23, 1936.

Chapter IX Notes

22. The Japan Times, December 26, 1936.

23. Then Wang relinquished his presidency of the Executive Yüan, but maintained the chairmanship of the Central Political Council, nominally the highest policy-making organ.

24. Ch'eng T'ien-fang, p. 38.

25. CWR, LXXIX, 4 (December 26, 1936), 118; Shen-pao, December 20, 1936; I Ming, p. 367.

26. Mayling Chiang, p. 34.

27. Ibid., p. 32.

28. The CC faction derived its name from the two brothers, Ch'en Kuo-fu and Ch'en Li-fu, nephews of Ch'en Ying-shih, Chiang Kai-shek's superior and sworn brother. Chiang put the Ch'en brothers in charge of the Kuomintang affairs roughly from 1926 to 1949. The Whompoa faction consisted of all graduates from the Whampoa Military Academy of which Chiang was Commandant. These graduates were almost exclusively in charge of the Central Army.

29. Mayling Chiang, p. 33; Kuo Ch'eng-kai, no. 37 (March 16, 1955), 7; Li Chin-chou, no. 118 (March 1972), 20-21; Ho, pp. 10-11.

30. Chang, "Confession," p. 52.

31. Mayling Chiang, p. 31.

32. Min-ch'üan chu-i [Doctrine of people's right or democracy] is the second part of the San-min chu-i.

33. The two polices were first spelled out by Sun in Shanghai on his way to North China in November 1924 and later included in his will.

34. Chiang Chien-yin, "Detailed Account of Chiang Kai-shek's Return to Nanking from Shensi," KWCP, XIV, 2 (January 4, 1936), 8-9.

Chapter IX Notes

35. Mayling Chiang, p. 37.

36. Ibid., p. 40. Madame Chiang did not mention Chou by name; instead she uses "the man." Also see Kuo Ch'eng-kai, no. 34 (February 1, 1955), 0-10. Kuo was a councilor of Yang Hu-ch'eng, and claimed that he took part in the negotiations.

37. Mayling Chiang, p. 41; Selle, p. 333.

38. Mayling Chiang, p. 42.

39. Snow, Random Notes, p. 12; Chang Kuo-t'ao, no. 55 (July 1970), 89.

40. Snow, p. 12.

41. Mayling Chiang, p. 43; Chiang, CTTC, II, 2430.

42. Kung, II, 704.

43. Chang, "Confession," p. 53; Chiang, CTTC, 2429.

44. See note 43.

45. Mayling Chiang, p. 45; New York Times, February 28, 1945, p. 4. This was Donald's interview with reporters in Luzon upon his release from concentration camp, where he had been detained since 1942.

46. Mao Tse-tung's immediate comments on the document only two days after its release attests to its authenticity (see Selected Works, I, 255-58). The Ta-kung pao (Shanghai) had an editorial to discuss the document on December 28, 1936. The document is reprinted in Kuo-wen chou-pao, XIV, 2 (January 4, 1937). It is important to note that in CTTC, I, 953-54, the "Admonition to Chang Hsüeh-liang and Yang Hu-ch'eng" is dated December 24, 1936, instead of December 25, 1936.

47. Mao, Selected Works, I, 255.

Chapter IX Notes

48. Ibid.

49. A slightly different translation is given in Mao's Selected Works, I, 257:

50. Interviews with Mao Shao-chou on September 3, 1971 and with Kuo Tsu chün on August 5, 1071; Li T'ien chih, p. 37.

51. Chiang, CTTC, II, 2430.

52. Mayling Chiang, p. 51.

53. Ibid.

54. Snow, Random Notes, p. 13; Chang Kuo-t'ao, loc. cit.; Kuo, III, 171.

55. See "The Sino-Japanese Question and the Sian Incident," p. 10 as cited in supra, chap. 7, note 1.

56. Li Chin-chou, no. 118 (March 1972), 21; Lu Pi, pp. 37-38.

Chapter X Notes

1. Royal Leonard, I Flew for China (New York, 1942), p. 109; "Chang Hsüeh-liang Also Arrived at Nanking Awaiting Punishment," KWCP, XIV, 2 (January 4, 1937), p. 10. Leonard was Chang's second pilot.

2. "Chang Hsüeh-liang Also Arrived at Nanking Awaiting Punishment," KWCP, XIV, 2 (January 4, 1937), p. 10; I Ming, pp. 17-18.

3. Selle, p. 336; Snow, Random Notes, p. 13; I Ming, pp. 23-25.

4. Mayling Chiang, pp. 18, 39; Kung, II, 664-65.

5. Ta-kung pao (Shanghai), January 5, 1937; I Ming, pp. 26-27.

244

Chapter X Notes

6. Ta-kung pao, January 7, 1937; Chiang, Soviet Russia in China, p. 79.

7. Ta-kung pao, January 5, 1937; Shen-pao, January 5, 1937.

8. Lu Pi, pp. 38-39; Sun Ming-chiu, p. 16.

9. Wan Yao-huang, no. 30 (January 10, 1974), p, 20; Sun Ming-chiu, p. 18; Shen-pao, December 28, 1936; Li T'ien-chih, p. 37.

10. Li Chin-chou, no. 118 (March 1972), 23.

11. Li T'ien-chih, p. 36.

12. Bertram, pp. 206-207.

13. Li T'ien-chih, p. 37.

14. Kung, II, 702-703. A partial translation appears in Bertram, p. 234.

15. Ta-kung pao, January 7, 1973.

16. Kung, II, 702; Bertram, p. 334.

17. Bertram, pp. 238-40. The Ch'ang-pai-shan [Long white mountain] and the Heilungchiang [Black dragon or Amur River] are the two prominent geographic features of Manchuria.

18. Ta-kung pao, January 12, 1973.

19. "The Right and Wrong Ways in the National Salvation and Reconstruction," Ta-kung pao, January 5, 1937.

20. Meng Chen, "The Popular Front after the Sian Incident," Wen-hua chien-she yüeh-k'an [Cultural construction], III, 6 (March 19, 1937), 1-2.

21. Ta-kung pao and Shen-pao, January 15, 1937.

Chapter X Notes

22. Ta-kung pao and Shen-pao, January 19, 1937.

23. Shen-pao, January 19, 1937. The Shanghai campaign was the Shanghai incident that erupted on January 28, 1932.

24. The First National Congress of the KMT was held at Canton in January 1924, at which Li Ta-chao, representing the CCP, issued the statement. Li's statement is reproduced in photographic facsimile in Lo Chia-lun (ed.), Ko-ming wen hsien [Revolutionary documents] (Taipei, 1957), IX, 37-48.

25. Shen-pao, January 23, 1937.

26. Ibid.

27. Ibid.

28. Ibid.; CWR, LXXIX, 9 (January 30, 1937), 299.

29. Snow, Random Notes, p. 14.

30. CWR, LXXIX, 6 (January 9, 1937), 299.

31. Immediately following the December 12 coup, the Northwest Anti-Japanese Military Council organized the First Army Corps with Sun Wei-ju as Commander and Wang I-che as Deputy Commander. The Council also inaugurated Ma Chan-shan as the Commander of the Anti-Japanese Vanguard Army. As the tension of war grew in January 1937, the recalcitrant forces were reorganized into five army corps: the 1st Army Corps (the Hsipei Army) was commanded by Sun Wei-ju, the 2nd Army Corps by Miu Cheng-liu, the 3rd Army Corps by Yü Hsüeh-chung, and the 4th Army Corps by Wang I-che, while the 5th Army Corps was composed of the troops of the Red Army. In addition, Ma Chan-shan was appointed the Commanding-General of Cavalry. See Li Chin-chou, no. 118 (March 1972), 25; Li T'ien-chih, p. 36; CWR, LXXIX, 9 (January 30, 1937); Shen-pao, February 7, 1937.

32. See Map 3.

Chapter X Notes

33. Shen-pao, February 2, 19, 1937; Bertram, pp. 294ff.

34. Shen-pao, January 24, 1937.

35. Shen-pao, January 21, 1937; Ta-kung pao, 21, 1937.

36. Ta-kung pao, January 24, 1937.

37. "Two Problems in the Shensi Settlement," Shen-pao, February 24, 1937; "Reminiscences of the Solution of the Shensi Affair," Shen-pao, February 28, 1937; CWR, LXXIX, 11 (February 13, 1937), 367.

38. Shen-pao, February 25, 26, 1937.

39. Shen-pao, January 29, 1937. The three-point settlement is based upon the report made by Ho Yin-ch'in at the Central KMT Headquarters on February 8. See CWR, LXXIX, 11 (February 13, 1937), 367.

40. Shen-pao, January 29, 1937.

41. Shen-pao, January 31, 1937.

42. For personal telegrams and newspaper editorials that urged Yü Hsüeh-chung to obey orders of the Central Government, see Ta-kung pao and Shen-pao, January 15, 23, 24, 26, 1937.

43. James M. Bertram, Crisis in China (New York, 1937).

44. Chang Kuo-t'ao, no. 56 (August 1970), 86; Snow, Red Star Over China, p. 447; CWR, LXXIX, 7 (January 16, 1937), 227.

45. Snow, Random Notes, p. 7.

46. Ibid., p. 8.

47. Bertram, loc. cit., p. 283.

48. Ibid., p. 291.

Chapter X Notes

49. "Reminiscences of the Solution of the Shensi Affairs"; Wang Sheng-t'ao, "Wang I-che, A Martyr after the Sian Incident," Chang-ku yüeh-k'an [Journal of historical records], no. 18 (February 19, 1973), 41-43; "Widow of General Wang I-che Asks Nanking to Punish Ringleaders," CWR, LXXIX, 12 (February 20, 1937), 410.

50. Snow, Random Notes, p. 9; Mao Shao-chou's interview with the writer on September 3, 1971.

51. Li Chin-chou writes that the list included ten names (March 1972, no. 118, 26); "Reminiscences of the Solution of the Shensi Affair" mentions two lists, one with 16 names and the other with 17.

52. Wang I-che was a graduate of the 8th class of the Paoting Military Academy. During the Mukden Incident on September 18, 1931, he was commander of the 7th Brigade stationed at Mukden and offered limited resistance to the Japanese even under the strict order of "nonresistance." He gained fame in fighting the Japanese in the Great Wall campaign in 1932, and was promoted to Commander of the 67th Army, a position which he had held until the Sian Incident.

53. Li Chin chou, no. 118 (March 1972), 26; "Recent Situation at Sian after the Coup," Shen-pao, February 20, 1937; Bertram, p. 296.

54. According to reports from Sian, the February 2 mutineers presented three demands to the Tungpei leading generals: (1) opposition to the Central Government, (2) offensive against the Central Army, and (3) no withdrawal of troops and nonacceptance of terms from the Central Government. See CWR, LXXIX, 11 (February 13, 1937), 367; "Recent Situation at Sian after the Coup"; "Reminiscences of the Solution of the Shensi Affair."

55. Li Chin-chou, loc. cit.; "Reminiscences of the Solution of the Shensi Affair"; Bertram, loc. cit., p. 298.

56. Li Chin-chou, p. 26; Bertram. p. 297.

Chapter X Notes

57. Snow, Random Notes, p. 10; Bertram, pp. 300-301. For Po Ku's account of the February 2 coup, see Nym Wales, "My Yenan Notebooks," p. 123.

58. Bertram, p. 298.

59. "Recent Situation at Sian after the Coup"; General Tung Yen-p'ing's interview with the writer on August 25, 1971. Tung was a brigade commander of the 105th Division then stationed at Hsien Yang.

60. Snow, Random Notes, pp. 9-10. Chou's position on the February 2 coup was confirmed by Po Ku (see Nym Wales, loc. cit.).

Chapter XI Notes

1. The manifesto was signed by six of the eight recalcitrant leaders of the Tungpei and Hsipei Armies, namely Yang Hu-ch'eng, Yü Hsüeh-chung, Sun Wei-ju, Ho Chu-kuo, Liu To-ch'üan, and Miu Cheng-liu. Tung Ying-pin, who signed the original December 12 Manifesto, now moved his headquarters to Pinhsien, some 80 miles northwest of Sian. The Chinese text of the February 4 manifesto is not available, but an English translation of the four demands set forth in the manifesto is given in the CWR, LXXIX, 11 (February 13, 1937), 368. The demands were: (1) that before the convocation of the third plenary session of the CEC of the KMT, General Chang Hsüeh-liang should be restored his civil rights and appointed to a new post in order to have a chance to serve the country; (2) that the terms for withdrawal and assignment of garrison areas of the Northwestern forces should be revised in accordance with the practical opinions of the Shensi officers; (3) that while the preliminary withdrawal had been completed, further withdrawal be postponed until General Chang Hsüeh-liang had returned to Sian and addressed his forces; and (4) that the National Government should protect the patriotic organizations in Sian and assure the personal safety of the persons who worked hard for the cause of national salvation. A partial translation is made in Bertram, pp. 297-98.

Chapter XI Notes

2. Ta-kung pao, February 9, 10, 1937; Shen-pao, February 10,
    11, 1937.

3. Shen-pao, February 14, 1937; CWR, LXXIX, 12 (February 20,
    1937), 410.

4. This information was made available by Li T'ien-lin, wife of
    T'ien Yü-shih. See "Speaking of General Wan Fu-lin's Rise
    from the Ranks," CCWII, no. 126 (November 1972), 59.

5. Shen-pao, February 15, 18, 1937.

6. Shen-pao, February 25, 27, 1937; Yao, Chen shih, I, 74-87.
    The six generals were Wu K'o-jen, Li Chen-t'ang, Huo Shou-i,
    Chou Fu-ch'eng, T'ang Chün-yao, and Chang Chih-huan.

7. "A Farewell Letter of the Tungpei Army to the Compatriots of
    the Northwest," in Wang Cho-yen, pp. 25-26; CWR, LXXX, 5
    (April 3, 1937), 168; Li Chin-chou, no. 119 (April 1972), 25.

8. "Reminiscences of the Solution of the Shensi Affair," loc. cit.;
    Bertram, pp. 308-309.

9. The Chinese text of the CCP telegram to the KMT Third Plenum
    can be found in T'an Ling (ed.), Kuo-Kung ho-tso K'ang-Jih
    wen-hsien; Yu Ch'i, pp. 330-331; Kuo, III, 182-83; Wang Chien-
    min, III, 102-103. An incomplete translation of the telegram
    is available in CWR, LXXIX, 13 (February 27, 1937), 442-43;
    Chiang, Soviet Russia in China, pp. 77-78.

10. Kuo, III, 183; Wang Chien-min, III, 103.

11. Both documents can be found in Lun K'ang-Jih min-chu t'ung-i
    chan-hsien chu wen-t'i [Discussion on questions of anti-Japa-
    nese national united front] in Yushodo, reel XIII. By far the
    second document, twelve pages long with the postscript date of
    March 13, 1937, is the most important available document that
    accounts for the CCP position on the peaceful settlement with
    the KMT.

Chapter XI Notes

12. The September 1936 Resolution is entitled "Resolution Concerning the Democratic Republic," a reprint of which is found in Yü Ch'i, pp. 243-49.

13. "Outline of Propaganda and Explanation Concerning the Meaning of the Peaceful Settlement of the Sian Incident and the Central's Telegram to the KMT Third Plenum," in Lun K'ang-Jih min-chu t'ung-i chan-hsien chu wen-t'i, p. 43.

14. Ibid., pp. 54-56.

15. Shen-pao, February 16, 1937.

16. CWR, LXXIX, 13 (February 27, 1937), 445.

17. Ibid., p. 465.

18. Ibid.

19. Ibid., p. 445. Li's anti-Japanese stand and his opposition to the resumption of the suppression campaign against the Communists was unequivocally enunciated in his article, "How Armed Resistance Will Bring Powerful Friends to China's Side," CWR, LXXIX, 9 (January 30, 1937), 294-96.

20. CWR, LXXIX, 13 (February 27, 1937), 442.

21. Shen-pao, February 20, 1937.

22. The full text of the declaration is reprinted in Shen-pao, February 23, 1937. A partial translation of it is given in CWR, LXXIX, 13 (February 27, 1937), 443-444.

23. See note 22.

24. For the resolution, see Shen-pao, February 23, 1937. It was reprinted in Wang Chien-min, III, 103-105.

25. See note 24. Also CWR, LXXIX, 13 (February 27, 1937), 445.

Chapter XII Notes

1. Mayling Chiang, p. 25.

2. <u>Ibid.</u>, p. 42.

3. <u>CWR</u>, LXXIX, 11 (February 13, 1937), 367; <u>Shen-pao</u>, January 21, 1973; "Reminiscences of the Solution of Shensi Affair."

4. In his meeting with the Japanese Ambassador Kawagoe in early March, Chiang said: "Rumors of such cooperation are absolutely false. No such cooperation will be possible unless the Communists accept the four conditions laid down by the recent Third Plenary session of the CEC of the KMT." A little later, Wang Ching-wei commented on the same subject: "If the Reds accept the policy as outlined in the manifesto of the Third Plenum, the Central Authorities will give the Communists a chance to start life anew. But this did not mean the outright admission of Communists into the KMT." See <u>CWR</u>, LXXX, 2, 4 (March 13, 27, 1937), 48, 144.

5. Wang Ming, "The Key to the Salvation of the Chinese People," <u>Communist International</u>, XIV, 5 (May 1937), 309.

6. To silence growing internal opposition to the capitulation policy and to urge the KMT leaders to accept its offer, the CCP leadership issued "A Letter to All Comrades of the Party" on April 15, 1937. For the letter, see <u>Yushodo</u>, reel XIV; a reprint with slight omissions is found in Wang Chien-min, III, 107-111.

7. <u>CWR</u>, LXXX, 9 (May 1, 1937), 326.

8. In his interview with Helen Snow at Yenan on June 22, 1937, Chou En-lai said: "Our demands now in negotiation are the same as the telgram sent to the plenum. . . . We want a special region and to organize an elected democratic government. We do not want an appointed governor and Chiang Kai-shek wants to appoint a governor here." See Nym Wales, "My Yenan Notebooks," p. 127.

Chapter XII Notes

9.   Following the Loukouchiao Incident, the CCP issued the "Dec-
      laration of the CCP Central for Proclaiming the Kuomintang-
      Communist Cooperation" on July 15, 1937, but it was not
      published by Nanking until September 22 when it was printed
      under the variant title "Declaration of the CCP for Meeting
      together with the National Exigency" along with "Generalissimo
      Chiang's Talk on the CCP Declaration," the latter being the
      acceptance of the KMT-CCP cooperation. Both documents are
      found in Yushodo, reel XIV; also reprinted in Wang Chien-min,
      III, 113-15.

10.   Foreign Relations, III (1937), 91.

11.   Nelson T. Johnson reported that according to one current re-
      port, "Chiang at one time almost decided to continue immediate-
      ly suppression of the Communists and other rebels at Sian by
      force and to execute Chang Hsüeh-liang as the rebel leader
      when he was visited at Fenghua by Soong, who bitterly criti-
      cized him for violating the pledges already mentioned and
      threatened to leave China and publicly announce Chiang's per-
      fidy." See Foreign Relations, vol. III (1937), 19. In discuss-
      ing this with the writer, Mao Ching-hsiang was of the opinion
      that the report was probably true.

12.   CWR, LXXX, 8 (April 24, 1937), 290. Yang Hu-ch'eng issued
      his farewell message to the Northwest people on May 1. See
      CWR, LXXX, 10 (May 8, 1937), 367.

13.   Foreign Relations, III, (1937), p. 385; Arthur N. Young, China
      and the Helping Hand, 1937-1945 (Cambridge, Mass., 1969),
      74-75.

14.   Lu Pi, pp. 34-112; Kuo Cheng-k'ai, no. 46 (August 1, 1955),
      11.

15.   Foreign Relations, III (1927), 90; CWR, LXXX, 5 (April 3,
      1937), 174.

16.   Yang went abroad in May 1937. Upon his return from Europe
      in August 1938, he was immediately put into custody, suffering

Chapter XII Notes

16. the same fate as the Young Marshal. By all accounts, he and
his family were executed by the KMT special secret service
in Chungking in September 1949. See Hsin Shen, "Tai Yü-
nung Seized Yang Hu-ch'eng aboard an Airplane," Hsin-wen
t'ien-ti [World news], no. 761 (September 1962); "The Murder
of Yang Hu-ch'eng," in Chiang Mei to nn Chung king to tin
sha tsui-hsing lu [Records of crimes of massacre committed
at Chungking by the special service of Chiang Kai-shek and
the United States] (Hong Kong, 1965), 24-32; Si-an shih-pien
chen-shih, II. 88-91; Kuo Cheng-k'ai, no. 46 (August 1, 1955),
12; Liu Mu-ning, "An Interview with Chou Yang-huo on the
Death of Yang Hu-ch'eng," Ch'i-shih nien tai [The seventies],
no. 70 (November 1975), 16-20.

BIBLIOGRAPHY

Books and Articles

"A Farewell Letter of the Tungpei Army to the Compatriots of the Northeast," in Wang Cho-yen, Chang Hsüeh-liang tao ti shih ko tsen-yang jen [What kind of person is Chang Hsüeh-liang?], (Peking, 1937?). China Weekly Review (hereafter CWR), LXXXI, 5 (April 3, 1937).

Abend, Hallett E. My Life in China, 1926-1941. New York, 1943.

Ballantine, Joseph W. "International Background: China's Intense Relations with the Power." Chien ku chien kuo ti shih nien [Strenuous ten years of nation building], Hsüeh Kuang-ch'ien (ed.). Taipei, 1971.

Bertram, James M. Crisis in China. New York, 1937.

_____. The Story of the Sian Mutiny. New York, 1938.

Bianco, Lucien. "La Crise de Sian." Unpublished Ph.D. thesis at Sorbonne, University of Paris, 1969.

Bisson, T.A. Japan in China. New York, 1938.

Borton, Hugh. Japan's Modern Century. New York, 1970, 2nd ed.

Chang Chün. "Chu Shao-chou's Great Skill to Save the Situation." Tzu-yu pao [Liberty news]. Hong Kong.

Chang Hsüeh-liang. Chang Hsüeh-liang chiang-yen chi [Collected speeches of Chang Hsüeh-liang]. N.p., preface dated November 11, 1936.

_____. "Chairman Chang's Radio Speech on December 14, 1936." K'ang-Jih chiu wang yen lun chi [Collected speeches on war of resistance against Japan]. N.p., 1936, vol. I, pp. 15-21.

_____. "Chairman Chang's Speech to All the Staff of the General Headquarters, December 13, 1936." K'ang-Jih chiu wang yen lun chi [Collected speeches on war of resistance against Japan].

N.p., 1936, vol. I, pp. 5-14.

_____. "Chairman Chang's Speech at the People's Rally, December 16, 1936." K'ang-Jih chiu wang yen lun chi [Collected speeches on war of resistance against Japan]. N.p., 1936, vol. I, pp. 26-30.

_____. Chung-kuo ch'u-lu wei yu k'ang-Jih [The only future of China is resistance against Japan]. N.p., June 1936.

_____. "Confession of the Sian Incident." Ming-pao yüeh-k'an. September 1968, no. 33, pp. 49-53.

Chang Kuo-t'ao. "My Memoirs." Ming-pao yüeh-k'an. February 1970, no. 50, pp. 85-86.

_____. The Rise of the Chinese Communist Party: The Autobiography of Chang Kuo-t'ao. Lawrence, 1971-1973, 2 vols.

Chang Ta-chün. Szu-shih nien tung-luan Sin-chiang [Forty years of chaos in Sinkiang]. Hong Kong, 1956.

_____. "Sinkiang Since the Founding of the Republic." Sinchiang yen chiu [Studies of Sinkiang]. Taipei, 1964, pp. 93-204.

Chang Ti-fei. "Recent Policies of the Chinese Communist Party Viewed from Marxism." Wen-hua chien she yüeh-k'an. March 10, 1937, III, 6, pp. 23-30.

Ch'ang Chiang (Fan Ch'ang-chiang). "A Journey to North Shensi." Ch'ang cheng shih-tai [During the long march], Huang Feng (ed.). Hankow, on microfilm in Yushodo Materials on Chinese Communist Party, reel VII.

Ch'en K'o-hua. Chung-kuo hsien-tai ko-ming shih shih [Historical facts of the modern Chinese revolution]. Hong Kong, 1965, 2 vols.

Ch'en Pu-lei. "Memoirs of Ch'en Pu-lei." Ch'uan chi wen-hsüeh (hereafter CCWH). August 1964, V, 2, 53.

Ch'eng T'ien-fang. "The Sian Incident." CCWH. July 1964, V, 1, pp. 35-40.

Chiang Chien-yin. "Detailed Account of Chiang Kai-shek's Return to Nanking from Shensi." Kuo-wen chou-pao (hereafter KWCP). January 4, 1937, XIV, 2, pp. 8-9.

Chiang Kai-shek. Si-an pan-yüeh chi [A fortnight at Sian]. Nanking, 1937.

_____. Chiang Tsung-t'ung chi [Collected works of President Chiang]. Taipei, 1961, 2 vols., 2nd ed.

_____. Soviet Russia in China. New York, 1957.

_____. "Admonition to Chang Hsüeh-liang and Yang Hu-ch'eng." KWCP. January 4, 1937, XIV, 2.

_____. "Generalissimo Chiang's Talk on the CCP Declaration." Kuo-Kung ho-tso k'ang-Jih wen-hsien [Documents on the Kuomintang-Communist collaboration and resistance against Japan], T'an Ling (ed.). Hankow, 1938, in Yushodo, reel XIV.

_____. "Talk at the Press Conference, February 23, 1937." CWR. February 27, 1937, LXXIX, 13.

Chiang, Mayling Soong. Sian: A Coup d'État. Shanghai, 1937.

Chiang Po-li. "Interview with Lung Yu-chün." Hsin-wen pao [News report]. December 27, 1936, in Historical Archives Commission of the KMT, no. 480/9.

Chien Yu-wen. "Reminiscences on Joining the Army in the Northwest." CCWH. July 1972, no. 121.

Chin Yao-t'an. "Recent Situation of the Northeastern Army Stationed in Lanchow." Pien-chiang t'ung-hsün. March 20, 1937, V, 4.

Ch'in Te-shun. "North Chahar Incident and Others." CCWH. February 1963, no. 9.

_____. "Reminiscences on the Period of the Hopeh-Chahar Political Council." CCWH. January 1963, no. 8.

258

Chinese Communist Party. "A Letter to All Comrades of the Party, April 15, 1937." In Yushodo, reel XIV.

_____. "Declaration of the CCP Central for Proclaiming the Kuomintang-Communist Cooperation, July 15, 1937." In Yushodo, reel XIV.

_____. "The Five Great Programs." Ch'en Ch'eng Collection. On microfilm at the Hoover Institution on War, Revolution and Peace, reel VII.

_____. "Outline of Propaganda and Explanation Concerning the Meaning of the Peaceful Settlement of the Sian Incident and the Central's Telegram to the KMT Third Plenum." Lun k'ang-Jih min-tsu t'ung-i chan-hsien wen-t'i [Discussion on questions of anti-Japanese national united front]. In Yushodo, reel XIII.

_____. "Questions and Answers Concerning the Party Central's Circular Telegram to the KMT Third Plenum." Lun k'ang-Jih min-tsu t'ung-i chan-hsien wen-t'i [Discussion on questions of anti-Japanese national united front]. In Yushodo, reel XIII.

_____. "The Six Great Programs." Ch'en Ch'eng Collection. Reel XVI.

_____. "Telegram to the KMT Third Plenum, February 10, 1937," in T'an Ling, Yushodo, reel XIV.

Chinese Communist Party, North China Bureau. "Declaration of the CCP North China Bureau on the Peaceful Solution of the Sian Incident," in Lucien Bianco, pp. 339-340.

Chou Ching-wen. Feng pao shih nien [Ten years' tempest]. Hong Kong, 1963.

Chu Shu-shou. "An Account of the Sian Incident Involving Loyang." CCWH. June 1972, no. 121.

Chu Teh and others. Ti pa-lu chün [The eighth route army]. Hankow, 1937, in Yushodo, reel VII.

Clubb, O. Edmund. Twentieth Century China. New York, 1967, 3rd ed.

Committee of the Chinese People's War against Japan. "Basic Plat-
form for the Chinese People's War against Japan." Hung-se
Chung-hua [Red China]. September 21, 1934, no. 236, in
Ch'en Ch'eng Collection, reel XVII.

Committe of Compilation for Commemorating Mr. Yen Hsi-shan.
Yen Po-ch'uan hsien-sheng chi-nien chi [Collection of writings
in commemoration of Mr. Yen Hsi-shan]. Taipei, 1963.

Eastman, Lloyd E. "Fascism in Kuomintang China: The Blue Shirts."
The China Quarterly. January/March 1972, no. 49.

Fang Shu-chung. "The Causes and Results of the Sian Incident."
In Historical Archives Commission of the KMT, no. 480/11.

"Final Turning Point of the Shensi Situation." Ta-kung pao. Shanghai, January 25, 1937.

Fu Pao-chen. "Biographies of German Military Advisors in China,
1928-1938." CCWH. January 1974, no. 140.

Fu Szu-nien. "Discussion on the Rebellion of Bandit Chang." Chung-
yang jih pao. Nanking, December 16, 1936.

Gillin, Donald G. Warlord Yen Hsi-shan, 1911-1949. Princeton,
1967.

Great Britain, Public Record Office. "Chang Hsüeh-liang Rebellion."
Ref. no. F7814/166/10.

Gunther, John. Inside Asia. New York, 1939.

Hane, Mikiso. Japan: A Historical Survey. New York, 1972.

Hanwell, Norman D. "The Course is Set in China." Asia. February 1937.

Ho Ching-hua. Shuang shih-erh yü min-tsu ko-ming [Double twelfth
and the national revolution]. Hong Kong, 1941.

Ho Kan-chih. Chung-kuo hsien-tai ko-ming yün-tung shih [A history
of modern Chinese revolution]. Hong Kong, 1958.

"How Armed Resistance Will Bring Powerful Friends to China's Side."
CWR. January 30, 1937, LXXIX, 9, 294-96.

Hsia Tsi-an. The Gate of Darkness: Studies on the Leftist Literary
Movement in China. Seattle, 1968.

Hsiang Nai-kuang. "Chinese Communist Strategy of Negotiations and
Historical Lessons." Chung-yang jih-pao. Taipei, July 21,
1972.

Hsin Shen. "Tai Yü-nung Seized Yang Hu-ch'eng Aboard an Airplane."
Hsin-wen t'ien ti [World news]. September 1962, no. 761.

Hsü Pin-wen. "Reminiscences of the National Salvation Movement in
the Northwest." Chieh-fang jih-pao [Liberation daily]. Sian,
December 20, 1936. As reprinted in Wang Chien-min, Chung-kuo
Kung-ch'an-tang shih-kao [Draft history of the CCP], Taipei,
1965, 3 vols, III, 85-86.

Hsu, U. T. Invisible Conflict. Hong Kong, 1958.

Hu Han-min. Hu Han-min hsien-sheng cheng lun hsüan-pien [Selected
political writings of Mr. Hu Han-min]. Canton, 1934.

_____. "The Rise and Fall of the Party and Military Powers and
Remedies for the Future." San-min chu-i yüeh-k'an. June 15,
1933, I, 6.

Hu Hua. Chung-kuo hsin min-chu chu-i ko-ming shih [A history of
Chinese new democratic revolution]. Peking, 1952, revised
edition.

_____ (ed.). Chung-kuo hsin min-chu chu-i ko-ming shih ts'an-
k'ao tzu-liao [Source materials on the history of Chinese new
democratic revolution]. Shanghai, 1951.

Hu Shih. "The Treason of Chang Hsüeh-liang." Ta-kung pao.
Tientsin, December 20, 1936.

I Ming (ed.). Si-an shih-pien shih-liao [Historical materials of the
Sian incident]. Taipei, n.d.

Institute of International Affairs. Survey of International Affairs, 1933-1939. London, 1939.

Iriye, Akira. "Chang Hsüeh-liang and the Japanese." Journal of Asian Studies. November 1960, XXX, 1.

Ishikawa Tadao. Chūgoku kyōsantō shi kenkyū [Studies on the history of the CCP]. Tokyo, 1960.

Israel, John. Student Nationalism in China, 1927-1937. Stanford, 1966.

"Japanese Press Urges War with China." CWR. December 19, 1936, LXXIX, 3.

Johnson, Nelson T. "Communist Situation in Northwest China," a report to the Secretary of State received by the Division of Far East Affairs on April 7, 1936, no. 893.00/13449.

K'ai Feng. "Discussions on the Various Problems of the Anti-Japanese National Front." Lun k'ang-Jih min-tsu t'ung-i chan-hsien chu wen-t'i [Discussion on problems of the national united front in resistance against Japan]. January 28, 1937. In Yushodo, reel XIII.

K'ang-Jih min-tsu t'ung-i chan-hsien chih-nan [Guide to resistance against Japan and people's united front]. Yenan, 1937-1939, 6 vols. In Yushodo, reel XIII.

Kapp, Robert A. "Provincial Independence versus National Rule: A Case Study of Szechwan in the 1920s and 1930s." Journal of Asian Studies. May 1971, XXX, 3.

Kiang, Wen-han. The Ideological Background of the Chinese Student Movement. New York, 1948.

Knatchbull-Hugessen, Sir. Diplomat in Peace and War. London, 1949.

Kuang Lu. "Sinkiang Question." Sin-chiang yen-chiu. Pp. 421-34.

K'un Chün and Shih Ta. "A Turning Point in History--Commemorate the Fortieth Anniversary of the Tsunyi Conference." Li-shih yen-chiu [Historical studies]. February 20, 1975, no. 1.

Kung, H. H. "Reminiscences of the Sian Incident." K'ung yung-chih hsien-sheng chiang-yen chi [Collected speeches of Mr. K'ung Yung-chih]. Taipei, 1960.

Kuo Cheng-k'ai. "Background of the Sian Incident." Je-feng. December 16, 1954, no. 31.

_____. "History is not Written with Lies." Je-feng. February 1, 1955, no. 34.

Kuo Hua-lun. Chung-Kung shih-lun [Analytical history of the Chinese Communist Party]. Taipei, 1969, 4 vols.

Lang Te-p'ei. "The Gloomy Shadow of the Sian Incident." Pien-shih yen-chiu. March 20, 1937, V, 3.

Leonard, Royal. I Flew for China. New York, 1942.

Li Chin-chou. "An Eyewitness Account of the Sian Incident." CCWH. December 1971-April 1972, nos. 115-119.

Li Fei. "The So-Called Village Ownership." Hsin wen-hua [New culture]. February 1, 1936, initial issue.

Li T'ien-chih. "One Month in Sian." KWCP. February 1, 1937, XIV, 6.

_____. "Record of One Month in Sian." Ta-kung pao. Shanghai, January 13, 1937.

Li T'ien-lin. "A Portrait of a Prominent Figure of North China, Hsiao Chen-ying." CCWH. January 1972, no. 116.

_____. "Speaking on General Wan Fu-lin's Rise from the Ranks." CCWH. November 1972, no. 126.

Li Yün-han. "The So-Called Ho-Umetsu Agreement." CCWH. November 1972, no. 126.

_____. "Sung Che-yüan Before and After the Establishment of the Hopei-Chahar Political Council." CCWH. July 1971, no. 110.

Liang Ching-tun. The Conspiracy of the Mukden Incident, September 18, 1931. New York, 1970.

"List of Martyrs of the Kansu Pacification Headquarters during the Sian Incident." Historical Archives Commission of the KMT, no. 480/10.

Liu Chien-ch'iu   Yin-ho i wang [Reminiscences from Yin-ho]. Taipei, 1966.

_____. "After Mr. Chiang's Return from Detention." Ta-kung pao. Shanghai, January 1, 1937.

Liu Po-ch'eng. "Reminiscences of the Long March." Hsing-huo liao yüan [A spark will start a prairie fire]. Peking, 1962.

Liu Po-ch'uan (ed.). Chiang wei-yüan chang Si-an meng-nan chi [Records of Generalissimo Chiang's being kidnapped at Sian]. Shanghai, 1937.

Lo Chia-lun (ed.). Ko-ming wen hsien [Revolutionary documents]. Taipei, 1953, 20 vols., vol. IX.

Lo Fu (alias Chang Wen-t'ien). "Strengthen Domestic Peace and Prepare War of Resistance Against Japan." Lun k'ang-Jih min-tsu t'ung-i chan-hsien chu wen-t'i. In Yushodo, reel XIII.

Lu Pi. Lun Chang Hsüeh-liang [Evaluation of Chang Hsüeh-liang]. Hong Kong, 1948.

Lung Fei-hu. Ken sui Chou fu-chu-hsi shih-i nien [Having followed Vice-Chairman Chou for eleven years]. Peking, 1960.

Lutz, Jessie G. "December 9, 1935 Student Nationalism and the Chinese Christian Colleges." Journal of Asian Studies. August 1967, XXVI, 4.

Ma Hung-k'uei. "Telegram to K'ung Hsiang-hsi, December 9, 1936," in H. H. Kung, II, 685.

Ma Pu-ch'ing. "The Annihilation Battle of the Western River Corridor." Chin-jih ta-lu [Mainland China today]. October 1961, no. 146.

"Major Events of the Week." KWCP. December 21, 1936, January
1, 4, 1937, XIII, 50, XIV, 1, 2.

Mao Tse-tung. "A Statement on Chiang Kai-shek's Statement, December
28, 1936." Selected Works of Mao Tse-tung. Peking, 1965,
4 vols., vol. I, pp. 255-58.

_____ and others. China: The March Toward Unity. New York,
1937.

_____ and Smedley. "The Sino-Japanese Question and the Sian
Incident." The Mao-Smedley Talk on March 1, 1937. In
Yushodo, reel. XIII.

Meng Chen. "The Popular Front after the Sian Incident." Wen-hua
chien she yüeh-k'an. March 10, 1937, III, 6.

Meng Po-chien. Tsou hsiang jen-tao [March toward humanity]. Hong
Kong, 1953.

Military History Bureau. Chiao-fei chan shih [A history of military
actions against the Communist rebellion during 1930-1945].
Taipei, 1967, 6 vols., vol. VI.

Mu Ching-yun. "Calamities of Szechwan Brought About by Chiang
Kai-shek." Chin-tai shih-liao [Materials of modern history].
Peking, 1962, vol. VI.

"The Murder of Yang Hu-ch'eng." Chiang-Mei t'e-wu Chung-king
ta t'u-sha tsui-hsing lu [Records of crimes of massacre
committed at Chungking by the special service of Chiang Kai-
shek and the United States]. Hong Kong, 1965.

"The New Appointment of Chiang Kai-shek." San-min chu-i yüeh-
k'an. October 15, 1935, VI, 4.

Northwestern Association for National Salvation. "A Letter to All
Parties and Groups, December 22, 1936." Chinese collection
at the Hoover Institution on War, Revolution and Peace.

Northwestern People's Convention. "Resolutions on Supporting Generals
Chang's and Yang's Policy for National Salvation, December 16,
1936," in Lucien Bianco, p. 294.

Ogata, Sadako N. Defiance in Manchuria. Berkeley, Calif., 1964.

"An Open Letter to the Military of Sian." Ta-kung pao. Tientsin and Shanghai, December 18, 1936.

Otsuka Reizō. Shina kyōsantō shi [History of the CCP]. Tokyo, 1940, 2 vols.

Pai Hsüeh-feng. Lan-chou shih-pien chi liao [A brief account of the Lanchow incident]. Historical Archives Commission of the KMT, no. 480/10.

Pao Tsun-p'eng. Chung-kuo chin-tai ch'ing-nien yün-tung shih [A history of youth movement in modern China]. Taipei, 1953.

Phelps, Dryden L. "Chiang Kai-shek Cleans Up in Szechwan." Asia. July 1936.

"The Policy of Indulgence to the Communists and Its Crisis." San-min chu-i yüeh-k'an. December 15, 1934, IV, 6.

"Recent Situation at Sian after the Coup." Shen pao. February 20, 1937.

"Reminiscences on the Real Situation of the Sian Incident." In Yushodo, reel X.

"Reminiscences of the Solution of the Shensi Affair." Shen pao. February 28, 1937.

"Resolution Concerning the Democratic Republic." In Yü Ch'i (ed.), Shih-lun hsüan-chi [Selected writings on current affairs]. Shanghai, 1937.

Rosinger, Lawrence K. China's Crisis. New York, 1945.

_____. China's Wartime Politics, 1937-1944. Princeton, 1944.

Scheindlin, Shira A. "The Political Career of Chang Hsüeh-liang, 1928-1936." Unpublished Master's thesis at Columbia University, 1969.

Selle, Earl Albert. Donald of China. New York, 1948.

Shen Po-shun. "Reminiscences of December 12." In Hu Hua (ed.), pp. 346-49.

Sheng Shih-ts'ai. "From Nanking to Sinkiang." CCWH. August 1970, no. 99.

Shu Liu. "Chang Hsüeh-liang and 'Confession of the Sian Incident.'" Ming-pao yüeh-k'an. August, September, October 1968, nos. 32, 33, 34.

"The Sian Incident." Tung-feng. July 1975, no. 9.

Smedley, Agnes. Battle Hymn of China. New York, 1943.

Snow, Edgar. Red Star Over China. New York, 1961, Black Cat ed.

_____. Random Notes on Red China, 1936-1945. Cambridge, Mass., 1957.

Ssu-ma Shang-tun. "A Biography of Chang Hsüeh-liang." Chung-hua yüeh-pao. June 1974, no. 705.

"A Student's Report on the Situation in Kansu and Shensi." Shen pao. February 1, 1937.

Sun Ming-chiu. Wo huo cho liao Chiang Chieh-shih [I caught Chiang Kai-shek alive]. Hong Kong, 1950.

"Suppress the Communists." San-min chu-i yüeh-k'an. May 15, 1935, V, 5.

Ta-ti Press (ed.). Si-an shih-pien san i [Three memoirs on the Sian Incident]. Macao, 1962.

Teeling, William. "Will South China Go Communist or Fascist?" Asia. July 1936.

Teng Ch'i. "Yen Po-ch'uan and the Sian Incident." CCWH. November 1966, IX, 5.

Teng Wen-i. Chung-kuo Kung-ch'an-tang chih shih pai [The failures of the CCP]. Nanking, 1947.

Thomson, James C. Jr. "Communist Policy and the United Front in China." Paper on China. 1957, XI.

T'ien Chiung-chin. "Reminiscences of Working in My Native Place." Chung-yang jih-pao. December 7, 1963.

Tong, Hollington K. Chiang Kai-shek--Soldier and Statesman. Shanghai, 1937, 2 vols.

Ts'ai Hsiao-ch'ien. "Reminiscences of the Red Army's Westward Flight." Chung-Kung yen chiu [Studies on Chinese Communism]. October 1970, no. 46.

_____. "Reminiscences of the Kiangsi Soviet." Chung-Kung yen chiu. April 1969, no. 28.

"Two Problems in the Shensi Settlement." Shen pao. February 24, 1937.

U.S. Department of State. Foreign Relations of the United States. IV (1936), III (1937).

_____. Nelson T. Johnson's Letter to the Department of State, May 11, 1937. Ref. no. 893.00/14126.

Van Slyke, Lyman P. Enemies and Friends: The United Front in China. Stanford, 1967.

Wales, Nym (Helen Snow). "My Yenan Notebooks." Unpublished manuscript, 1961.

_____. Notes on the Chinese Student Movement, 1935-1936. Stanford, 1959.

Wan Yao-huang. "Diaries on the Long Journey of Pursuing Campaigns." Hu-pei wen-hsien. December 1973, no. 29.

Wang Chi. "The Young Marshal Chang Hsüeh-liang, 1928-1931." Unpublished Ph.D. thesis at Georgetown University, 1969.

268

Wang Ching-wei. "How to Achieve National Salvation and Survival." Shen pao. January 23, 1937.

_____. "Opening Speech at the KMT Third Plenum." Shen pao. February 16, 1937.

Wang Kuan-ying. Chiang Tsung-t'ung yü Chung-kuo [President Chiang and China]. Taipei, 1966.

Wang Ming (Ch'en Shao-yü). "The Key to the Salvation of the Chinese People." The Communist International. May 1937, XIV, 5.

_____. "The Struggle for the Anti-imperialist United Front and the Immediate Tasks of the Communist Party of China." The Communist International. February 1936, XII, special issue.

Wang Sheng-t'ao. "Wang I-che, A Martyr after the Sian Incident." Chang-ku yüeh-k'an [Journal of historical records]. February 10, 1973, no. 18.

Wang T'ieh-han. "A Brief History of the Tungpei Army." CCWH. May, June 1971, nos. 108, 109.

_____. "Resistance in the Non-resistance Policy." Chung-yang jih-pao. January 9, 11, 1964.

Whiting, Allen S. and Sheng Shih-ts'ai. Sinkiang: Pawn or Pivot? Ann Arbor, 1958.

"Widow of General Wang I-che Asks Nanking to Punish Ringleaders." CWR. February 20, 1937, LXXIX, 12.

Williamsen, Thomas M. "The Development of German-Chinese Military Relations, 1928-1936." Unpublished Master's thesis at Duke University, 1967.

Wu Chih. "The Tendency of Thought of the Shensi Youths during the Previous Ten Years." KWCP. January 1, 1937, XIV, 1.

Wu T'ieh-ch'eng. "The Right and Wrong Ways in the National Salvation and Reconstruction." Ta-kung pao. Shanghai, January 5, 1937.

Yang Hu-ch'eng. "Vice-Chairman Yang's Broadcast Speech, December 15, 1936." K'ang-Jih chiu-wang yen-lun chi. Pp. 22-25.

_____. "Vice-Chairman Yang's Speech at the People's Convention, December 16, 1936." K'ang-Jih chiu-wang yen-lun chi. Pp. 31-35.

_____. "The January 5, 1937 Circular Telegram of Yang Hu-ch'eng and Others." In H. H. Kung, pp. 702-703.

_____. "Farewell Message to the Northwestern People, May 1, 1937." CWR. May 8, 1937, LXXX, 10.

Yang Ping-wen. "A Brief Account of the Punitive War of General Training Division against the Rebels during the Sian Incident." April 29, 1953. Historical Archives Commission of the KMT, no. 480/31.

Yang Tzu-lieh. Chang Kuo-t'ao fu-jen hui-i lu [Memoirs of Mrs. Chang Kuo-t'ao]. Hong Kong, 1970.

Yao, L. F. (ed.). Si-an shih-pien chen shih [Precious history of the Sian Incident]. Hong Kong, 1967-1969, 3 vols.

Yeh Ch'ing (Jen Cho-hsüan). "The Road to the Unification of China." Wen-hua chien-she yüeh-k'an. February 10, 1937, III, 5.

Yen Hsi-shan. "Telegram to Chang Hsüeh-liang." KWCP. December 21, 1936, XIII, 50.

_____. Product Certificate and Distribution According to Labor. Nanking, 1936.

Young, Arthur N. China and the Helping Hand, 1937-1945. Cambridge, Mass., 1969.

Yü Kuo-hsün. "Reminiscences of Liu Chien-ch'ün and An Explanation of the 'Blue Skirt Club.'" CCWH. September 1972, no. 124.

Yueh Sheng. Sun Yat-sen University of Moscow and the Chinese Revolution. Lawrence, Kansas, 1971.

Interviews

Hsiang Nai-kuang, July 10, 1971.

Kuo Tzu-chün, July 20, August 5, 1971.

Ma Shao-chou, September 3, 1971.

Mao Ching-hsiang, April 3, August 12, 1974.

Miu Cheng-liu, July 15, August 10, 1971.

Tung Yen-p'ing, July 25, August 12, 1971.

Wan Yao-huang, September 6, 1971.

Newspapers

Chung-yang jih-pao [Central daily], Nanking, Taipei.

The Japan Times, Tokyo.

New York Times.

Shen-pao [The Shanghai newspaper].

Ta-kung pao [Great public paper], Tientsin, Shanghai.

Periodicals

Asia.

China Weekly Review.

Chung-hua yüeh-pao [The China monthly].

Ch'uan chi wen-hsüeh [Biographical literature].

The Communist International.

Hu-pei wen-hsien [Documentary literature of Hupeh].

Je-feng [Hot wind].

Kuo wen chou-pao [National news weekly].

Ming-pao yüeh-k'an [Ming-pao monthly].

Pien-chiang t'ung-hsün [Frontier newsletter].

Pien shih yen-chiu [Study of frontier affairs].

San-min chu-i yüeh-k'an [Three principles of the people's monthly].

Tung-fang tsa-chih [Eastern miscellany].

Tung feng [East wind].

Tung-nan feng [Southeast wind].

Wen-hua chien she yüeh-k'an [Cultural construction monthly].

An-nei jang wai	安內攘外	Chao Kuo-p'ing	趙國緩	屏光
Chang Chao-lin	張兆麟	Chao Shou-kuang	趙綬	文
Chang Chen	張貞	Chao Tai-wen	趙戴	時
Chang Cheng-te	張正德	Chao Yü-shih	趙雨	誠
Chang Chi	張繼	Ch'en Ch'eng	陳	承
Chang Chi-luan	張季鸞	Ch'en Chi-ch'eng	陳繼	棠
Chang Ch'ien-hua	張潛華	Ch'en Chi-t'ang	陳濟	東
Chang Ch'ün	張羣	Ch'en Hsü-tung	陳旭	博
Chang Ch'ung	張沖	Ch'en Kung-po	陳公	夫
Chang Hao	張浩	Ch'en Kuo-fu	陳果	夫
Chang Hsüeh-liang	張學良	Ch'en Li-fu	陳立	君
Chang Kuo-t'ao	張國燾	Ch'en Pi-chün	陳璧	寬
Chang Nai-ch'i	張乃器	Ch'en Shao-k'uan	陳紹	元
Chang Tso-lin	張作霖	Ch'en Tiao-yüan	陳調	士
Chang Tsung-ch'ang	張宗昌	Ch'en Ying-shih	陳英	光
Chang Wen-t'ien	張聞天	Ch'en Yü-kuang	陳宇	門
Chang Yin-hsiang	張印相	Cheng-yang-men	正陽	潛
Ch'ang Yin-huai	常蔭槐	Ch'eng Ch'ien	程	放
Ch'ang En-to	常恩多	Ch'eng T'ien-fang	程天翼	翹
Chao I	趙毅	Chi I-ch'iao	戢翼	

273

Chiang Chien-jen 蔣堅忍

Chiang Ching-kuo 蔣經國

Chiang Hsiao-hsien 蔣孝先

Chiang Kai-shek 蔣介石

Chiang Meng-lin 蔣夢麟

Chiang Pin 蔣斌

Chiang Po-ch'eng 蔣伯誠

Chiang Po-li 蔣百里

Chiang Soong Mayling 蔣宋美齡

Chiang Ting-wen 蔣鼎文

Chiang T'ing-fu 蔣廷黻

Chiang Tso-pin 蔣作賓

Chiang Wei-kuo 蔣緯國

Chiang-wu t'ang 講武堂

Chieh Ju-chuan 解如川

Ch'ien Ta-chün 錢大鈞

Chihlochen 紫羅鎮

Ch'in Pang-hsien 秦邦憲

Chou En-lai 周恩來

Chou Fu-ch'eng 周福成

Chou Kuang-lieh 周光烈

Chu P'ei-te 朱培德

Chu Shao-chou 祝紹周

Chu Shao-liang 朱紹良

Chu Teh 朱德

Ch'ü Cheng 居正

Ch'u-chih 處置

Chung-nan-hai 中南海

Chung Yung-tan 仲容誕

Fan Sung-pu 樊嵩甫

Feng Yü-hsiang 馮玉祥

Fu-shih 膚施

Fu Tso-i 傅作義

Han Chih-cho 韓志琢

Han Ch'ing 漢卿

Han Fu-ch'ü 韓復渠

Ho Chu-kuo 何桂國

Ho Ying-ch'in 何應欽

Hsi-pei hsiang tao 西北嚮導

Hsieh K'o 謝珂

Hsien-yang 咸陽

Hsü Fang 徐方

Hsü Hsiang-ch'ien 徐向前

Hsü Shih-ying 許世英

Hsü Yung-ch'ang 徐永昌

Hu Ching-i 胡景翼

Hu Han-min 胡漢民

Hu Jo-yü 胡若愚

Hu Shih 胡適

Hu Tsung-nan 胡宗南

Hua-ch'ing-ch'ih 華清池

Hua-yin 華陰

Huang Chieh 黃杰

Huang Fu 黃郛

Huang Hsien-sheng 黃顯聲

Huang Hsü-ch'u 黃旭初

Huang Jen-lin 黃仁霖

Huang Ta-ting 黃大定

Huo-lu 活路

Huo Shou-i 霍守義

Jen Pi-shih 任弼時

K'ai Feng 凱豐

Kanchuan 甘泉

K'ang-Jih t'ung-chih hui 抗日同志會

Kao Ch'ung-min 高崇民

Kao Fu-yüan 高福源

Kao Kuei-chih 高桂滋

Ken chüeh ch'ih-huo an 根絕赤禍案

Ku Chu-t'ung 顧祝同

Kuan Hsiang-ying 關何應

Kuan Lin-cheng 關麟徵

Kuei Yung-ch'ing 桂永清

Kung Ping-fan 公秉藩

K'ung Hsiang-hsi 孔祥熙

Kuo Hsi-p'eng 郭希鵬

Kuo Sung-ling 郭松齡

Kuo T'ai-ch'i 郭泰祺

Kuo Tzu-chün 郭紫峻

Liang Han-ts'ao 梁寒操

Liao Chung-k'ai 廖仲凱

Li Ch'ang-hsin 李昶新

Li Chen-t'ang 李振唐

Li Chi-shen 李濟琛

Li Chih-kang	李	志	剛	Liu Kuei-wu	劉	桂	武
Li-chih she	勵	志	社	Liu Lan-po	劉	瀾	波
Li Chin-chou	李	金	洲	Liu Shang-ch'ing	劉	尚	清
Li Kung-pu	李	公	僕	Liu Shao-ch'i	劉	少	奇
Li K'o-nung	李	克	農	Liu To-ch'üan	劉	多	荃
Li Lieh-chün	李	烈	鈞	Liu Wen-tao	劉	文	島
Li Mo-an	李	黙	庵	Lo Chia-lun	羅	家	倫
Li Shou-hsin	李	守	信	Lu Hsun	魯		迅
Li T'ien-ts'ai	黎	天	才	Lu Kuang-chi	盧	廣	績
Li Tsung-jen	李	宗	仁	Ma Chan-shan	馬	占	山
Li Tu	李		杜	Ma Ch'ao-chün	馬	超	俊
Li Wen-fan	李	文	範	Ma Chih-ch'ao	馬	志	超
Li Yen-nien	李	延	年	Ma Hung-k'uei	馬	鴻	逵
Li Yu-wen	栗	右	文	Ma Pu-ch'ing	馬	步	青
Lin Shen	林		森	Ma Shao-chou	馬	紹	周
Lin-t'ung	臨		潼	Mao Ching-hsiang	毛	慶	祥
Lin Yü-ying	林	毓	英	Mao Pang-ch'u	毛	邦	初
Liu Che	劉		哲	Mao Ping-wen	毛	炳	文
Liu Chen-huan	劉	振	寰	Mao Tse-tung	毛	澤	東
Liu Ch'ih	劉		峙	Mei I-chi	梅	貽	琦
Liu Hsiang	劉		湘	Mi Ch'un-lin	米	春	霖

Mi Tsan-ch'en	米暫沈	
Miao Chien-ch'iu	苗劍秋	
Miao Po-yen	苗勃然	
Miu Cheng-liu	繆徵流	
Mo Te-hui	莫德惠	
Mou Chung-hsing	牟中行	
Nan Han-ch'en	南漢辰	
Ning Ku-shih	甯古石	
Nu Yüan-feng	牛元峯	
Niu Yung-chien	鈕永建	
O-Yü-Wan	鄂豫皖	
Pai Ch'ung-hsi	白崇禧	
Pai Feng-hsiang	白鳳翔	
Pailingmiao	百靈廟	
Pao-ting	保定	
P'eng Shao-hsien	彭紹賢	
San-yüan	三原	
Sha Ch'ien-li	沙千里	
Shao Li-tzu	邵力子	
Shao Yüan-ch'ung	邵元冲	
Shen Chün-ju	沈鈞儒	

Shen Hung-lieh	沈鴻烈	
Shen K'o	沈克	
Shen Po-shun	申伯純	
Sheng Shih-ts'ai	盛世才	
Shih Liang	史良	
Shih Yu-shan	石友三	
Si-ching jih-pao	西京日報	
Sun Ch'uan-fang	孫傳芳	
Sun Feng-ming	孫鳳鳴	
Sun Fo (K'o)	孫科	
Sun Lien-chung	孫連仲	
Sun Kuang-te	孫廣德	
Sun Ming-chiu	孫銘九	
Sun Wei-ju	孫蔚如	
Sun Yüan-liang	孫元良	
Sung Che-yüan	宋哲元	
Sung Hsi-lien	宋希濂	
Sung Hsüeh-li	宋學禮	
Sung I-yün	宋綺雲	
Sung Li	宋黎	
Szu-wei hsüeh hui	四維學會	

Tai Chi-t'ao	戴 季 陶	Tungpei	東 北
Tai Ch'uan-hsien	戴 傳 賢	Wan Fu-lin	萬 福 林
Tai Li	戴 笠	Wan Yao-huang	萬 耀 煌
T'an Chen	覃 振	Wan Yi	萬 毅
T'an Tzu-hsin	檀 自 新	Wang Chao-shih	王 造 時
T'ang Chün-yao	唐 君 堯	Wang Chia-lieh	王 家 烈
T'ang En-po	湯 恩 伯	Wang Ching-chiu	王 敬 久
T'ang Sheng-chih	唐 生 智	Wang Ching-wei	汪 精 衛
Teh Wang	德 王	Wang-Ch'ü	王 曲
Teng Fa	鄧 發	Wang Ch'ung-hui	汪 寵 惠
Ting Wei-fen	丁 惟 汾	Wang Hua-i	王 化 一
Ts'ai Hsi-ch'ang	蔡 錫 昌	Wang I-che	王 以 哲
Tseng K'uo-ch'ing	曾 擴 清	Wang Lu-i	王 陸 一
Tseng Wan-chung	曾 萬 鍾	Wang Ming	王 明
Tso Ti-ju	左 迪 如	Wang Ping-nan	王 炳 南
Tsou Ta-p'eng	鄒 大 鵬	Wang Po-ch'ün	王 伯 羣
Tsou T'ao-fen	鄒 韜 奮	Wang Shu-ch'ang	王 樹 常
Tu Wei-kang	杜 維 綱	Wang Shu-ming	王 叔 銘
Tung Yen-p'ing	董 彥 平	Wang Ying	王 英
Tung Ying-pin	董 英 斌	Wang Yü-chang	王 玉 章
Tungkuan	潼 關	Wei Li-huang	衛 立 煌

Wei-nan	渭	南		Yü Yu-jen	于 右 任
Wu Chia-hsiang	吳	家	象	Yüan T'ung-li	袁 同 禮
Wu Ching-heng	吳	敬	恆
Wu Han-t'ao	吳	瀚	濤
Wu I-fang	吳	貽	芳
Wu P'ei-fu	吳	佩	孚
Wu T'ieh-ch'eng	吳	鐵	城
Yang Hu-ch'eng	楊	虎	城
Yang Kuei-fei	楊	貴	妃
Yang Yung-t'ai	楊	永	泰
Yang Yü-t'ing	楊	宇	霆
Yeh Chien-ying	葉	劍	英
Yeh Ch'u-ts'ang	葉	楚	傖
Yen Hsi-shan	閻	錫	山
Yen Pao-hang	閻	寶	航
Yen Tao-kang	晏	道	剛
Yin Ju-keng	殷	汝	耕
Ying Te-t'ien	應	得	田
Yü Chi-shih	俞	濟	時
Yü Hsüeh-chung	于	學	忠
Yü Wen-chün	余	文	俊

INDEX

Abend, Hallett, 95

Bertram, James M., 58, 157, 158, 175

Central Government, 90, 96, 97, 141, 159

Chang Chao-lin, 53

Chang Chi-luan, 67, 123

Chang Ch'ün, 54, 60, 63, 140, 141, 159

Chang Han-ch'ing, see Chang Hsüeh-liang

Chang Hsüeh-liang, early life, 1-3; Mukden Incident, 4; European trip, 5, 6; in charge of O-Yü-Wan, 6, 7; on the united front, 7, 26, 30, 31, 38–40; anti-Japanese theory, 38-40; negotiations with the CCP, 27, 28, 31, 32, 59; meeting with Chou En-lai, 31, 32; aid to the CCP, 34, 59; aid to Suiyuan, 60; the pension issue, 42, 56; interview with Helen Snow, 56; support for national salvation movement, 55, 56, 61, 62; allying with Yen Hsi-shan, 47-49, 113, 114, 136; last appeal to Chiang, 72; plans for the coup, 71, 76; eight demands, 82, 83; the Chiang diaries, 86, 87; talk with Donald, 94; speech at the people's rally, 97, 98; rebuttal to Ho Ying-ch'in, 98; talk with Wan Yao-huang, 84; speech to his staff, 85; arrival of T. V. Soong, 136; the Chiang-Chang talk, 135, 136; the coming of Madame Chiang, 139; final negotiations, 145, 146; return to Nanking, 153; visit of the six generals, 181; assistance in the settlement, 166, 180; trial, 155, 156, 166; as a prisoner, 208

Chang Hao, 19

Chang Kuo-t'ao, 19, 101, 102

Chang Mu-t'ao, 175

Chang Tso-lin, 2

Chang Wen-t'ien, 102, 108

Ch'en Ch'eng, 75, 79, 143, 159, 167

Ch'en Li-fu, 21, 34, 96, 143, 145

Ch'eng T'ien-fang, 142

Chiang Chien-jen, 146

Chiang Ching-kuo, 148, 203

Chiang Kai-shek, policy toward Japan, 3, 9; negotiations with the CCP, 34, 145; 50th anniversary, 49; first trip to Sian, 57; second trip, 62, 63; interviews with the Sian generals, 68, 69; interview with Chang Chi-luan, 67; capture, 78; life in captivity, 82; move to the new abode, 95; visit of Donald, 95; Chiang Ting-wen's mission, 97; arrival of T. V. Soong, 136; will, 136; arrival of Madame Chiang, 139; meeting with Chou En-lai, 147, 148; release, 149; admonition to Chang and Yang, 149, 150; triumphant return, 155; in retirement, 155, 161; meeting with Wang Ching-wei, 170; receiving

MICHIGAN PAPERS IN CHINESE STUDIES

No. 1. The Chinese Economy, 1912-1949, by Albert Feuerwerker.

No. 2. The Cultural Revolution: 1967 in Review, four essays by Michel Oksenberg, Carl Riskin, Robert Scalapino, and Ezra Vogel.

No. 3. Two Studies in Chinese Literature, by Li Chi and Dale Johnson.

No. 4. Early Communist China: Two Studies, by Ronald Suleski and Daniel Bays.

No. 5. The Chinese Economy, ca. 1870-1911, by Albert Feuerwerker.

No. 6. Chinese Paintings in Chinese Publications, 1956-1968: An Annotated Bibliography and an Index to the Paintings, by E. J. Laing.

No. 7. The Treaty Ports and China's Modernization: What Went Wrong? by Rhoads Murphey.

No. 8. Two Twelfth Century Texts on Chinese Painting, by Robert J. Maeda.

No. 9. The Economy of Communist China, 1949-1969, by Chu-yuan Cheng.

No. 10. Educated Youth and the Cultural Revolution in China, by Martin Singer.

No. 11. Premodern China: A Bibliographical Introduction, by Chun-shu Chang.

No. 12. Two Studies on Ming History, by Charles O. Hucker.

No. 13. Nineteenth Century China: Five Imperialist Perspectives, selected by Dilip Basu, edited by Rhoads Murphey.

No. 14. Modern China, 1840-1972: An Introduction to Sources and Research Aids, by Andrew J. Nathan.

No. 15. Women in China: Studies in Social Change and Feminism, edited by Marilyn B. Young.

No. 16. An Annotated Bibliography of Chinese Painting Catalogues and Related Texts, by Hin-cheung Lovell.

No. 17. China's Allocation of Fixed Capital Investment, 1952-1957, by Chu-yuan Cheng.

No. 18. Health, Conflict, and the Chinese Political System, by David M. Lampton.

No. 19. Chinese and Japanese Music-Dramas, edited by J. I. Crump and William P. Malm.

No. 20. Hsin-lun (New Treatise) and Other Writings by Huan T'an (43 B.C.-28 A.D.), translated by Timoteus Pokora.

No. 21. Rebellion in Nineteenth-Century China, by Albert Feuerwerker.

No. 22. Between Two Plenums: China's Intraleadership Conflict, 1959-1962, by Ellis Joffe.

No. 23. "Proletarian Hegemony" in the Chinese Revolution and the Canton Commune of 1927, by S. Bernard Thomas.

No. 24. Chinese Communist Materials at the Bureau of Investigation Archives, Taiwan, by Peter Donovan, Carl E. Dorris, and Lawrence R. Sullivan.

No. 25. Shanghai Old-Style Banks (Ch'ien-chuang), 1800-1935, by Andrea Lee McElderry.

No. 26. The Sian Incident: A Pivotal Point in Modern Chinese History, by Tien-wei Wu.

Prepaid Orders Only

MICHIGAN ABSTRACTS OF CHINESE AND JAPANESE WORKS ON CHINESE HISTORY

No. 1. The Ming Tribute Grain System, by Hoshi Ayao, translated by Mark Elvin.

No. 2. Commerce and Society in Sung China, by Shiba Yoshinobu, translated by Mark Elvin.

No. 3. Transport in Transition: The Evolution of Traditional Shipping in China, translations by Andrew Watson.

No. 4. Japanese Perspectives on China's Early Modernization: A Bibliographical Survey, by K. H. Kim.

No. 5. The Silk Industry in Ch'ing China, by Shih Min-hsiung, translated by E-tu Zen Sun.

NONSERIES PUBLICATION

Index to the "Chan-kuo Ts'e", by Sharon Fidler and J. I. Crump. A companion volume to the Chan-kuo Ts'e, translated by J. I. Crump (Oxford: Clarendon Press, 1970).

Michigan Papers and Abstracts available from:
Center for Chinese Studies
The University of Michigan
Lane Hall (Publications)
Ann Arbor, MI 48109 USA

Prepaid Orders Only
write for complete price listing